Hellenistic, Roman and Byzantine Settlement Patterns of the Coast Lands of Western Rough Cilicia

Richard E. Blanton

BAR International Series 879
2000

Published in 2016 by
BAR Publishing, Oxford

BAR International Series 879

Hellenistic, Roman and Byzantine Settlement Patterns of the Coast Lands of Western Rough Cilicia

© R Ξ Blanton and the Publisher 2000

ISBN 9781841710808 paperback
ISBN 9781407352190 e-format
DOI https://doi.org/10.30861/9781841710808
A catalogue record for this book is available from the British Library

BAR Publishing is the trading name of British Archaeological Reports (Oxford) Ltd.
British Archaeological Reports was first incorporated in 1974 to publish the BAR
Series, International and British. In 1992 Hadrian Books Ltd became part of the BAR
group. This volume was originally published by Archaeopress in conjunction with
British Archaeological Reports (Oxford) Ltd / Hadrian Books Ltd, the Series
principal publisher, in 2000. This present volume is published by BAR Publishing,
2016.

BAR

PUBLISHING

BAR titles are available from:

    BAR Publishing
    122 Banbury Rd, Oxford, OX2 7BP, UK
EMAIL info@barpublishing.com
PHONE +44 (0)1865 310431
FAX +44 (0)1865 316916
    www.barpublishing.com

Table of Contents

Figures

Tables

Plates

Preface

The aims of the archaeological settlement pattern survey of the coast lands of western Rough Cilicia are three-fold. The first is to "populate the countryside" (in the words of Wallace-Hadrill [1991: xiv]) by identifying and studying rural settlements in a region known primarily from its urban architecture and inscriptions. The second goal is to provide more detailed information regarding the nature of local urbanism by investigating cities as communities, including such topics as population history and economic activity; combined, these two approaches contribute to the elucidation of rural-urban interactions. Lastly, our goal is to contribute to an understanding of how this region influenced, and was influenced by, larger social formations of the greater Mediterranean region.

The coast lands of western Rough Cilicia presented both advantages and disadvantages for the researcher wishing to employ the method of systematic archaeological settlement pattern survey. Field conditions for pedestrian survey were challenging, owing to the rugged terrain, dense and spiny ground cover, the intensive modern agricultural development, and the debilitating midday heat, but they were not inherently limiting. Rural households in the survey area were gracious and hospitable, and generally allowed us to work unimpeded. In one important respect the archaeology of the study region itself presents difficulties for the survey archaeologist. During the Roman Period, the survey area experienced considerable urban population growth. These large sites are characterized by substantial remains of public buildings and spaces, some previously recorded, as well as dwellings and other features never before recorded in prior architectural surveys. Hence, many of the project's resources went to the recording of urban architectural remains (these will be reported on by the project architects, Rhys Townsend and Michael Hoff). By necessity, the demands of urban investigation limited the amount of terrain we were able to cover away from cities.

The most serious limitations on our ability to work productively were imposed by Turkish Government. Aerial photographs were not made available, and the only topographic map series we were able to purchase covered just a narrow coastal strip. These 1:5,000 maps, dating from the mid-1970s, have minimal information, and in some cases displayed obvious errors in contour lines. Delays in the issuance of permits, restrictions on our movements across the countryside, and failure to provide two service representatives (as originally agreed), limited the number of productive work days, particularly on the rural survey as opposed to the architectural recording. During the second field season (1997) Dr. Ismail Karamut, director of the Alanya Archaeological Museum, abruptly and unexpectedly informed us he would not store our

pottery collections over the winter of 1997-1998. Our intention had been to return to Rough Cilicia during the summer of 1998 to complete the tabulation and study of the ceramic collections, so that we would be able to devote the entire 1997 field season to the survey. Instead, we were forced to quickly complete the ceramic tabulation in 1997 in anticipation that our hard-won and quite interesting collections would be thrown out (which they were, minus a small study collection). This is very unfortunate, since one of the main goals of the anticipated 1998 season was to complete a detailed study and technical description of the dozens of local pottery types not previously recognized or studied. Fortunately, Dr. Richard M. Rothaus was available late in the summer of 1997 and was able to complete a preliminary tabulation of the surface collected pottery, and to develop a preliminary typology of the local pottery (Rothaus n.d.). We are very thankful for his diligent and competent completion of this daunting task, and under time pressure.

I thank those persons who participated in the settlement pattern survey. During the summer of 1996, this included Helene Marie Thibault, Mette Korsholm, Jennifer Tobin, Rhys Townsend, Stephen Tracy, Jason DeBlock, and Nicholas Rauh. I might mention that Tracy's efforts possibly represent the first time that a (somewhat) older and prominent epigrapher engaged in systematic pedestrian survey, but I am able to report that Steve acquitted himself well until his knees finally gave out. During the 1997 season, I am grateful for the persistence and hard work of Cindy Bedell and Zac Laugheed on the rural survey. Jason DeBlock, Nicholas Rauh and Paige Rothaus also participated in the 1997 pedestrian survey on a few occasions. Levant Vardar served as the project's Turkish representative for part of July 1997. His substitute, Sultan Tutar, was a devoted and hard-working representative who did much to facilitate the settlement pattern survey. Dr. Seher Turkman and Gülcan Kücükkaraaslan, both of the Alanya Archaeological Museum, facilitated our project. I thank the people of Gazipasa, particularly the staff of the Muz Deniz ("Bananas by the Sea") apartments, who made our stay in Turkey so enjoyable. I thank my colleague Stephen Kowalewski, who joined the survey for a week in 1997. He reminded me how great it is to work with an archaeologist devoted to the goals and methods of settlement pattern survey.

Funding has come from the Purdue University School of Liberal Arts and from the National Science Foundation Program for Archaeology, Archaeometry, and Systematic Collections, Grant 9600617 (Nicholas Rauh, co-PI). I thank John Yellen for his aid in administering this grant. Verenice Heredia Heather Fuller, and Elizabeth Hopper contributed to the preparation of this report.

Chapter 1

Introduction to Theory and Method

To a greater degree, perhaps, than is true in other areas, Mediterranean civilizations reflect the pervasive influences of the long-distance movement of people, goods, and cultures. Hence a geographical approach provides a powerful analytical tool (Braudel 1972). Long-distance interactions figured into social, cultural, and technological change at the scale of the Mediterranean and its major subdivisions, as well as at the more localized level, where regions often display "nodal" properties (e.g., Haggett 1966: Ch. 1). Nodal regions are not defined by a uniformity of culture. Instead, they are defined by the system of interactions along routes of interchange between multiple cultural groups. This is especially apparent in the many cases of interactions between adjoining populations based on an economic symbiosis and cultural differentiation between the "backward" peoples of the mountains, with their economies of seasonally transhumant animal herding (among other mountain specializations), and the more "civilized" residents of intensively cultivated alluvial plains (Braudel 1972: Part One). Fairs and periodic markets along the junctures of mountain and plain were among the institutions that evolved to mediate between diverse groups, for example in Roman North Africa (de Ligt 1993), but social interactions in nodal regions had other social and technological outcomes, including those related to the necessity to develop strategies for defense and offense. In spite of the economic importance of the inter-cultural division of labor, between-group antagonisms were frequently expressed, as in the example of the "explosive" markets of the highland Berber (Benet 1957); hence, the presence, in several areas, of fortifications noted by archaeologists in these same zones of intercultural intercourse (Whittaker 1978: 336). The coast lands of Rough Cilicia are part of one such nodal region. Below I discuss how regional-scale interactions impacted on past residents of this region.

Social interactions and population movements at larger scales, between regions, have also been recurrent themes as causal factors in the evolution of social, cultural, and technological systems of the Mediterranean, evidently since the Neolithic (van Andel and Runnels 1988). In the historical and archaeological literatures, long distance interaction has been addressed under many rubrics, including commerce, trade and exchange (e.g., Carandini 1989; Garnsey, Hopkins, and Whittaker, eds. 1983; Renfrew 1972: Ch. 20; Rostovtzeff 1941), imperialism, especially Roman imperialism and Romanization (e.g., Alcock 1993; Mattingly, ed. 1997; Whittaker 1994), and migration, colonization, and slavery (e.g., Brunt 1971; Descoeudres, ed. 1990; Hopkins 1978a: Ch. 1). In this report, I hope to contribute in some small way to the elucidation of the nature of long-distance processes of these kinds. The survey region was powerfully impacted by Rome after about 65 BCE, and previous to that some degree of Hellenistic influence is present.

While a number of historical sources have investigated the impact of imperial systems in particular instances, recently some scholars have adopted a more comparative and theoretical approach to macroregional interaction and its outcomes that incorporates and evaluates ideas from world-systems theory (Bintliff 1997; Kardulias, ed. 1999; Woolf 1990). In many of its current applications world-systems theory retains Wallerstein's (1974) original terminology of core, semi-periphery, and periphery (and some of his key insights, for example, that forms of labor control will vary between core and periphery), but today analysts recognize more kinds of world systems than Wallerstein proposed, recognize more variation around the theme of core-periphery hierarchy than he conceived of, and they use an expanded terminology to describe the varied types and consequences of periphery incorporation (Hall 1986; cf. Chase-Dunn and Hall 1991; Chase-Dunn and Hall 1997). The emerging world-system theory thus retains the potential for comparison and generalization across space and time inherent in the original theory, while allowing more leeway for understanding how social actors in specific situations responded to both opportunities and costs of participation in larger social fields (e.g., Kardulias, ed. 1999). In what follows, I hope to contribute to a refined understanding of the Roman world system by describing a type of periphery formation previously not well studied archaeologically.

This project's methodology, systematic archaeological settlement pattern survey, represents an important approach potentially able to contribute to a comparative understanding of world-systems. In its most developed forms, settlement pattern archaeology promotes comparison by making use of a commonly-accepted suite of field and analytical methods, as well as a shared language for the characterization of settlement patterns drawn from the literature of regional analysis. For example, in agriculturally marginal localities such as Melos (Renfrew and Wagstaff, eds. 1982), the Nemea Valley (Wright et al. 1990), and Keos (Cherry, Davis, and Mantzourani, eds. 1991), episodes of expanded external ties resulted in, variously, the establishment of powerful centralized polities, "feeder" (dendritic) market systems, and primate (highly nucleated) settlement patterns (e.g., Cherry, Davis, and Mantzourani, eds. 1991: Ch. 22). By contrast, in the comparatively agriculturally rich southern Argolid region of the mainland Peloponnese region of Greece, heightened external contacts brought more dispersed settlement patterns reflecting population growth and rural economic development based on increased production for export (Jameson, Runnels, and van Andel 1994; van Andel and Runnels 1987). These Greek and Aegean patterns, however, are not likely to represent all we would want to know about periphery development in Mediterranean world systems, although as yet no systematic comparative study has been done along these lines. For example, it seems unlikely that the emerging settlement patterns of the Roman province of Africa Proconsularis, with its system of share-tenancy on vast government-owned estates (Kehoe 1988) will approximate patterns identified in Greece and the Aegean, where such estates were absent. However, surveys conducted in North Africa (summarized in Mattingly 1997) have not made use of either the field procedures or analytical methods that would facilitate comparative discussion of periphery incorporation as a social process.

Field Methods

Systematic all-period pedestrian surface survey is now widely accepted as a valid approach in Mediterranean archaeology, and, especially in Greece, the Aegean, and Crete, has already made an imprint on the archaeological literature (Alcock 1994; Alcock, Cherry, and Davis 1994; Barker and Lloyd, eds. 1991; Bintliff and Snodgrass 1985; Bintliff 1997; Cherry 1982, 1983, 1994; Dyson 1982; Gregory 1986; Kardulias, ed. 1994; Keller and Rupp, eds. 1983; Snodgrass 1990). In the coast lands of western Rough Cilicia, I found it possible to adapt many aspects of survey methodology I had previously used in highland regions of Mesoamerica (Blanton 1978: 7-12; Blanton et al. 1982: 6-10; Kowalewski et al. 1989: 24-26), but at the same time I was influenced by local factors that make Mediterranean surveys slightly different from their Mesoamerican counterparts.

The comparatively high density of off-site remains frequently encountered in Mediterranean (and other Old World) surveys (Barker 1991: 5-6; Bintliff and Snodgrass 1988; Cherry 1983: 396; Cherry et al. 1988; Gallant 1986), more than any other factor, necessitated a survey strategy slightly modified from my prior practice. To monitor off-site pottery, I identified units of data recording and surface collection, called survey tracts, ranging in size from 10 ha to 1 km^2. These are naturally bounded topographic units such as small valleys, alluvial plains or segments of ridge line. In the survey of each tract, survey teams noted the density and nature of off-site remains, and took collections of diagnostic sherds. Upon completion of a tract, I noted its location on the topographic map, photographed it, bagged the collection, and wrote a description of its environmental and off-site artifact characteristics. Environmental variables recorded included elevation range, soil type(s) and depth, vegetation, drainage characteristics, availability of water for irrigation, and modern land use. However, we found little in the way of off-site pottery overall, at least by comparison with regions such as Northern Keos (Cherry, Davis, and Mantzourani, eds. 1991: 37-54). Sites are, for the most part, highly discrete patches of pottery and other artifacts whose densities far exceed those encountered in the surrounding terrain. Tract surface collections typically were small and not highly diagnostic. In several areas we did note very small patches

of scattered sherds, lacking construction stone or roof tiles, that might represent the remains of nomadic herding camps. I describe these scatters in Chapter 3.

My goal was to cover an area of at least 100 contiguous kms^2 in two field seasons, thus allowing for the possibility using regional analytical methods (e.g., Kowalewski 1990), while at the same time not overlooking even small sites such as isolated farmsteads. The demands of a regional theoretical orientation, coupled with limited financial resources and time, required a method that would allow us to cover more ground than some projects reported in the literature, in which only a few square kilometers are surveyed each field season (e.g., Bintliff and Snodgrass 1985: 130-7), but suitably intensive and systematic so as to derive information comparable to other similar survey projects (cf. the discussions in Bintliff and Snodgrass 1985: 130-32; Cherry 1983: 396; and Cherry, Davis, Mantzourani, and Whitelaw 1991: 18). I settled on an approach in which survey crews, usually consisting of between 3 and 7 persons, walked across the landscape spaced between 20 and 30 m apart, so even the smallest sites are not likely to be missed. Given the complex terrain in much of the area, regular spacing was often impossible. Very steep slopes were not surveyed (many in the area could not be done except with mountaineering equipment), so that in some instances the spacing between persons walking along adjoining ridge lines, or between two persons, one on a ridge, the other in an adjacent gully or valley, exceeded the usual spacing. On complex ridge lines, which were common in this area, two or more persons walked side by side along the ridge top, but split into smaller teams which would walk down subsidiary ridges, either to their base or to a point where the terrain becomes too steep, then back to the central ridge to rejoin the team.

As I mentioned, sites were generally highly discrete patches of sherds, building stone, roof tiles, and other artifacts, and thus identifying site limits typically was rather straightforward (except in a few instances where modern settlement and/or modern agricultural features obscured sherd scatter). Upon encountering a site, I first identified its maximum limits and recorded them on the topographic map. In the case of smaller sites (of about 1 ha or less), a surface collection was taken from the whole site; for larger sites, multiple discrete collection areas were identified, usually defined by field boundaries or topographic features. A sketch map was made of each collection area, and its dimensions noted. We used a "grab-bag" method of surface collection (i.e., we selectively picked up only diagnostic sherds). Our goal was to collect 50 to 100 diagnostic sherds from each site or collection area, but often this was difficult. Especially on small rural sites, where much of the pottery consists of the locally-made vessels for which we had no chronological knowledge, we could not find this many diagnostics. Finally, the site was photographed and I wrote notes describing its immediate natural environment, modern land use, the density of non-collected artifacts such as roof tiles, and evidence of specialized production or other activities. Features such as reservoirs, defensive walls, and other public constructions were paced or tape-measured and sketched, but, given the limited resources at our disposal, typically not all remains of stone architecture, especially houses, could be recorded in detail.

3

Comparative Methods

In addition to reporting on the results of the surface survey, this volume describes the results of a comparative analysis of coded data from similar projects done in other parts of the Mediterranean. The purpose of this limited comparative exercise is to throw additional light on the settlement patterns of the survey area. While I found the comparative task at times challenging, it did prove both enlightening and stimulating. However, what I report on here has to be considered a first, small, step towards comparative analyses that should be carried out on a much larger scale. To date, few comparative efforts have been published that could have served as exemplars for my research, although I benefited from the pioneering efforts of Alcock (1993, 1994), Bintliff (1997), and Lloyd (1991).

Cross-regional comparison of archaeological settlement patterns is problematic in some key respects. Site preservation may differ from region to region. Between-region comparison of ceramic sequences is sometimes not straightforward. More importantly, survey methods tend to vary somewhat from project to project. For example, variation in the degree of intensity of coverage (i.e., the closeness of spacing of survey crew members), influences the likelihood that all small sites will be located (cf. Bintliff 1997: 2), and could influence comparative statistics such as sites per square kilometer of surveyed area. To minimize the possibility that observable variation between reported survey data might reflect methodological differences rather than behavioral differences between regional social systems, the studies I selected by and large are similar to the Rough Cilicia coast lands survey in their intensity of ground coverage, although some between-survey differences are found in my sample. In some analyses that follow, I exclude cases where low density values might be attributable to survey method. An additional challenge to comparison is to be found in the fact that some of the pioneering surveys of the 1950s to the 1970s were done before settlement pattern archaeology emerged as a methodologically self-conscious branch of archaeological method in general (e.g., the South Etruria projects, described below; cf. Lloyd 1991: 234). In such cases, because field methods were not described in detail, it was difficult to judge the value of the published data for answering comparative questions. But I included several key projects done during an earlier phase of development of methodology because they provide useful data, and in many ways appear methodologically similar to more recent projects.

Selection of Cases

In my analysis I wanted to address primarily two issues. First, I wanted to know how site densities by period in the coast lands of western Rough Cilicia compared with other Mediterranean regions. Hence, I required survey reports that accurately report the number of sites by period found within a systematically surveyed region of known size (permitting a calculation of sites per square kilometer of surveyed area). Further, I selected cases where I could code numbers of sites according to the broad periodization found in Table 1-1 (in cases where a report gives site numbers for phase subdivisions of a period, I coded the largest number of sites for the period).

My second concern was variation in Early and Late Roman settlement patterns, which I hoped to analyze in greater detail than just sites per square kilometer. For this aspect of the analysis, I required site-by-site descriptions for the Early and Late Roman Periods, preferably including site sizes in hectares and site functional information. Several surveys which were suitable for the all-period site density comparison were included in the coded data even though they did not meet the latter requirement (or did not subdivide Early and Late Roman).

Survey reports that did include site-by site descriptions but did not report Early and Late Roman site sizes presented coding problems. The critical variables for my Roman Period settlement pattern analyses are the number of and sizes of residential sites of four categories: farmsteads, villas, villages, and towns/cities (see below). Particularly in the South Etruria survey reports, I had difficulty identifying a cut-off point for small residential sites; in some cases the small sherd scatters described might represent only off-site debris, or possibly other non-residential activity areas. Also, a small sherd scatter given a site number in a survey report might represent some of the sherd "halo" usually found around larger sites, rather than a separate site. Fortunately, for South Etruria, I was able to compare my coding from the original sources with the summary maps provided by Potter (1979). This source was also useful in providing a more complete chronological breakdown of Early and Late Roman sites than was found in the original reports. The following lists the surveys I selected for coding, with references and comments on issues pertaining to possible methodological problems for comparative analysis; Figure 1-1 shows the locations of the survey regions, and Appendix 3 includes the coding scheme and coded data:

1. **Capena and the Ager Capenas** (Jones 1962, 1963; Potter 1979). Survey methodology not described in detail; Roman Period emphasis, but earlier sites were reported.

2. **Sutri** (Duncan 1958; Potter 1979). Survey methodology not described in detail; Roman Period emphasis, but earlier sites were reported.

3. **Ager Faliscus** (Frederiksen and Ward Perkins 1957; Potter 1979). Survey methodology not described in detail; Roman Period emphasis, but earlier sites were reported.

4. **Ager Veientanus** (Kahane, Threipland, and Ward-Perkins 1968; Potter 1979). Survey methodology not described in detail; Roman Period emphasis, but earlier sites were reported.

5. **Guadalquivir** (Ponsich 1974). Like surveys 1-4, this report makes it difficult to distinguish between small residential sites and other sherd scatters, and also makes it difficult to know if two or more adjacent scatters might pertain to one larger site. Survey methodology is not described in detail; Roman Period emphasis. The chronology of Roman sites is in some cases uncertain owing to the small sizes of most surface collections, hence I assumed that all sites date to the period of maximum population density, Early Roman (1st to 4th centuries AD)(Ponsich 1974: 293).

6. **Ager Cosanus** (Dyson 1978). This is a much larger area than usual for Mediterranean survey projects (450 kms^2), suggesting less intensive coverage than other surveys, but survey methods are not described in detail; Roman Period emphasis, but earlier sites were reported. Dyson includes

an elaborate typology of farms and villas (p. 257). In order to facilitate comparison with other surveys, I coded his two most elaborate villa types (A and B) as villas, while coding his C and D categories as farmsteads (villas are defined in Chapter 4).

7. **Rieti Basin** (Coccia and Mattingly, eds., 1992; Coccia et al. 1995).

8. **Melos** (Renfrew and Wagstaff, eds., 1982). Combines data from intensively surveyed sample transects with that from known sites.

9. **Lasithi Plain** (Watrous 1974, 1982). Survey method not described in detail.

10. **Kavousi-Thriphti** (Haggis, 1996).

11. **Western Mesara Plain** (Watrous, Vance, and Blitzer, eds., 1993).

12. **Vrokastro** (Hayden, Moody, and Rackham 1992).

13. **Southern Euboea** (Keller 1985).

14. **Ayiofarango Valley** (Blackman and Branigan, eds. 1977).

15. **Northern Keos** (Cherry, Davis, and Mantzourani, eds. 1991).

16. **Southern Argolid** (Jameson, Runnels, and van Andel 1994).

17. **Pylos** (Davis et al. 1997).

18. **Palaipaphos** (Rupp et al. 1984).

19. **Western Coast Lands of Rough Cilicia.**

Table 1-1. Periods used for coding from published survey data, with approximate chronology.

Period	Date
	650
Late Roman	
	AD 300
Early Roman	
	50 BCE
Republican Roman/Hellenistic	
	333
Classical	
	500
Orientalizing/Archaic	
	700
Protogeometric/Geometric	
	1000
Late Bronze	
	1600
Middle Bronze	
	2000
Early Bronze	
	3300
Ceramic Neolithic	
	6500

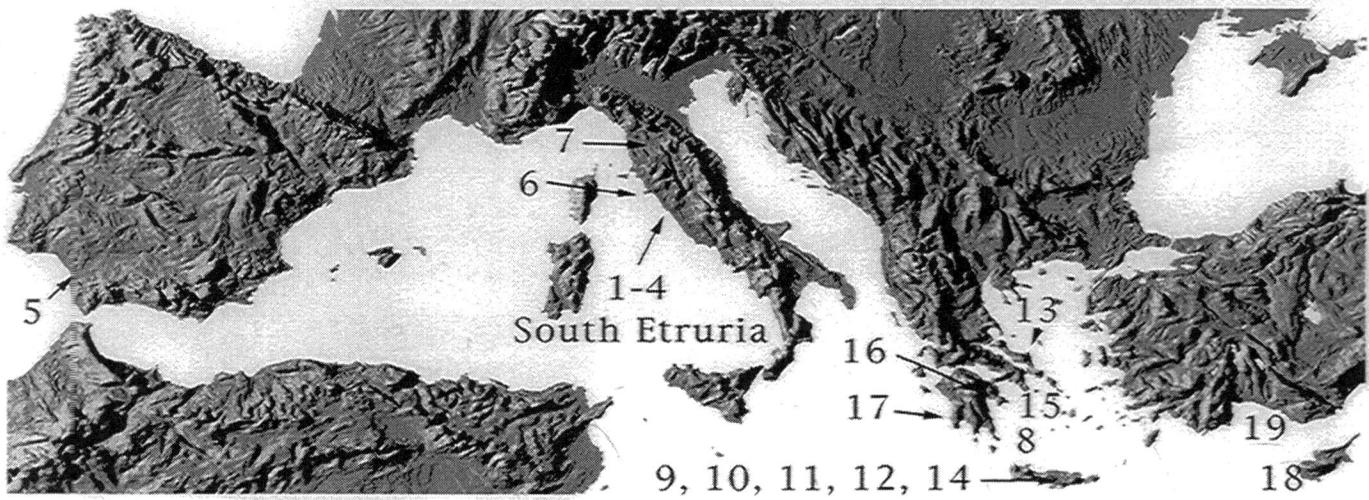

Figure 1-1. Locations of coded survey regions. 1=Ager Capenas, 2=Sutri, 3=Ager Faliscus, 4=Ager Veientanus, 5=Guadalquivir Valley, 6=Ager Cosanus, 7=Rieti Basin, 8=Melos, 9=Lasithi Plain, 10=Kavousi-Thriphti, 11=W. Mesara, 12=Vrokastro, 13=S. Euboea, 14=Ayiofarango Valley, 15=N. Keos, 16=S. Argolid, 17=Pylos, 18=Palaipaphos, 19=western coast lands of Rough Cilicia.

Chapter 2

Description of the Survey Area, Its History and Resources

The survey area extends along the western coast lands of a region called Rough Cilicia (or Cilicia Tracheia) in the vicinity of the modern Turkish town of Gazipasa, and includes an area of approximately 45 km² (Figures 2-1 to 2-3). The systematic survey was restricted to this coastal strip because the only topographic maps available to us at a scale suitable for survey (1:5,000) are a series of Turkish Government map grids (from the Mapping and Cadastral Central Administration) made to facilitate coastal economic development (the map grids and their identification numbers are shown in Figure 2-4). Site field numbers consist of a grid square designation plus a number (in order of discovery). In addition to the lack of suitable map coverage, other factors precluded carrying the systematic survey further inland. The urban area of Gazipasa and its immediate surrounds (shown as a darkened zone in Figure 2-3) cannot be systematically surveyed owing to the abundance of recent construction and agricultural development projects. This area, covering some 35 km², was surface surveyed, although less intensively than the remainder of the survey area, by systematically driving every road, and looking for sherds and structures in adjacent fields, yards, and road cuts. No sites older than early modern were found during the course of this "vehicular" survey. It is feasible to extend the pedestrian survey to the high ridges and valleys of the Taurus to the north and east of the survey area, but to do this, a methodology different than ours would be required. Logistically, such a survey would require multi-day survey sweeps into highly inaccessible terrain, for which this project simply was not equipped, and for which detailed topographic maps were not available.

Five major archaeological sites are located within the survey area (Figure 2-5). From north to south they are Iotape, Selinus, Cestrus, Nephelion, and Antiochia. These five sites form a comparatively compact cluster of coastal centers spaced from about 5 to 7 kms apart. To the north and west of the survey area, Syedra is the next large coastal center (Bean and Mitford 1962: 191-4, 1970: 106-7) (Figure 2-6), some 16 kms from Iotape. Charadrus (Bean and Mitford 1965: 42-3) is located some 13 kms southeast of Antiochia. Several nearby mountain sites are known, located on high ridges inland from the survey area, and separated from it by rugged terrain, including Lamus (Bean and Mitford 1970: 172-5)(the Roman administrative center of the Lamotis district, which included Antiochia of the survey area), and Asar Tepe (Bean and Mitford 1970: 170-1)(Figure 2-6).

For many purposes of organizing and analyzing the archaeological, environmental, and agricultural data, I grouped sites by what I call city hinterlands. As defined here, a hinterland is the area contiguous to a city and most likely to have contained rural communities involved in its polity and economy, and where city-dwelling farm families are most likely to have grown their crops. It is also possible that coastal cities controlled larger territories in upland forested terrain further inland, but this cannot be confirmed. The surveyed area has five hinterland areas, each centered around one of the major sites (Figure 2-5). The hinterland boundary locations shown in the figure are estimates, drawn midway between centers. The gray shaded areas of Figure 2-5 indicate the uncertain positions of the hinterland boundaries in the direction of the Taurus uplands, and the boundaries of Iotape and Antiochia in relation to other coastal cities (the next adjacent centers in both cases are far from the survey area). The north boundary of the Iotape hinterland was estimated by placing it the same distance from the center as its distance from the south boundary. The same procedure was used to estimate a south boundary of the Antiochia hinterland.

Resources of Coastal Rough Cilicia and the Survey Region

Lack of access to significant land routes to upland Anatolia, minimal potential for agricultural development, and an uncertain military and political environment were among the factors limiting human occupation of the coast lands of western Rough Cilicia during some periods (these factors are discussed in more detail below). However, certain local resources were valued by outside interests, particularly the forest products of the Taurus (Broughton 1975: 616-17; Bean and Mitford 1962: 187; Jones 1971: 198; Magie 1975: 267). Locations featuring a proximity of densely forested slopes and coastal inlets minimized the costs of moving forest products from harvest to shipping (Magie ibid.); all of the major sites in the survey area are advantaged in this way, especially Iotape, Nephelion, and Antiochia. Forest products exported from Rough Cilicia included cedar (for ship construction), dwarf oak for kermes-dye, storax gum, and liquorice (Magie ibid.). Ptolemaic interests in this area reflected the desire for wood (Ormerod 1978: 202), and, possibly, mercenaries (Jones 1971: 198). Hopwood (1989) suggests a symbiosis developed between coastal and upland populations of Rough Cilicia in a manner analogous to other nodal regions of the Mediterranean, with the upland peoples producing the wool and goat's hair cloth for which this area was famous in Roman times (Hopwood 1989: 192), while coastal communities specialized in agricultural products. Later I evaluate this hypothesis.

Figure 2-1. Major topographic features of Asia Minor, showing three regions of the south coast mentioned in the text.

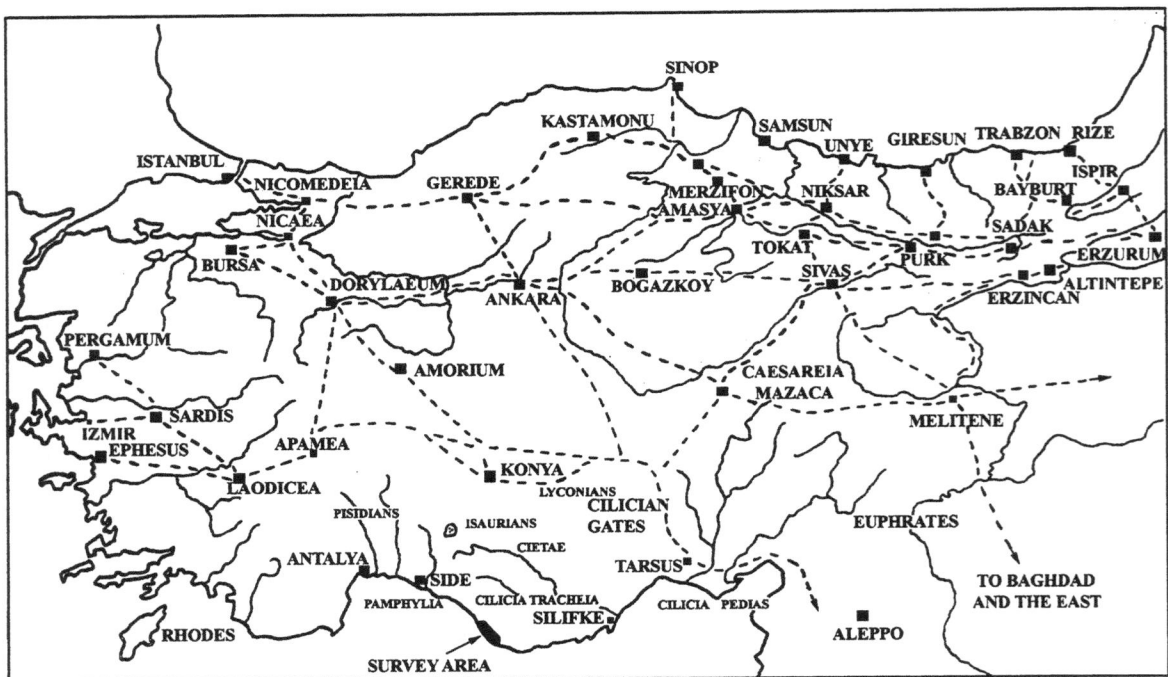

Figure 2-2. Location of the survey area in relation to important sites and regions of Asia Minor. Dashed lines are major ancient routes. Modified from Winfield (1977: Figure 1).

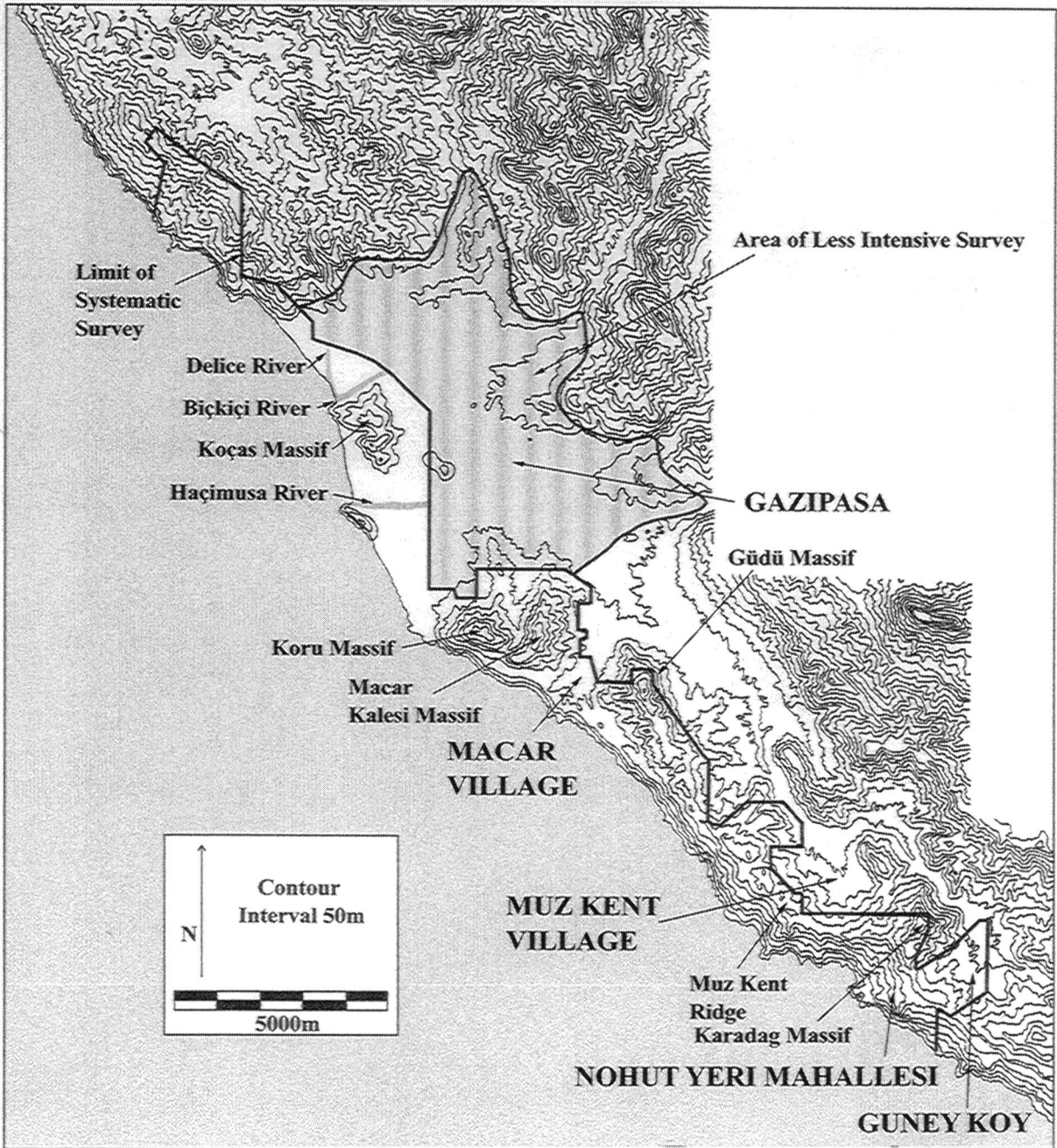

Figure 2-3. Survey limits, modern communities (capitalized) and major natural features of the survey region.

Labels on the map:

Area of Less Intensive Survey

Limit of Systematic Survey

Delice River

Biçkiçi River

Koças Massif

Haçimusa River

GAZIPASA

Güdü Massif

Koru Massif

Macar Kalesi Massif

MACAR VILLAGE

MUZ KENT VILLAGE

Muz Kent Ridge

Karadag Massif

NOHUT YERI MAHALLESI

GUNEY KOY

N

Contour Interval 50m

5000m

9

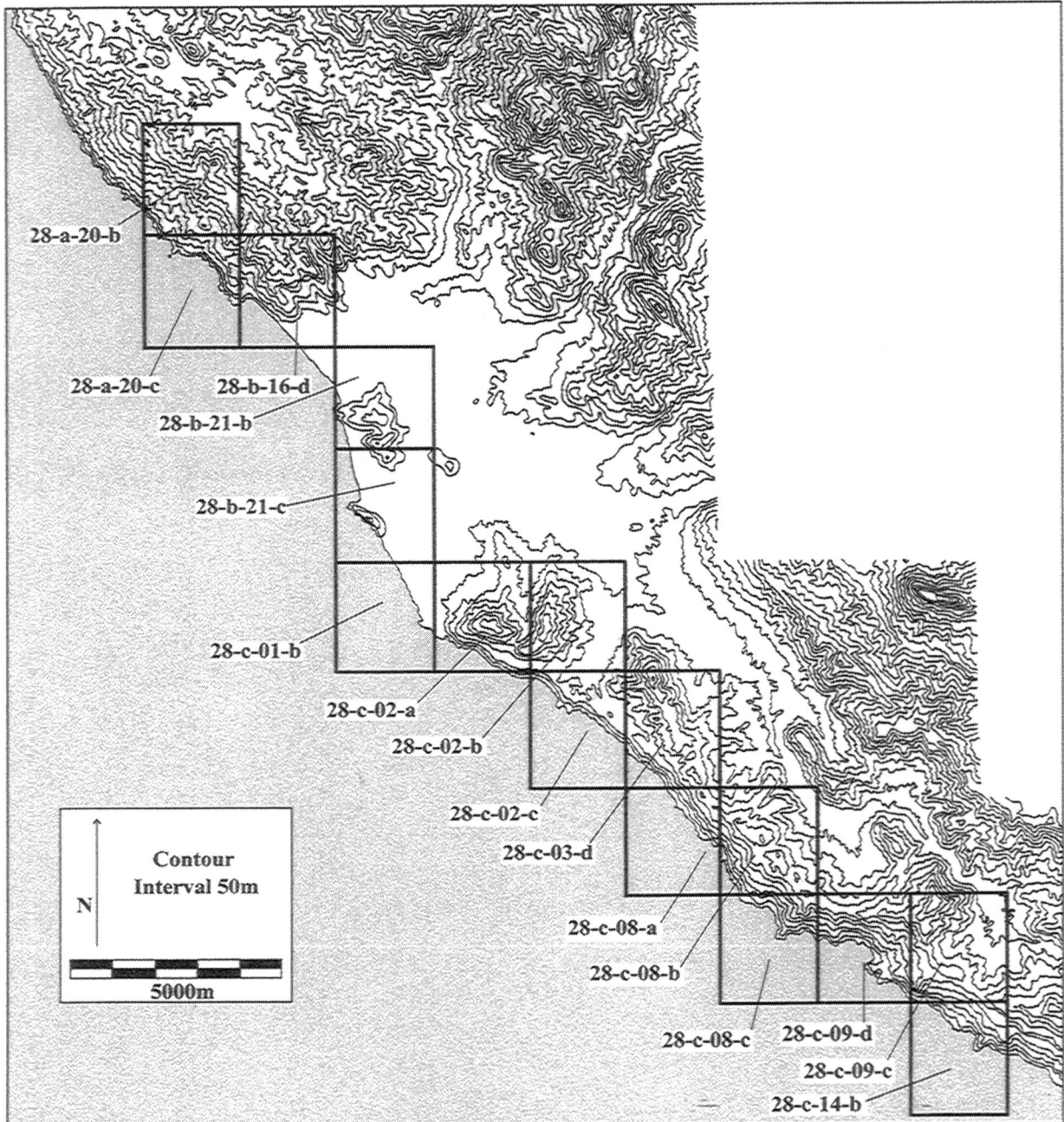

Figure 2-4. Survey grid squares and their identification numbers.

28-a-20-b

28-a-20-c   28-b-16-d

28-b-21-b

28-b-21-c

28-c-01-b

28-c-02-a

28-c-02-b

28-c-02-c

28-c-03-d

28-c-08-a

28-c-08-b

28-c-08-c   28-c-09-d

28-c-09-c

28-c-14-b

N

Contour
Interval 50m

5000m

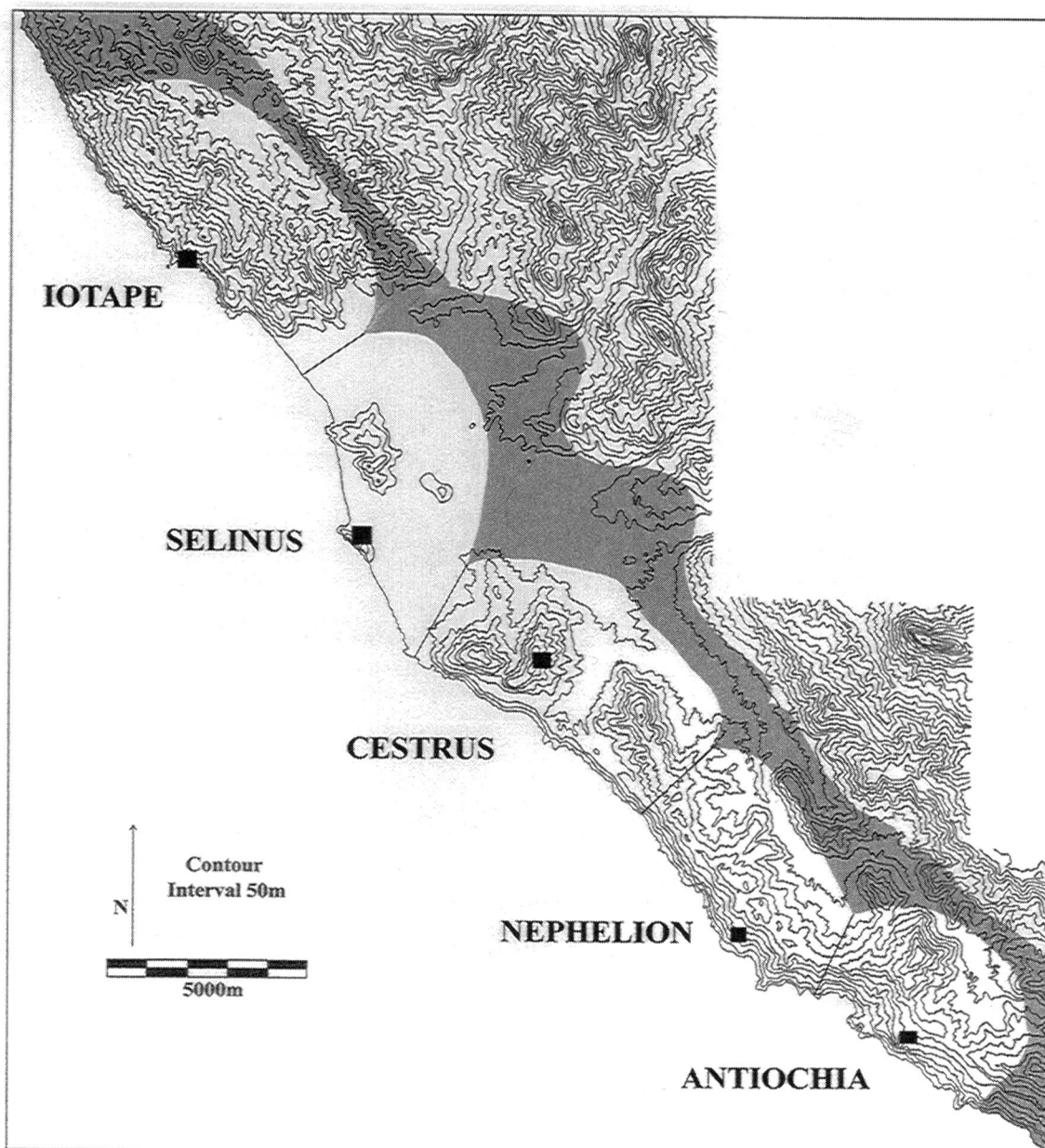

Figure 2-5. Major sites and city hinterlands of the survey area.

Variables Related to Agricultural Production

Given the generally rugged terrain of the survey area, it would not have been capable of producing vast surpluses of agricultural commodities. But it is reasonable to ask: To what extent could a local population here be self-supporting or even capable of producing an agricultural surplus for exchange? Or would it have been necessary to import food supplies? Answering this question will throw light on how local communities were tied into larger interactive networks of commodity trade and other exchanges. To address this issue, I now turn to a consideration of the nature of the local environmental variables as they relate to the potential for agricultural production, and attempt to calculate an agricultural carrying capacity of the survey area and each of the city

hinterlands. Population estimates by site for the various periods of occupation are given in the next chapter (and in Appendix 1) and discussed in more detail in the concluding chapter.

Diverse sources from soil studies (Oakes 1957), geography (Dewdney 1971), and agronomy (e.g., Erinç and Tunçdilek 1952; Stratil-Sauer 1933) identify a distinct environmental zone of Turkey extending from the Pamphylian plain to south and east of the survey area (e.g., the "Mediterranean Region" in Dewdney [1971: Ch. 12], and the "subregion of Mediterranean agriculture" in Erinç and Tunçdilek [1952: 194-6]). Although annual average precipitation here is higher than the semi-arid interior plateau (with Antalya receiving an estimated 665-1056 mm/year [FAO 1959: Table I/2; Oakes 1957: Table 1]), agricultural production is limited by the extremely hot

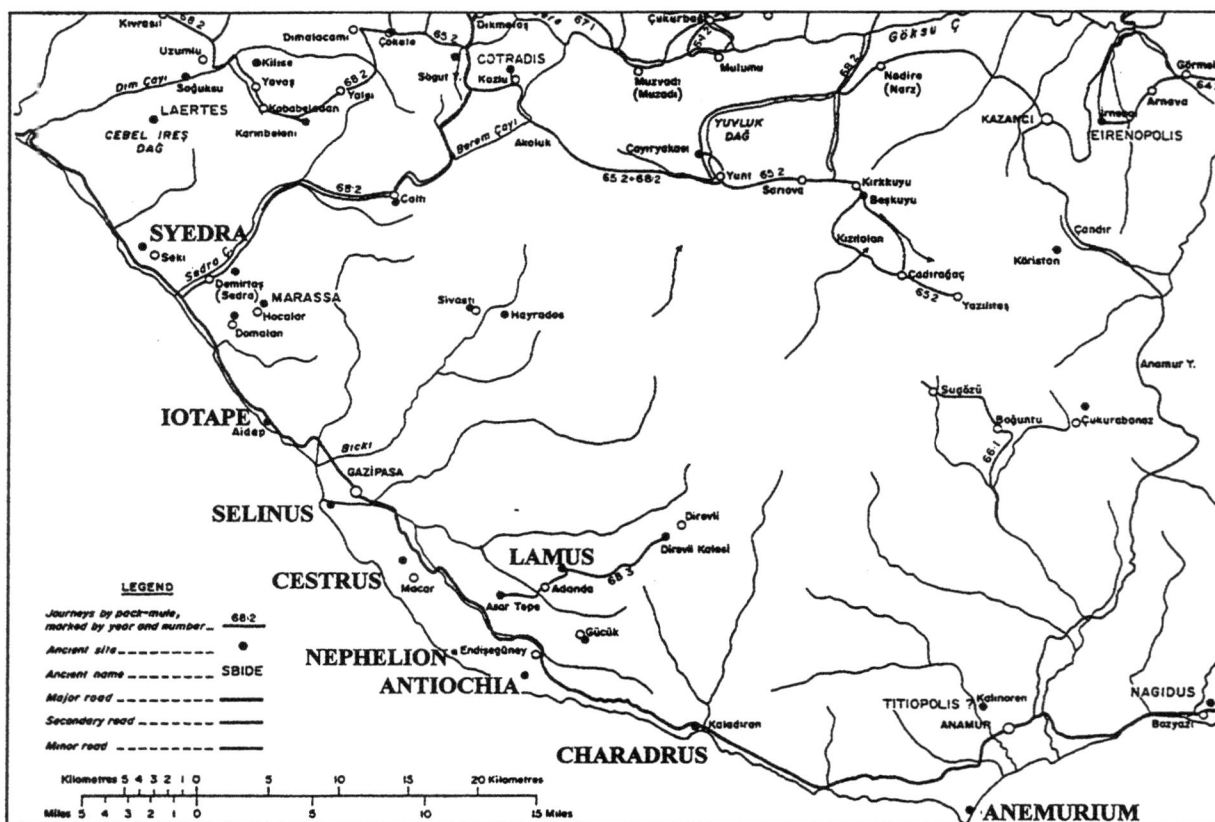

Figure 2-6. Western Rough Cilicia, showing sites in and adjacent to the survey area. Modified from Bean and Mitford 1970: Map B.

Table 2-1. Summary of estimates for agricultural variables.

	A	B	C	D	E
Household Size	5	6	5	n.d.	3.25 (1)
Productivity (2)	240-400	680	612	686	n.d.
% Fallowed	50	50	50	50	50
Ha/Person (3)	1	.77	.4	n.d.	1.08 (4)
Ha Cultivated (5)	n.d.	3.2-10	9.11	7.8	5.4 (6)

Key:
A. Jameson et al. (1994: 283, 550). Argolid, Greece.
B. Stirling (1965: 16, 44, 48, 85, and Table 3). Kayseri Vilayet, Central Turkey
C. Morrison (1939: 1, 14, 16, Table 4). Yozgat Vilayet, Central Turkey.
D. Helburn (1955: 384, Table I). Semi-arid Central Turkey.
E. White (1970: 336). Roman Period, Italian Peninsula.
Footnotes:
(1) This value seems small in comparison with most known agrarian households (e.g., Goody 1972: Table 3.1; cf. Jameson et al. 1994: 550).
(2) In kgs/ha, for dry-farmed wheat fields actually in cultivation (excluding fallow fields). The amount indicated is available for household consumption and surplus (i.e., after deducting reserved seed and other seed requirements such as feeding oxen). The values for Morrison and Helburn were estimated based on calculations in Stirling (1965: 85).
(3) Land required for basic subsistence only.
(4) Uses the value of 5 persons per household.
(5) By an average farm family using primarily household labor.
(6) This would be a minimal value for subsistence-only farming (White 1970: 336).

summers (with between 24.8 and 28.2 degrees centigrade average for the months of June through September) and the pronounced summer drought (precipitation values for June through September are 13.2, 1.3, 1.3, and 15.7 mm)(rainfall and temperature values are from Oakes 1957: Table 1).

One product of this climate regime is the development of Terra Rossa soils. These soils develop over hard limestone bedrock (like other brown soils that develop on sloping land), in a regime of hot dry summers and mild wet winters. They are comparatively low in potential productivity owing to some degree of laterization and a poor ability to retain water (Bintliff 1977: 92; Oakes 1957: 66, 79), but along the tops of ridge lines in the survey area, these soils are cultivated, primarily for wheat production. In addition to the Terra Rossa soils, the survey area does contain a limited amount of higher productivity alluvial soils (Oakes 1957: 48, 155). But these soils are often found (for example, as they are in the vicinity of Selinus) adjacent to the mouths of rivers draining the Taurus, where they are subject to flooding and may remain marshy and malarial until reclaimed (Dewdney 1971: 178). Heberdey and Wilhelm (1896: 149), early archaeological explorers of Rough Cilicia, found the alluvial plain north of Selinus to be "boggy." Even as late as the early 1960s, when Bean and Mitford did their epigraphic survey of Rough Cilicia, they described the area around Selinus as "mosquito-infested" (Bean and Mitford 1962: 206).

On the plus side for agricultural production, the Mediterranean region is characterized by mild winters. Thus, the potential loss in productivity due to excess cold during the early period of plant growth is not found here as may occur in the central plains of Anatolia (e.g., Morrison 1939: 23). However, the early-arriving spring and summer heat would preclude the spring sowing that is feasible, owing to the milder spring and summer temperatures, in the central plains (and which can serve to make up for a poor winter crop)(ibid.: 21-23). While in the central highlands the harvest continues through most of the summer (ibid.), I never observed any grain harvesting taking place even during the month of June in the survey area (in the central plains, it routinely extends throughout the summer months). I assume from this that the local agronomic regime is based on an autumn planting and an early spring harvest that would avoid the onset of damaging high temperatures and dry conditions of the spring.

Estimates of Potential Agricultural Productivity

No ethnographic or similar source describes current agricultural practices in the survey area, so I must make use of comparative data to throw light on the probable nature of production in the periods of relevance to the survey data (Classical Greek through Roman Periods). Recent advances in irrigation technology, especially electric and gasoline powered pumps drawing water from shallow wells, drip irrigation systems for banana plantations, and large-scale greenhouses that permit winter vegetable production have revolutionized agriculture in the survey region in the past few decades, but the agriculture of the past was quite different. Several of the sources summarized in Table 2-1 describe Turkish methods of wheat production, from the early decades of this century,

that are incredibly similar to those of the Greek and Roman Periods (e.g., as described in White 1970). This includes a fifty percent fallow cycle, the use of oxen-pulled wooden plows, hand sowing, hand weeding, scythe harvesting, threshing and straw chopping with an animal-drawn sledge studded with flints, and winnowing in the wind (e.g., Stirling 1965: 46). Thus the production values summarized in Table 2-1 are more relevant than would be the data of modern mechanized and chemical-based farming, but the comparative data are still difficult to interpret in some respects for what they might imply about ancient farming in the survey region.

Some recent agriculture, even that done before the widespread use of mechanization, chemical fertilizers, and pesticides, may be more productive than 2,000 years ago. For example, Stratil-Sauer (1933: 325) reports a Turkey-wide average production for wheat (the main crop) of 172 tons per km^2 (1560 kg/ha). This is comparable to the range from 907.5 to 2467.5 kg/ha reported for contemporary Cyprus reported in Wagstaff (1979: Table 3), but is far higher than the range from 240 to 400 kg/ha estimated for smallholder production in the Argolid, Greece, that Jameson et al. (1994: 283) think might be a reasonable proxy for the Classical Period (140-200 kg/ha for all land, considering that one-half of a family's fields are in fallow each year). The values given by Jameson et al. are after reserving of seed, and evidently represent the amount actually available for human consumption, while the modern Turkish values are total production, but this discrepancy could not account for the vast difference. One possible reason for the higher value for Turkey for the 1930s might be that production measures reflect primarily larger commercial farms, rather than small-holder farms whose productivity would be more like that of the past, and more like the Argolid (data sources for the Turkey agricultural census reported in Stratil-Sauer are not described in detail). Clearly, some highly commercialized districts adjacent to major urban areas had achieved quite high levels of production, pulling up the national average (ibid.: Figure 1).

Stratil-Sauer (1933: Fig. 1) does indicate that the district of Antalya (which would include the survey area) has an average productivity far lower than the national average, at about 26-50 tons per km^2 (an estimated 345 kgs/ha on average), similar to the Argolid estimates described above. Another productivity value that may be useful for understanding coastal Rough Cilician archaeological periods comes from Helburn (1955), who provides data from farms that are definitely small-holder farms (he calls them "subsistence-based" farms), although they are located in the semi-arid central plains of Central Turkey rather than the south coast. While it was evident that by 1955 a minor amount of farm mechanization had already been adopted, Helburn mentions that plowing was still done with oxen, and that plowing represents one of the critical limiting factors facing this primitive production system. While there was a two-week optimal period for plowing (I assume, just after, or just before, the start of the fall rains, but not so late as to cause a late planting, cf. White [1970: 103, 116, 178]), some farmers plowed for up to 56 days. According to Helburn, one man, with two oxen, can plow .1 ha per day. Jameson et al. (1994: 388) suggest that one man can plow .3 ha per day, but base this on one informant.

Sources for the Roman Period (e.g., Duncan-Jones 1974: 330) are consistent with about .1 ha/day for first plowing, implying 50 days of fall plowing for a family cultivating 5 ha, close to the maximum mentioned by Helburn.

Helburn (1955: 384) indicates that productivity of fields actually in production (rather than for farm holdings as a whole) was found to "vary downward" from 15 bushels/acre (37 bushels/ha, or an estimated 1009 kgs/ha). After removing reserved seed and seed used for other purposes, this probably represents in the neighborhood of 686 kgs/ha for the most productive farms, still somewhat higher than the estimate for the Argolid (Table 2-1)(I base my estimates on seed use from the detailed accounting provided by Stirling [1965: 85]). According to Stratil-Sauer (1933: Fig. 1) Helburn's study area has, on average, equal or higher productivity than the south coast in the vicinity of Antalya, so is not a perfect comparative situation, in part because the long growing season permits both fall and spring crops.

It is difficult to know what productivity estimates should be used for the coast lands of Rough Cilicia in the absence of any direct measures of small-holder production there. While the survey area's rainfall (at an estimated 665-1056 mm/year [FAO 1959: Table I/2; Oakes 1957: Table 1]) is higher than the Argolid (which is 520 mm in Jameson et al.: 157), the survey area is characterized by a hotter, drier summer than the Argolid (cf. Jameson et al. 1994: 157 and Oakes 1957: Table 1). The extreme hot dry summers may be a factor limiting not only grain agriculture, but also many kinds of perennial production. While the fig is a commonly occurring tree in the coast lands region, very little olive or grape production is recorded for this century (Erinç and Tunçdilek 1952: Fig. 2), and olive trees and vines are not numerous in the survey area today. This same table indicates that the major production of the area in the 1950s was wheat (primary crop), maize, and citrus, with some barley and grapes.

I make use of the varied, if not always useful, comparative information available to me to make the following assumptions about several key parameters of agricultural production in the archaeological periods of most interest to the survey area (Table 2-1), using wheat as the key crop. For the Argolid, Jameson et al. (1994: 283) infer that for the Classical and Roman periods it is likely that the amount of arable land required per person for subsistence production would be slightly more than 1 ha, or 5 ha per farm family, assuming the productivity values mentioned above (140-200 kgs/ha) and a per capita consumption of 175 to 200 kgs of wheat equivalent per person per year (cf. Foxhall and Forbes 1982). I use these figures below for the survey area. The smallholders described by Helburn (1955) in Central Turkey conform roughly to these same values for land required per person. From his Table I, the estimated average cultivated land per farm family is 7.8 ha (ranging from 5.9 to 11.2 ha), but some production is for market sale, up to 50% (ibid.: 384); specific data on per farm production are not provided. Presumably the farms in the 5.9 ha range are closer to being subsistence-oriented, and thus conform to the estimates for subsistence-oriented farm sizes for both Greece (Argolid) and Roman Italy (Table 2-1).

Assuming it was normal for farms in the survey area to produce at least some surplus for sale (cf. Engels 1990: Ch. 2), and to meet tenancy obligations and taxes, I make use of a value of 10 ha per agricultural producer household as an estimate of arable land cultivated per farm family on average (cf. Jameson 1977/78: 131 for Classical Greece; Kehoe 1988: 14 for the Roman Period, who suggest similar values). This would be an estimate of surplus production that seems well within the parameters of the ethnographic data described above. A farm of this size would entail the plowing of 5 ha per year (cf. Kehoe 1988: 16), requiring an estimated 50 days for first plowing from the onset of autumn rains until planting. Such farms would produce an estimated 2000 kgs/ha of wheat, while the producer household would consume 1000 kgs, leaving a surplus of 1000 kgs. That surplus would support an estimated 5 consumers (cf. Engels 1990: 41; Wagstaff, Augustson, and Gamble 1982: 179).

It is impossible to know what proportion of farms would have cultivated 5 ha per year. It would appear to be the case that without labor subsidies the 50 day plowing requirement might delay planting to an unacceptable degree, but the risks of late planting are not known with certainty. I take it from Helburn's (1955: 380) comments that 8 weeks, or 56 days, is some kind of an upper limit for time committed to plowing, which would place a limit on the area of land cultivated by small holders who only make use of household labor. Borrowing from White's calculations (1970: 181), the farm cultivating 5 ha would face at least 100 additional days of field work over the crop cycle for hoeing, weeding, and harvesting (not counting threshing and winnowing) out of an estimated production cycle of 240 days from October 1 through May.

Other crops would have been cultivated in addition to wheat. In the survey area this is not likely to have included wine production in significant quantities, judging from current practice in the survey area, where vines are rare. Rough Cilicia was not known for wine exports in the Roman Period (Broughton 1975: 609-10). Olives could be cultivated at the lower elevations of the survey area (as they were elsewhere on the lower slopes of Rough Cilicia [ibid.: 611]). Given that olives do not grow well above about 600 masl (ibid.: 611; cf. Mee et al. 1991: 225), one could conjecture that coast-based oil production could have supplied consumers in the adjacent uplands of the Taurus, and could have been a product exchanged for forest and animal products. Mitchell (1993: 257) indicates that olive oil was imported from coastal zones into Central Anatolia, but it is not clear whether this would include the survey area specifically. More likely, this is in reference to Pamphylia and its "extensive olive culture" (Mitchell 1993: 247). Olives might have been intercropped in grain fields as they are now in a few instances we noted on terraced hillside fields, however, the late fall harvest period for olives (e.g., Wagstaff and Gamble 1982: Fig. 10.7) would have interfered with fall plowing, perhaps limiting the potential for large-scale olive production. Kitchen gardens would have been another potential form of agricultural production, but, given that these are likely to have required irrigation (White 1970: 246), I doubt if they would have been of much importance to farm families living well up on high ridges with no access to irrigation water, as many were in the survey area. Vegetables could have been produced in irrigated plots in some localities, particularly in the alluvial plain near Selinus, but it is impossible to know how many families were involved in such specializations.

The environmental characteristics of city hinterlands are described in more detail in the next chapter, but here I introduce some elements of between-hinterland variation as

14

they pertain to potential agricultural productivity. For each hinterland, I measured the areas of three soil/slope categories: (1) alluvial, (2) moderate slopes with arable brown soils, and (3) slopes too steep to cultivate (although usable for animal grazing). In the absence of information on productivity by soil type, I assume an equal potential productivity for arable slopes and alluvium. Table 2-2 summarizes the total estimated area of each hinterland, the percentage of soil/slope categories, and the estimated carrying capacity based on the data summarized in Table 2-1, from which it is assumed that each person requires roughly one hectare of cultivated land.

Table 2-2. City hinterlands environmental characteristics and estimated carrying capacity.

	Area (ha)	% Alluvial	% Steep Slope	% Arable Sloping	Estimated Carrying Capacity
Iotape	2800	10	56	34	1200
Selinus	2275	82	8	10	2100
Cestrus	2285	31	30	39	1600
Nephelion	1800	8	32	60	1200
Antiochia	1125	2	41	57	650
				Total	6750

Chronology of Human Occupation of the Coast Lands of Western Rough Cilicia Compared With Other Regions

Although earlier periods of human settlement are known from adjacent regions, including Neolithic, Chalcolithic, and Bronze Age sites in Cilicia Pedias (Seton-Williams 1954), the survey area does not appear to have been settled until the Iron Age. The earliest diagnostic pottery we found in our surface collections consists of four sherds of Classical Black Glaze (500 to 333 BCE) at Selinus and one at Nephelion (see Appendix 2 for the ceramic tabulations). Following this probable initial period of occupation, there was population growth continuously from Hellenistic through Late Roman Periods. I wondered how unusual it might be for a regional sequence to be missing several major chronological periods, and turned to my comparative data to answer the question. Between survey areas, the density of sites of various periods is highly variant, although every survey included in my sample has at least some Roman sites. Other periods, however, may not be represented, suggesting a more patchy population distribution prior to the Roman Period (Tables 2-3 and 2-4). This is in spite of the fact that some earlier periods (Middle and Late Bronze, and Archaic to Hellenistic) have comparatively high mean density values for all the survey areas considered together (Table 2-3).

The nature of patchiness of settlement distribution can be clarified somewhat by grouping survey areas by what I call sectors. This method gives a preliminarily view of macroregional variation for those areas of the Mediterranean where systematic surveys have been completed. For this discussion, I identified four sectors comprised of 1) east (coast lands of Rough Cilicia and Cyprus); 2) Crete; 3) Greece and the Aegean; and 4) west (Italy and Spain)(Table 2-5). Grouping the survey data in this way is made problematic by the relative concentration of recent, methodologically sophisticated all-period settlement pattern projects primarily in Greece, the Aegean and Crete. Hence this exercise is of limited validity for comparative analyses, but nonetheless is suggestive regarding macroregional factors that may have influenced site densities.

Figure 2-7 shows the mean and one standard deviation values for number of sites per square kilometer of surveyed area for all periods, by sector. The Neolithic displays a generally spotty distribution (cf. Cherry 1985: 18), but the central two sectors have comparatively higher site density values from the Neolithic through Geometric, while from the Archaic through the remainder of the sequence, somewhat less variation is found sector to sector (the east sector, based on only two surveys, has lower site densities even in peak periods). Crete, and Greece and the Aegean, as expected, show substantial increases in site densities during those periods corresponding to the growth of Bronze Age Minoan-Mycenean civilization (Renfrew 1972). The site density data suggest that this system was strongly localized in Crete, Greece, and immediately adjoining areas, roughly corresponding to the comparatively higher density distribution of Bronze Age tholos tombs (Renfrew, ibid.: Figure 4.2), and did not strongly transform the social systems of my east and west sectors, at least insofar as this is evident from site density data. This need not imply that the east and west sectors were not in some ways tied in to the Bronze Age systems. For example, Cyprus was a significant source of copper by the Late Bronze Age (Keswani 1993). Rather, the data suggest that a Neolithic-

Table 2-3. Descriptive statistics for numbers of sites by period for the coded survey areas.

	neo/km2	EB/km2	MB/km2	LB/km2	Geo/km2	Arc/km2	CL/km2	HLN...	ER/...	LR/...
Mean	.073	.181	.321	.300	.124	.434	.523	.762	.688	.465
Std. Dev.	.118	.235	.636	.478	.178	.419	.665	.878	.655	.443
Std. Error	.028	.057	.159	.120	.042	.099	.157	.207	.159	.111
Count	18	17	16	16	18	18	18	18	17	16
Minimum	0.000	0.000	0.000	0.000	0.000	0.000	0.000	0.000	.030	.005
Maximum	.409	.727	2.524	1.429	.571	1.611	2.222	2.500	2.273	1.295
# Missing	1	2	3	3	1	1	1	1	2	3

Table 2-4. Survey areas with no sites (indicated by '0'), by period. Blanks indicate sites present or no data.

	Neo	EB	MB	LB	Geo	Arc	CL	HLN	ER	LR
Caperas	0	0	0							
Sutri	0	0	0	0	0					
Faliscus	0	0								
Veientanus	0									
Guadalquivir										
Cosanus	0	0	0	0	0		0			
Rieti	0									
Melos			0	0	0					
Lasithi										
Kavousi							0	0		
W Mesara										
Vrokastro										
S Euboea				0						
Ayiofarango	0				0	0				
N Keos										
S Argolid	0									
Pylos	0									
Palaipaphos	0	0								
W C R Cilicia	0	0	0	0	0	0	0			

Table 2-5. Survey areas grouped by sector.

West   Ager Capenas, Sutri, Ager Faliscus, Ager Veientanus, Lower

            Guadalquivir, Ager Cosanus, Rieti Basin

Greece and the Aegean   Melos, Southern Euboea, N. Keos, S.   Argolid, Pylos

Crete   Lasithi Plain, Kavousi, W. Mesara, Vrokastro, Ayiofarango Valley

East   Palaipaphos, Coast Lands of W Rough Cilicia

like patchiness in settlement distributions persisted in marginal areas well beyond the Neolithic.

A subsequent major cycle of   sociocultural evolutionary change, evident from increasing site densities, followed the Geometric Period in Greece and the Aegean (Bintliff 1997: Figure 6), but is also evident in a parallel but less-pronounced growth phase in Crete (Figure 2-7). This second growth cycle can be linked to rapidly increasing site numbers as far afield as my west sector, particularly in Italy (Potter 1979: Chapter 4). While settlement density of my east sector remained low, and was patchy, following the Geometric Period, it is the case that the survey collections from the coast lands of Rough Cilicia found a few sherds attributable to the Classic Period. Clearly the second major cycle of sociocultural evolutionary change following the Geometric Period took place in a larger arena than had the first, but still did not substantially reorganize all the sectors.

In Figure 2-7, all sectors show increased mean values for site densities during and after the Hellenistic Period, reflecting the vastly increased scale and degree of integration of political, commercial, and cultural systems that developed beginning in the 4th century BCE (Rostovtzeff 1941). However, the persistent large standard deviations of site densities even into the Hellenistic and Roman Periods indicate a continuation of between-region differences in site densities. Variance in these later periods is due in part to low densities in scattered cases (e.g., the coast lands of Rough Cilicia in the Hellenistic Period, and in Early Roman Lasithi), but is also due to exceptionally high densities--among the highest values in the whole sample--in others, for example Rieti and W. Mesara for both Hellenistic and Early Roman (Appendix 3). However, the likelihood of finding whole periods missing in a regional sequence is greater for the periods prior to Hellenistic, and greater in the earlier periods in the East and West sectors that were distant from the emerging Bronze Age and Early Iron Age civilizations of Crete, Greece, and the Aegean. The coast lands of western Rough Cilicia can be included in the list of areas marginal to the major foci of pre-Hellenistic sociocultural and demographic change.

An Uncertain Political and Military Environment

The survey area is in the western coastal portion of Rough Cilicia (also called Cilicia Aspera or Cilicia Tracheia)(Figure 2-6). The vast and agriculturally productive alluvial plain of Cilicia Pedias (or Campestris) bounds Rough Cilicia on the east (Figures 2-1, 2-6). By contrast, Rough Cilicia is a rugged mountainous zone, some 217 kms (EW) by 117 kms (NS), dominated topographically by the Taurus range, that separates a coastal fringe from highland Anatolia. The abrupt descent from the heights of the Taurus to the coast leaves little in the way of flat alluvial land suitable for agricultural development, and the rugged ridges and deep canyons dominating the Rough Cilician landscape inhibit human interaction from coast to the highlands, as well as along the coast (cf. Magie 1975: 266-8), although the Roman Empire did eventually build and maintain a minor coastal road (Magie 1975: 270). As is evident from Figure 2-2, Rough Cilicia is far removed from the major terrestrial routes and trade centers of Roman Period (and earlier) Anatolia. The major route from Syria to the Anatolian highlands was through Cilicia Pedias and the Cilician Gates north of Tarsus (Figure 2-2), far to the east of the survey area. To the west, minor coastal-inland routes extended from Side and from the vicinity of Antalya in the Pamphylian Plain, leaving Cilicia Tracheia without significant connections from the sea to the north. Sea routes, on the other hand, were important to coastal residents. The major sea-route from Greece and Rome to Syria and Egypt skirted the Cilician coast (Broughton 1975: 857; Rostovtzeff 1941: 228-9).

Rough Cilicia's paucity of land routes was a significant factor explaining the comparative lack of development of complex social institutions by local upland populations and the patchy distribution of various autonomous or semiautonomous tribal peoples named, variously, Pisidians, Homanadeis, Lyconians, Kennatai, Qodi, Que, Hue, Hume, Hiluku, and Cietae (or Cetae, the Egyptian Kedi)(Shaw 1990). Shaw (ibid.) refers to upland Rough Cilicia as Isauria, while its dominant language was Luwian. The Assyrian, Persian, Egyptian, Hellenistic, Roman, and Byzantine states that attempted to establish hegemony here regarded Rough Cilicia, particularly the inland Isauria, as a backward area of primitive, contentious, and dangerous tribal peoples (e.g. Jones 1971: 212; Levick 1967: 16, 17; Shaw 1990) that represented a persistent knot of resistance to imperial control; Cilician revolts are recorded for AD 6, 36, 52, 354, 355, 367-8, 375, 403, and 469 (Hopwood 1986: 344). Some of these groups were thought to have been active in the piracy emanating from Rough Cilicia during the Late Hellenistic Period (Ormerod 1978: 193). Although the tribes resided deep in the mountains of Cilicia Tracheia, they could make life along the coast risky through their persistent raiding of the more Hellenized and Romanized coastal settlements (Hopwood 1986: 345).

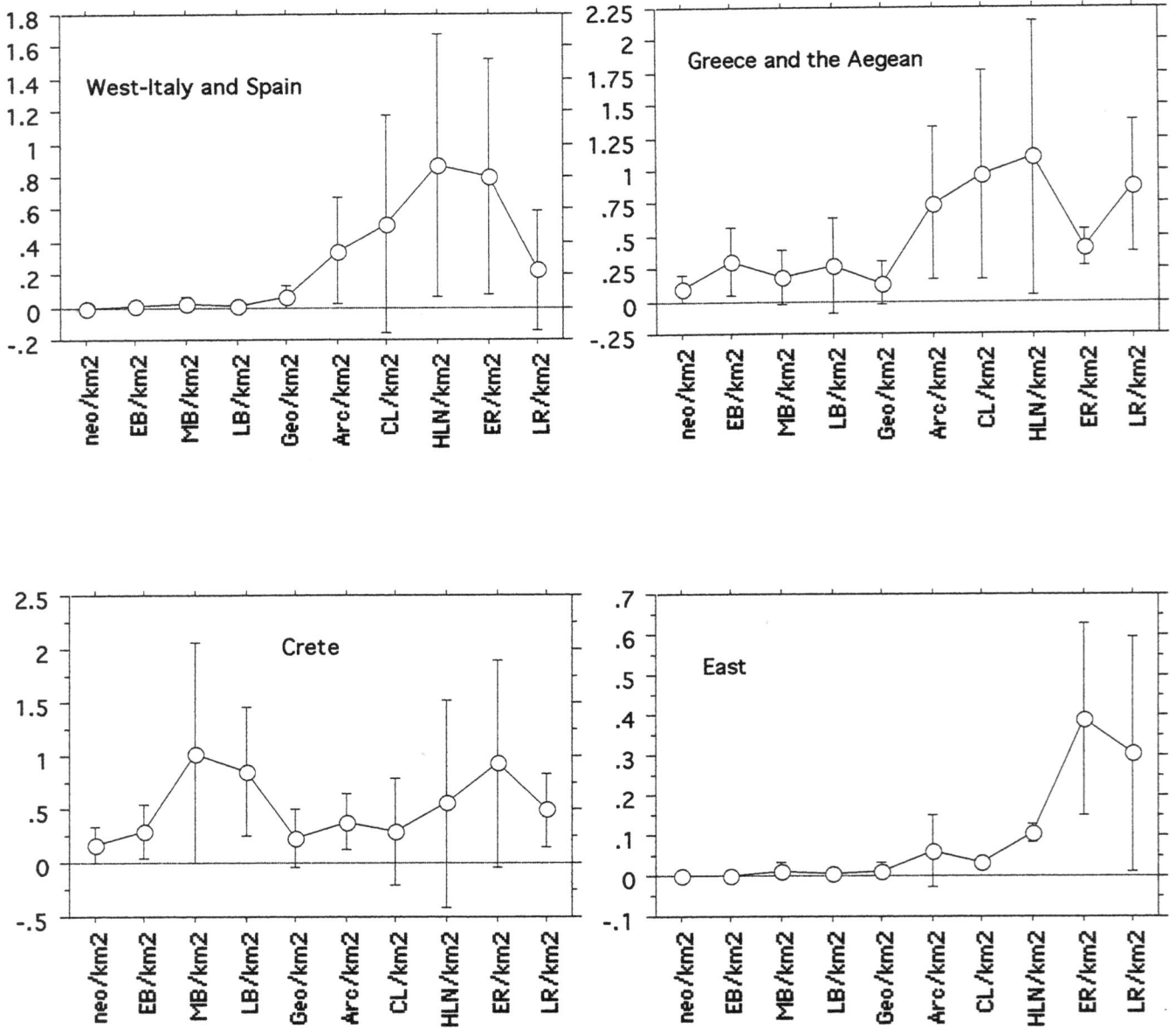

Figure 2-7. Mean number of sites per square kilometer of surveyed area by sectors (error bars=one standard deviation).

Major tribal wars against outside forces are recorded in 193 BCE, on two occasions in the first century AD, and later in the fourth century (Jones 1971: 211, 213; Levick 1967: 17).

Greek Colonies and the History of Imperial Involvement

Owing to the comparative lack of agricultural potential, and the dangers of tribal raiding, Greek colonizing of the coast of Rough Cilicia was meager by comparison with areas both to the east and west of it (Graham 1982: 92, 93; Levick 1967: 16; Magie 1975: 268; Shipley 1987: 41). What little there was extended primarily along a narrow coastal fringe. According to Jones (1971: 194), Selinus, a site within the survey area, may have a Greek origin, although the chronology of Greek migration is not clear from historical records. Judging from inscriptions of the

Roman Period, few Greeks lived within the survey area. Local names (or names that are unrecognizable) make up some 80% of names on inscriptions, based on my count from those published by Bean and Mitford (1962: 206-7, 211-16; 1965: 24-9, 34-42; 1970: 149-70, 184-86; cf. Karamut and Russell 1999: 369-70). These names indicate a largely Luwian cultural ancestry for coastal residents, while at the same time they adopted many Hellenistic and Roman cultural elements (Hopwood 1986: 345), as indicated, for example, by the coins minted in the area under the rulership of Antiochus IV of Commagene (AD 38-74), and again in the Imperial Period from Trajan to Philip (Head 1911: 728). Greek was the predominant language for inscriptions, even during the Roman Empire. Only two Latin inscriptions are recorded from the survey area (Bean and Mitford 1970: 155), one a funerary monument at Selinus, the other a milestone at Antiochia.

The earliest historical record of a settlement in the survey area pertains to Selinus, which is mentioned in the Periplus of Scylax, done for Darius I in the late fourth century BCE (Jones 1971: 197). Selinus is recorded as having had a Ptolemaic garrison in 197 BCE (ibid.: 198), reflecting Egyptian interest in the local forest resources, and the region may have been a source of mercenaries serving the Ptolemies (ibid.: 198). Seleucid power was reinstated by Antiochus III in 197 BCE, and Selinus is one of the localities recorded as having been taken by Antiochus III from Ptolemy V (Bagnall 1976: 115). After the death of Antiochus IV, Seleucid royal power was weakened and a period of civil wars ensued. Beginning during this period of weak state control of Rough Cilicia, about the middle of the second century BCE, piracy became a prominent feature of the social scene in Cilicia and adjacent coastal regions, although no pirate bases or communities are definitely known to have been located within the survey area itself. The nearest well-documented pirate center is at Coracesium (modern Alanya), some 40 km west of Selinus, and even further west, another is known at Side (Bean and Mitford 1965: 22; Levick 1967:20; Ormerod 1978: 203, 205).

The Romans attempted to exercise control of piracy in a newly-formed "Province of Cilicia" but their efforts seemed to emphasize areas more to the west of Rough Cilicia (including Lycia, the Milyas, Phrygia, Pisidia, and Pamphylia)(Jones 1971: 201). After 67 BCE, Pompey was given extraordinary powers to deal with the pirates and after their defeat he made Cilicia a Roman province (ibid.: 202), although his specific organizational strategy in Cilicia Tracheia is unknown (ibid.). After the reorganization, the western portion of Cilicia became a separate principality that included most of Tracheia, and Antiochus IV of Commagene the most significant and active ruler. In the survey area, he founded Antiochia, and named Claudiopolis at Ninica (very likely Nephelion) and Iotape (Jones 1971: 211). During this period, from AD 38-74, Selinus issued coins (Head 1911: 728). Under Vespasian, the principality was divided into districts of the province of Cilicia, in which Selinus was made the chief town of the Selinitis district (Bean and Mitford 1962: 209; Jones 1971: 208, 210). From the reigns of Trajan to Philippus, Selinus again issued coins (Rosenbaum 1967a: viii), as did other cities within the survey region, detailed below.

Chronological Summary

The ceramic tabulations from our 85 surface collections are found in Appendix 2. The periods represented in these collections span Classical to Byzantine, with strong peaks in Early and Late Roman. Table 2-6 summarizes the chronological scheme used below in the site descriptions and data analyses. Dates for the Classical and Hellenistic Periods are based on diagnostic pottery (Appendix 2). The end date for Hellenistic (66 BCE) corresponds to Pompey's establishment of a Roman province. Consistently, evidence from public architecture (Huber 1967), tombs (Rosenbaum 1967b), and inscriptions (Bean and Mitford 1962, 1965, 1970), indicate a period of rapid sociocultural change from the first to third centuries AD (summarized by site, below), hence the end date for Early Roman used here of about AD 250. Karamut and Russell (1999: 370-1) suggest the area may have suffered decline from the mid third century onward, after the Persians advanced against the Romans as far as Antiochia and Selinus. Below I evaluate this suggestion, but clearly conditions had changed after about AD 250, hence our identification of a Late Roman Period lasting from about AD 250 to about AD 700, the latter date derived from well-dated diagnostic pottery types (Appendix 2), as is Early and Late Byzantine. Due to a paucity of suitable diagnostics in our surface collections, it was not possible to subdivide sites by Early and Late Byzantine.

Table 2-6. Chronology of the survey area.

Late Byzantine (LBYZ)	AD 970 to 1071
Early Byzantine (EBYZ)	AD 700 to 969
Late Roman (LR)	AD 250 to AD 699
Early Roman (ER)	65 BCE to AD 249
Hellenistic (HLN)	332 BCE to 66 BCE
Classical (CL)	500 BCE to 333 BCE

Chapter 3

Descriptions of City Hinterlands and Their Sites

Iotape Hinterland

The grid square maps we had available for the survey of Iotape and its hinterland include 28-a-20-b, 28-a-20-c, and 28-b-16-d (Figures 3-1, 3-2, 3-3). The hinterland area (with an approximate radius of 4 km) was estimated by drawing a boundary line half-way between Iotape and Selinus (Figure 2-5); this same distance was used to estimate its northern boundary. No major site is found along the coast to the north and west of Iotape any closer than Syedra, which is located at a distance of 16 kms (Fig. 2-6). Under the Empire, the Roman administrative boundary between Cilicia Tracheia and Pamphylia was located somewhere between Syedra and Iotape (Bean and Mitford 1962: 196), but it is not clear how important this boundary would have been to the local polity and economy of Iotape. In Figure 2-5, Iotape's hinterland boundary towards the Taurus is shown at approximately the base of the first high ridge that reaches a much higher elevation than the coastal range, but it is not known how far Iotape's hinterland might have extended. Bean and Mitford (1970: 107-8) found no significant sites in the hills behind Iotape, which to them would have been sites with inscriptions. Our map grids did not extend all the way to the proposed hinterland boundary, so we did not survey some portions of the designated area. Given the fact that there is one village in the survey area on a ridge above Iotape, it is possible more could be found further inland.

Overall, this hinterland offers few opportunities for agricultural production, particularly in terms of the kind of arable soils suitable for grain production. The major topographic feature is a steep and rugged slope rising directly from the water's edge to a high ridge line some 2 kms north and east of Iotape, that reaches over 400 masl in some places. Directly to the north of this ridge is a small elevated plain, beyond which an even higher and densely forested mountain range is found, beyond the estimated north and east boundaries of the hinterland. One of the advantages of Iotape's location compared with the other surveyed hinterlands is its comparatively easy access to the dense forests of these higher ridges. The other coastal ridges in the survey area are separated from the higher elevations to the north and east by an intervening alluvial plain or low-lying valley, but Iotape has direct access by way of the elevated plain behind the first ridge. A pass through the ridge behind Iotape has evidence of a fortification wall of some sort (described below), perhaps indicating the importance of regulating traffic between the higher elevations and the Iotape site.

The higher elevations of the first ridge line immediately north of Iotape feature a dense forest of oak and pine, with some grassy areas, but few agricultural fields presently (Plate 3-1). On the lower slopes, closer to the coastal highway, scattered farms can be found whose residents cultivate primarily wheat, vegetables, and fruit, particularly irrigated bananas on terraced fields. The small-scale drip irrigation systems feeding the latter fields derive small quantities of water from springs higher up on the ridge line, transported in plastic and metal pipes to holding tanks. Overall, however, water for irrigation is in short supply throughout this whole hinterland. Given the steepness of the slopes, numerous agricultural terraces have been constructed in this area, but most appear quite recent, in fact, many are currently in use. None of the terraces could be definitely associated with the periods of occupation of Iotape, and only a very sparse off-site sherd scatter was noted around Iotape or the other sites in its hinterland; the few localities with evidence of human activity away from the district's residential sites are described below.

Of the approximately 2800 ha of primarily rugged terrain making up this hinterland, only 10% is alluvial soil, found in a small patch over 3 km south and east of Iotape, north of the flood plain of the Delice River (Figure 2-3). Another 56% of the area is steep slope, while the remaining 34% is moderately sloping arable soils, particularly along the ridge line just north of Iotape, as well as in a region of shallow slopes on the opposite side of this ridge, away from Iotape, and measuring 3 km or more from the city. The closest patch of arable soil near Iotape is along the top of the first high ridge line, but I estimate that this entire area (and more) would have been cultivated by residents of a village located at the top of the ridge. Given this, and the fact that the nearest alluvial soil is over 3 kms from Iotape, it is doubtful whether the city's population would have had any access to highly productive land for grain agriculture. And, given the area's (evident) lack of an extensive ancient terrace system, it is unlikely that the population of Iotape was self-sufficient in terms of food. However, forest product export could have been an important economic activity.

Site Descriptions

28-a-20-b-1 (ER-1, LR-1)

This site is located where a rugged ridge line north and east of Iotape takes the form of a small peak, at 375 masl (Plates 3-1 and 3-2). Vegetation in this area is oak, pine, weeds, and grass, with modern agricultural fields noted primarily 100 m or more lower than the site. Near its summit, the ridge line has some relatively gentle slopes that are potentially arable, but bedrock outcrops are found in places all along it. The site's location at a high point of the ridge appears to have been chosen with defense in mind. A wall fragment at the site's northern edge may have had a defensive function or served simply as a terrace wall.

The central part of the site has abundant remains of houses built of substantial but roughly dressed stone (Plate 3-3)(no obvious non-residential construction was noted); in the field I estimated a total of 30 houses, and possibly 20 more in the area of a halo of sherds that extends some 25 to 75 m beyond the area of stone construction (however, the latter area might have been simply a zone of discarded

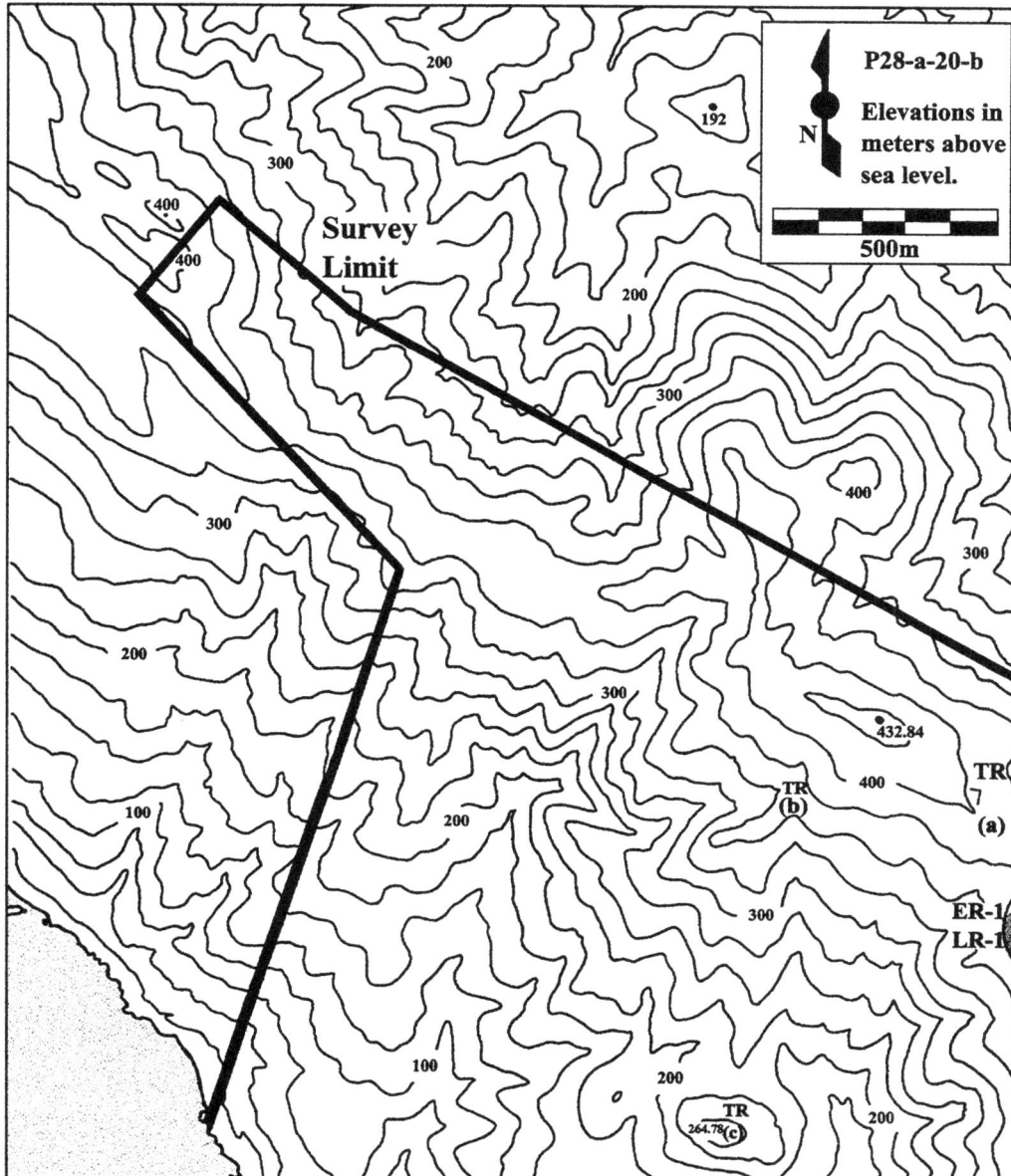

Figure 3-1. 28-a-20-b.

pottery along the edges of the residential area). The site is located in part off the map, and so its surface area was determined through pacing, although this was not a straightforward methodology as I was impeded by the site's rugged setting, the abundant stone remains of houses, and the generally dense vegetation. The total site area, estimated at .92 ha, would imply a population of about 115 (or 23 households)(site data, including population estimates, are tabulated in Appendix 1). Population estimates are made from site area using two conversion values widely used in Mediterranean survey archaeology (Cherry et al., eds. 1991: 280; Jameson, Runnels, and van Andel 1994: 542-50). For hamlets and villages, the conversion value is 125/ha, while for urban settlements it is 210/ha.

Off site pottery was noted in several localities near the site (marked as a, b, and c in Figure 3-1). At location (a), in addition to a trace of pottery, we noted the fragmentary remains of a stone wall. Location (a) faces a pass leading to a broad plain of moderate sloping terrain north and east of the ridge line on which the site is located (beyond our map coverage). Given the shortage of gently sloping land I

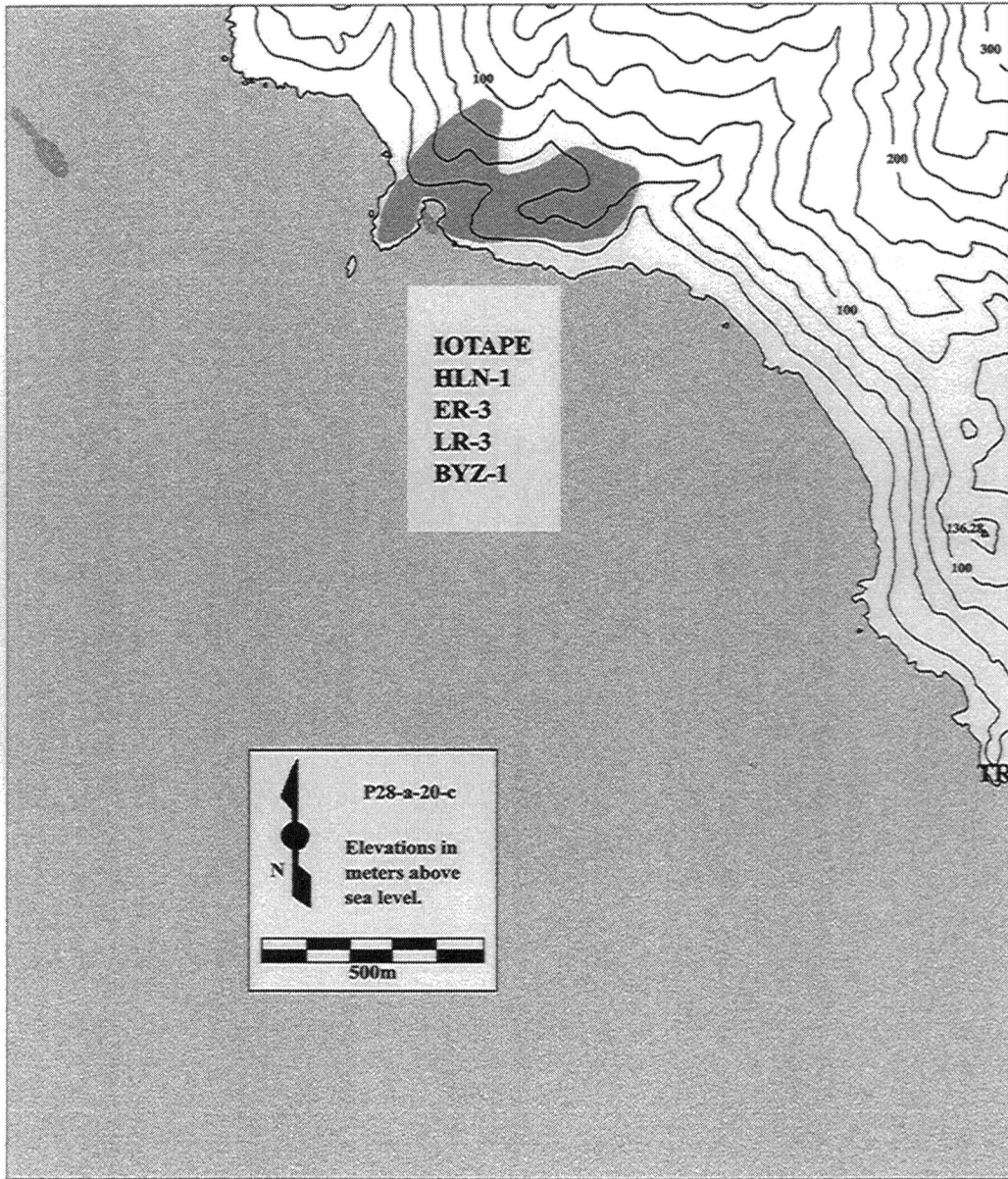

IOTAPE
HLN-1
ER-3
LR-3
BYZ-1

P28-a-20-c

Elevations in
meters above
sea level.

N

500m

Figure 3-2. 28-a-20-c.

estimate this would have been part of the area cultivated by the site's population (even though the minimum distance from the site to this area is over 2 km), as well as serving as a route connecting this hinterland to the higher forested slopes. Perhaps the wall served a defensive or traffic regulating function. At location (b) we noted the remains of a 4 by 5 m mortar and rubble structure on a narrow ridge at about 350 masl; very little pottery was noted around this structure. Location (c) was simply a scatter of non-diagnostic sherds near the summit of a small peak overlooking Iotape.

The whole surface of 28-a-20-b-1 was collected. Early Roman is present (ceramic tabulations are found in Appendix 2). Late Roman is possibly indicated by 1 Aegean Transport Amphora, and one of the sherds collected from location (a) just to the north and east of the site is a Wheel Ridged Amphora, and 6 Cypriot Red Ware sherds may be ER or LR. Besides pottery, few artifacts were noted; no millstones were observed, and roof tiles were comparatively infrequent.

28-b-16-d-1 (ER-2, LR-2)

Located just 40 m from the beach dunes in an area of abundant sandy alluvial soil. No features were noted near

22

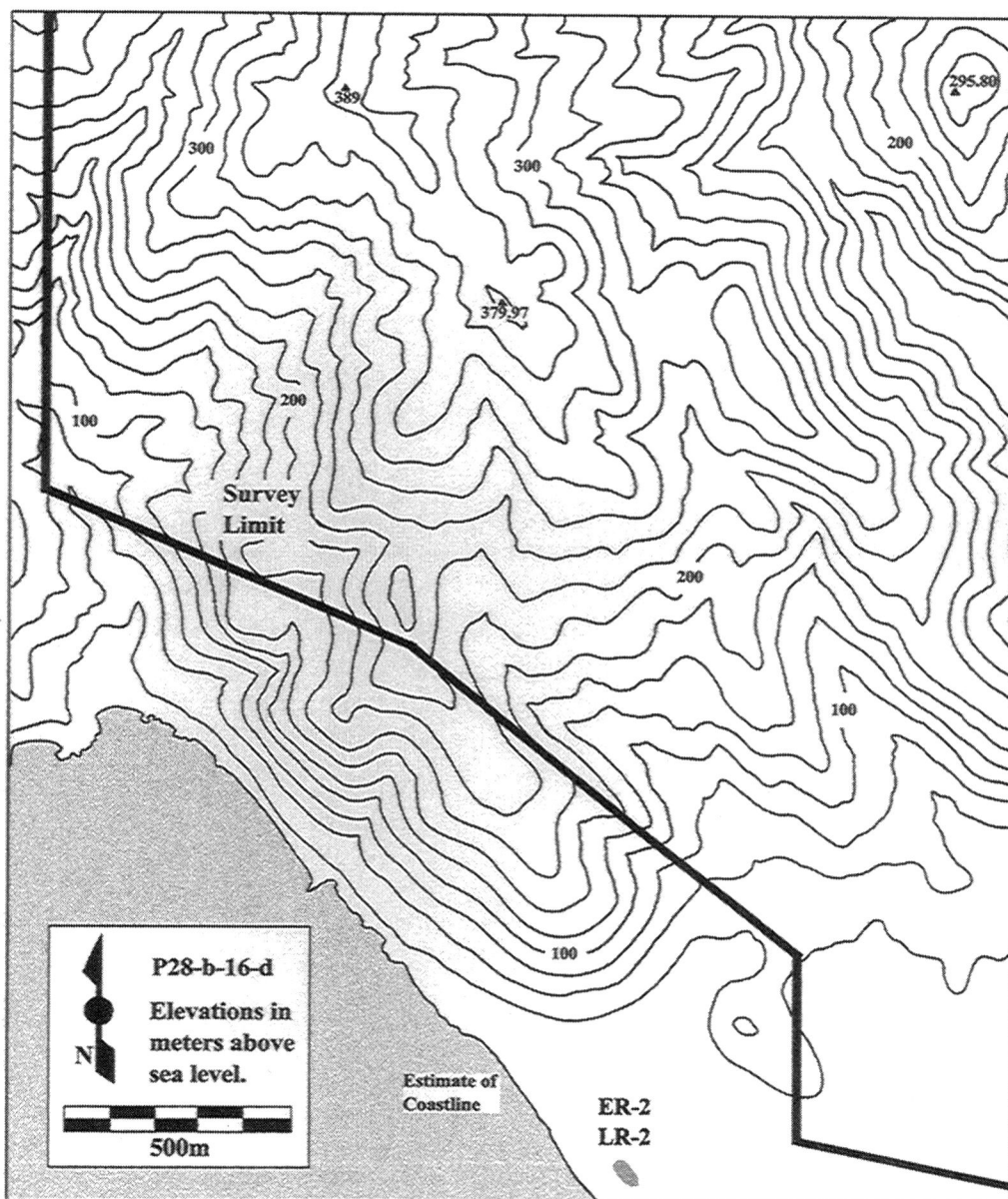

Figure 3-3. 28-b-16-d.

the adjacent beach, although a few off-site sherds can be seen. The site is an area of comparatively dense pottery measuring roughly 90 m N-S by 70 m E-W. The remains of a structure were found along the northeast edge of the site (Figure 3-4). Roof tiles were noted in the structure area and in other parts of the site, although no architectural evidence for additional residential structures was noted. The large size of the sherd scatter may imply a resident population living in more ephemeral structures outside the main structure. The area of the site, estimated to be .6 ha, would imply a population of 79, or 16 households; this number might be inflated if a substantial portion of the site

area had been devoted to facilities related to ceramic production, as we suspected while collecting the site. The latter inference is based on the presence of many sherds that are oddly colored, and perhaps were kiln wasters. One clear amphora waster was noted, and four pieces of clay slag were collected. These data suggest the presence of a firing operation of some kind, although no evidence of kilns could be seen on the surface. Five Late Roman Transport Amphora (and an additional 16 that could be ER or LR), as well as 7 local W. Cilicia Zemer 41 amphora, make up the bulk of the diagnostic sherds in the surface collection. The field crew inferred that the site was a villa (judging from the large structure) or hamlet with a specialized production/exchange function involving transport amphora and perhaps other ceramic production. This is the one locality within Iotape's hinterland providing access to clay soils suitable for ceramic manufacture. While the soils in the immediate vicinity of the site are quite sandy, clayey soils were noted within the surveyed area south of the site, in the alluvial zone between the Delice and Biçkiçi Rivers (Fig. 2-3).

While I included the site within the district of Iotape, it is of interest to note the site's approximate equal distance to Iotape (3.7 km) and Selinus (5 km), which would have provided commercial advantages for supplying ceramic products to both centers.

28-a-20-c-1 (HLN-1, ER-3, LR-3, BYZ-1) Iotape (Figure 3-5)

Iotape extends from the sea up along two ridges that join at a small inlet defined on its west edge by a rocky promontory rising some 30 masl (Plate 3-4). This promontory features a series of now fragmentary defensive walls (shown only impressionistically in Huber 1967: Plan 4), as well as a dense complex of residential and other structures that will be described in more detail in this project's architectural report. A formal avenue, lined with inscribed statue bases (Bean and Mitford 1965: 24-9, 1970: 149-53; Paribeni and Romanelli 1914: 174-83), is situated in a saddle between the promontory and a steep rise to the north and east, above which is found one of the community's main residential areas distributed along the top of a nearly north-south trending ridge (collection area 2 in Figure 3-5). Although it was difficult to determine the northern site boundary along this ridge with great accuracy (given the absence of suitable landmarks on the topographic maps), I was able to pace up slope to the limit of sherd scatter from a medieval church mapped by Huber (1967: Plan 4). The area of most dense sherd scatter and stone architecture extends for approximately 60 to 100 m north of the church (Blanton and Rauh 1997: Plan 2, based on the architectural recording of Rhys Townsend).

A large area of sherd scatter and stone architecture can be found also along a ridge trending east-west from the inlet, extending to a small valley to the east (Figure 3-5). Two farm houses, a series of outbuildings and numerous banana terraces obscure the summit of this ridge east of our collection area 3, as well as obscuring the slopes north of the ridge. The farm owner, although a gracious host when we called on him, gave us permission to inspect and to surface collect only those parts of the site closer to the main complex of public buildings, hence the clustering of our collection areas 1 through 4. The complex of tombs to the north of the east-west ridge (Rosenbaum 1967b: 58-65) is shown in my figure as outside the area of sherd scatter. However, the lack of surface pottery around what was the cemetery may be an artifact of the extensive terrace construction along these slopes that has obliterated nearly all traces of the tombs, and may have removed or obscured surface pottery as well. These same banana terraces have largely obscured an aqueduct that Huber describes coming into the site from the small valley to the east (Huber 1967: Plan 4).

Based on my limited inspection of the site along its easternmost boundary, I infer that the eastern extension dates primarily to the Early and Late Roman periods, with possible occupation as late as the Byzantine Period, based in part on the construction and dates of the cemetery. According to Rosenbaum (1967b: 62, 66), while one earlier tomb in this area may date to the first century AD, the great majority of tombs were constructed in the second and no later than the third century, although the cemetery may have been in use into the Byzantine Period. A chapel in this eastern area of the site is Byzantine in date (ibid: 66).

The extensive modern occupation and use of the site, coupled with the restrictions on surface collection, make it difficult to estimate site size by period. Based on the presence of both Early and Late Roman pottery in collection areas 1 through 4, and (limited) inspection of sherds in the eastern end of the site, I propose that the site's maximum limits pertain to the Early and Late Roman Periods. This conclusion is supported by other data. Iotape was named by Antiochus IV of Commagene after he was granted the principality of Cilicia Tracheia in AD 38 (Jones 1971: 211). His benefaction may have produced an increased regional importance for the community; for example, after this time it issued coins (as well as during the empire, from Trajan to Valerian [Head 1911: 721]). From their analysis of inscriptions, Bean and Mitford (1970: 150) conclude that the community flourished during the reign of Trajan (in his last years), and did well also under Hadrian and the Antonines. A large bath structure in collection area 1 incorporates a lintel referring to the emperor Trajan, dating to AD 115, perhaps acknowledging his generosity during a visit to the site in approximately AD 114 (Bean and Mitford 1965: 29). And the study of the public architecture indicates that the Early Roman period was a time of substantial architectural elaboration of the site (Huber 1967: 38-41, 61-2, 66, 77), although major buildings were probably continuously in use from that time into the Byzantine Period (Onurkan 1967: 85).

The maximum extent of the site from the study of sherd scatter is estimated at 10.4 ha, implying a population for the Early and Late Roman Periods of between 1300 (at 125 per ha) and 2,184 (at 210 per ha). I use the larger of the two estimates to remain consistent with the accepted density for towns and cities used elsewhere in Eastern Mediterranean survey archaeology. Rhys Townsend's detailed recording of surface architectural remains should provide additional insights regarding the probable density of settlement. The Byzantine Period is represented by only 10 fine ware sherds from the four collections. Given the occurrence of these sherds in collection areas 1 and 4, and given the church construction dating to this period on the eastern ridge, I infer a maximum extent of the site from the area of public buildings east along the ridge, for a total of 7.5 ha (or 1575 persons), but this estimate must be regarded as highly provisional.

The role of Antiochus IV is evident in the history of the community between AD 38, when this part of the Cilician dominion was granted to him, and AD 72, when Vespasian reorganized this area from principality to Roman province (Jones 1971: 208). However, the presence of Hellenistic pottery in our surface collections testifies to the presence of a small community prior to AD 38 (Rosenbaum [1967b: 61-2] also identifies a probable Hellenistic Period tomb). Hellenistic pottery was found in collection areas 1, 2, and 4, suggesting a community smaller than the Roman Period, clustered primarily around and north of the inlet. I estimate a minimum extent of Hellenistic pottery of 4.5 ha, giving a population estimate of 945, or 189 households. However, the extensive masking of the earlier period by the extensive Roman Period remains leaves this estimate in considerable doubt.

Earlier, I commented on the paucity of agricultural resources within the district of Iotape. This would have been particularly acute for the population of the center itself, since what little arable land is available was probably being cultivated by residents of smaller communities in its hinterland. And these two rural communities could not have provided anywhere close to the grain requirements of the center, even if we assume they were cultivating close to the maximum surplus possible (i.e., 2 ha per person). At this level of surplus production, the rural population we located in Iotape's hinterland could have supported approximately 200 persons, or approximately 10% of the maximum population of the center. Of course, other rural communities beyond the survey limit might have been tied into the economy of Iotape, but even so the potential for surplus production in this hinterland is seriously limited.

Another element of the local Iotape economy was specialized production of olive oil. A *mortarium* (stone cup) section of an olive crushing *trapete* (cf. Drachmann 1932: Fig. 1) now sits adjacent to the modern highway (Plate 3-5 and 3-6). Its size (with a diameter of slightly more than 1 m) is similar to examples described in Drachmann (ibid.: pp. 11-17, Table 1) that are clearly intended for commercial or other large-scale production uses.

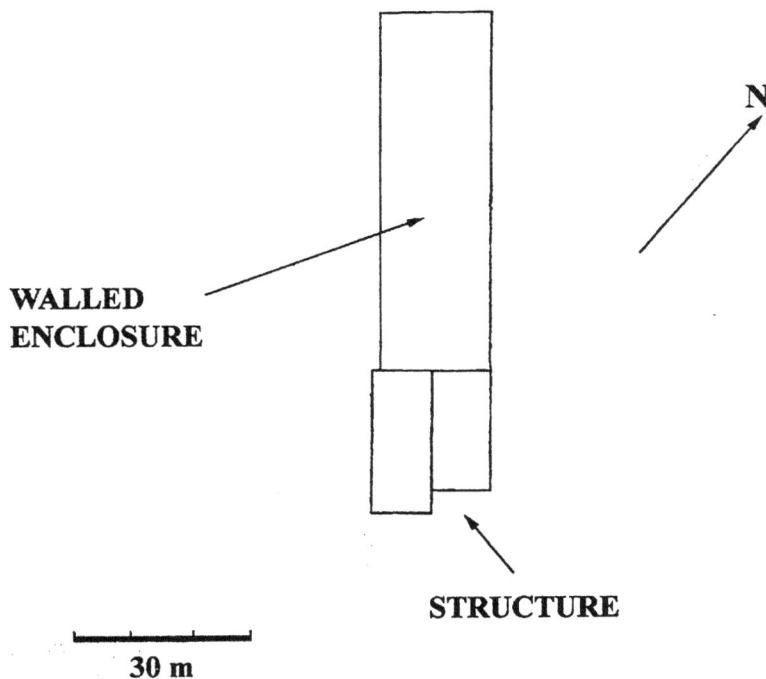

Figure 3-4. Sketch of a structure at 28-b-16-d-1 (ER-2, LR-2).

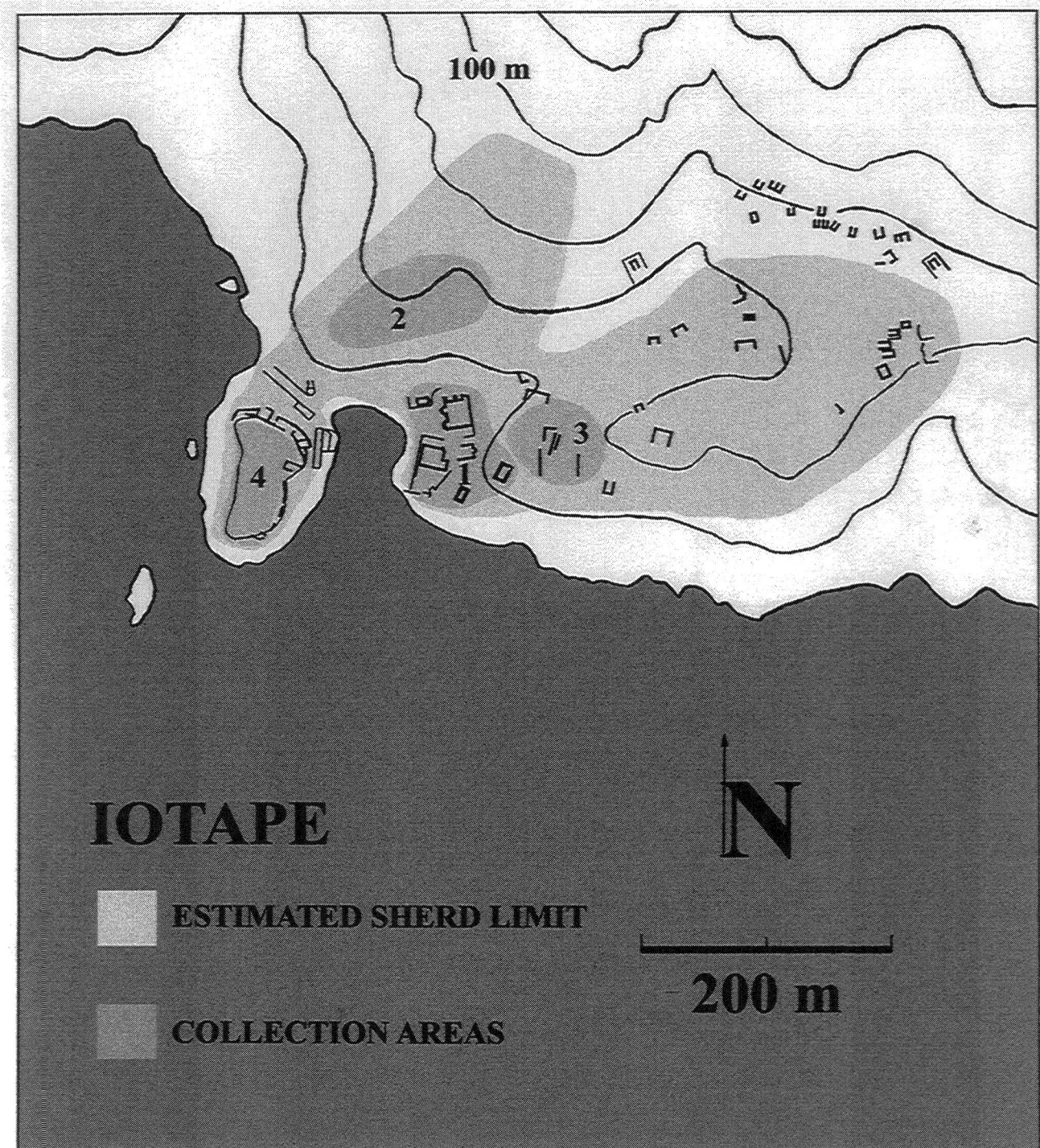

Figure 3-5. Iotape, showing sherd limits, collection areas (numbered) and approximate locations of public buildings (the latter from Huber 1967: 35-44, Plan 4).

Selinus Hinterland

The hinterland of Selinus includes the area in and near the modern town of Gazipasa, and includes grid squares 28-b-21-b, 28-b-21-c, and 28-c-01-b (Figures 3-6, 3-7, 3-8). It includes all or parts of the alluvial zones of three rivers, which are, from north to south, the Delice, the Biçkiçi, and, passing by the main site, the Haçimusa (Figure 2-3). In contrast with the other city hinterlands, that of Selinus consists almost entirely of alluvial plain (making up 82% of the 2300 ha area), with steep slopes accounting for 8%, and 10% consisting of cultivable but sloping terrain (Plates 3-7, 3-8, 3-9). The small Koças massif (maximum elevation 194 masl) divides the area into a northern alluvial zone of the Delice and Biçkiçi Rivers, and a southern zone of the Haçimusa River and the coastal plain south of the river. The site of Selinus is located on and at the base of a smaller but steeply sloped rise, interrupting the otherwise flat terrain, that reaches a maximum elevation of just over 150 masl.

While the Selinus hinterland includes a larger proportion of alluvium than others in the survey area, not all of this generally flat terrain is equally valuable for agricultural use. The areas shown in pale gray in the figures indicate the extent of the river floodplains, which are not cultivated. In areas directly adjacent to the floodplains, and adjacent to the beach line, soils are sandy and poor in nutrients. Further away from the floodplains and beaches, soils become more clayey and darker in color, but poor drainage can be a problem for agricultural use. Systems of recent drainage canals were noted in the area between the Delice and Biçkiçi Rivers, in the area west of the the Koças massif (just south of the Biçkiçi River), and in the plain north of the Haçimusa River. The process of drainage of swampy lowland is ongoing; some areas of the alluvium north of the Biçkiçi River were described in the field notebooks as "swampy and almost impassable" (cf. Heberdey and Wilhelm 1896: 149). Another area that is swampy and densely vegetated is found across the Haçimusa River from the Selinus site. Drainage has probably always been an obstacle to the agricultural use of the Selinus hinterland's alluvial soils.

Contemporary agricultural use of this alluvial zone is quite dense, and emphasizes irrigated vegetables (mostly drawing water from shallow wells or from the drainage canals), some in greenhouses, and wheat production is found in better-drained fields. The moderate to steep slopes of the Koças massif and the Selinus hill are used to a minor degree for herding animals, but over-grazing has left these mountain zones so choked with spiny weeds and brush that grazing potential is limited. Systems of terracing, not now in use, were noted on the lower ocean-facing slopes of the Koças massif, but these could not be dated with certainty. One system of terraces, Feature 2 of site ER-6 and LR-6, does seem to have been built and used in association with the occupation of the site (described below).

Site Descriptions

28-b-21-b-1 (ER-4, LR-4)

This is a small patch of sherds of less than 1 ha scattered along a piedmont ridge adjacent to a gully. The irrigation of olive and fruit trees in the site area is based on water pumped from the Gazipasa water system, but a drainage canal in the adjoining alluvium to the east is also a source of water. A light scatter of sherds and one roof tile were noted. Surface collection was problematic due to recent terrace, road, and house construction. The collection contained two probable ER or LR coarse wares and 2 Zemer 41 transport amphora.

28-b-21-b-2 (ER-5, LR-5)

A .2 ha sherd scatter in an area of terraced wheat fields and houses whose surface area was difficult to estimate owing to recent domestic construction. The site is situated in gently sloping piedmont, grading into alluvium within about 200 m to the west and south. ER possible, from 2 ER/LR transport amphora sherds, one micaceous water jar, and a West Cilicia Zemer 41 that may be ER. LR is well represented.

28-b-21-b-3 [collection area 1] and -5 [collection area 2] (ER-6, LR-6)

The site is situated along a N-S trending ridge line of the Koças massif. The main part of the site (28-b-21-b-5) occupies an area where the ridge flattens out at about 100 m elevation (collection area 2), covering an estimated 2.6 ha. The ridge spine north of the main settlement is covered with a light scatter of sherds, culminating in a denser patch just above the 25 m contour line (28-b-21-b-3, collection area 1). This smaller patch covers an area of .2 ha. At approximately 150 m down slope from the main settlement, and roughly midway between the two sherd concentrations, there is a large flat circular feature now behind a high fence and mostly covered by a radio transmission station (Feature 1). From outside the fence, the feature appears to be a grain threshing floor. On the comparatively steep slope north and west from the main part of the site, there is a large, well-preserved system of stone-faced terraces covering an area estimated to be at least 2 ha (the lower courses of the terrace system have been damaged by recent house construction)(Feature 2). The total area of the site, including the terrace complex and the off-site sherd scatter between collection areas 1 and 2, is 6 ha.

A continuous scatter of sherds between collection area 2 and the terraces suggests they might have been built and used during the occupational history of the site. Given the steepness of the slope here, these are narrow terraces (3-5 m wide) that may have supported olive production. A large (1.16 m diameter) circular olive press bed, with channel, was noted in the main part of the site, atop a small elevation dominating the site, and adjacent to a complex of 4 structures (now nearly destroyed), the largest measuring roughly 13 m N-S by 10 m E-W, with walls .65 to .8 m thick. A partial threshold block was found in this complex. Evidence of firing, perhaps a kiln, was noted in a recent road cut near the north edge of collection area 2. One loom weight was noted.

The main settlement area has a dense cover of thorny

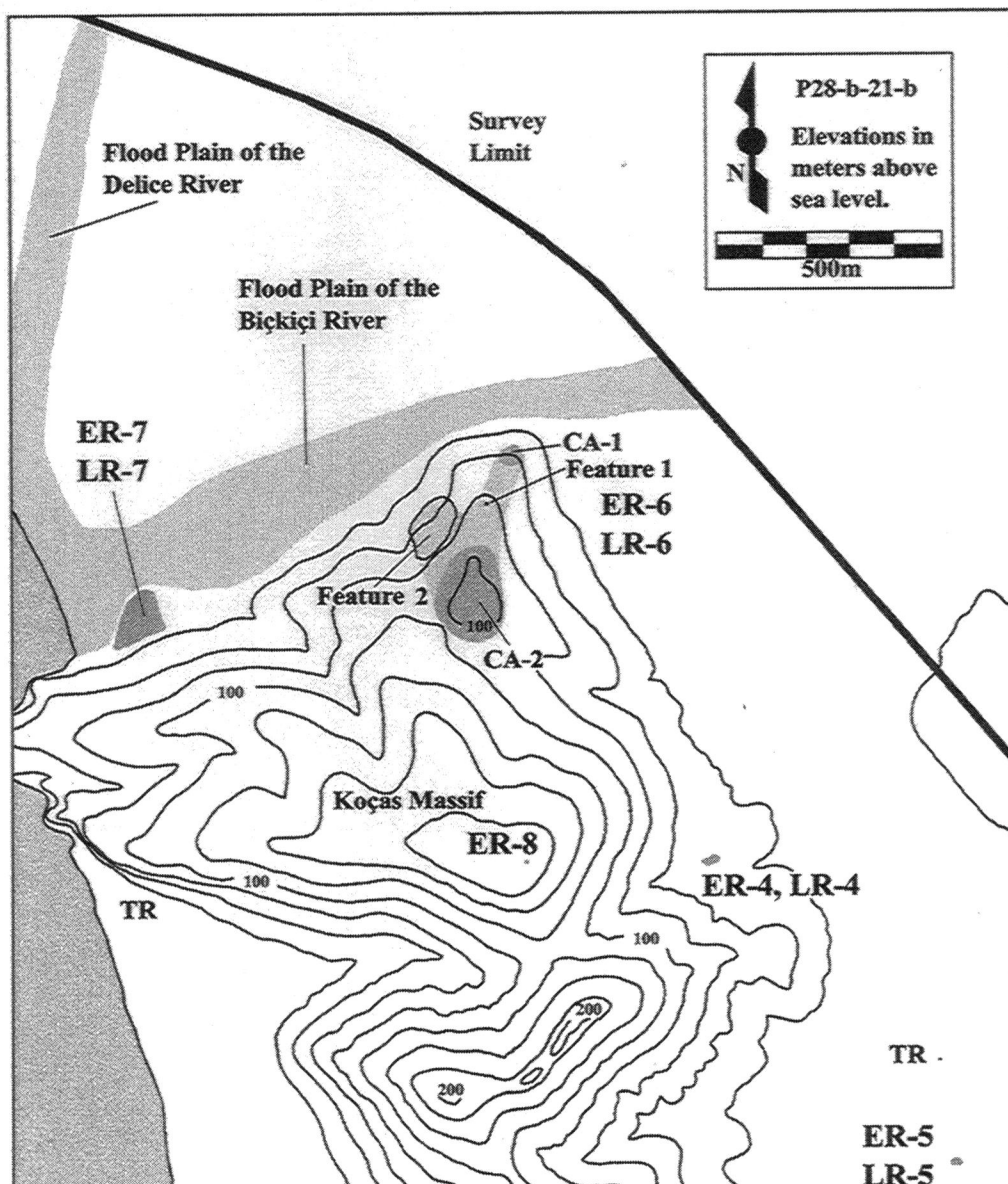

Figure 3-6. 28-b-21-b.

brush, making ceramic collection and architectural recording difficult. Patches of roughly shaped stone represent house remains, but were not recorded in detail. In the vicinity of the previously-mentioned structure complex, several wall fragments constructed of large roughly-shaped stones may have served as terrace walls, but may have had defensive functions. With an estimated population of 350, the agricultural catchment of the site by necessity would have extended well north of the floodplain of the Biçkiçi River. Given an assumption of 10 ha

cultivated per farm family, I estimate the required 700 ha catchment would have extended somewhat less than 2 kms to the north into this alluvial zone, or very close to the estimated boundary between Selinus and Iotape, and just to the south of 28-b-16-d-1 (ER-2, LR-2).

Dating of the site is somewhat problematic except for the presence of several definite LR types. One "Classical-Hellenistic" fine ware sherd was noted from collection area 1, but other evidence of pre-ER settlement is equivocal. One Pseudo-Coan amphora might date to either Late

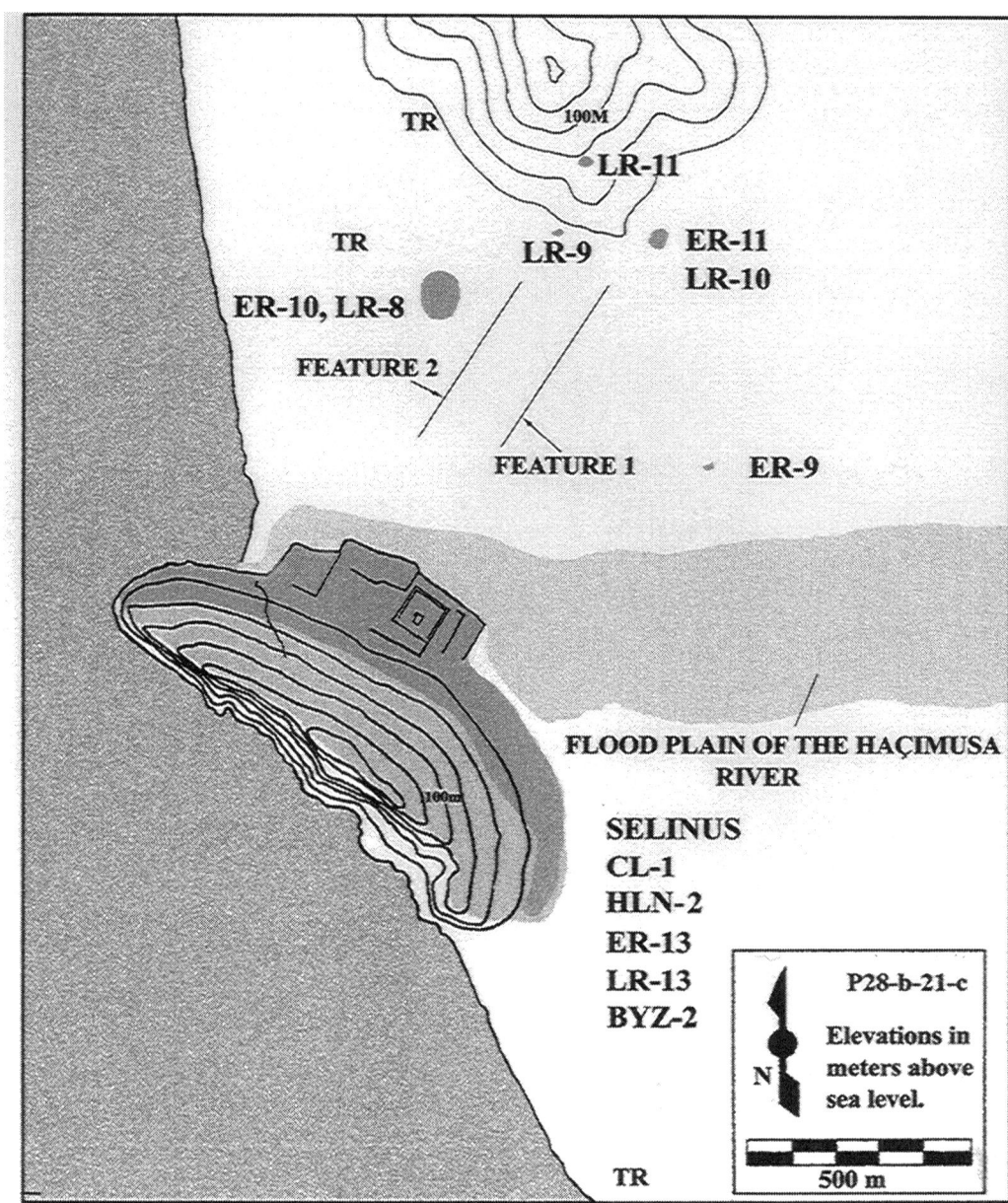

Figure 3-7. 28-b-21-c.

Hellenistic or ER; one Roman Red ware and two amphora types could date to ER or LR (including 7 sherds identified as Zemer 41 amphora). Otherwise, no good ER diagnostics were collected.

28-b-21-b-4 (ER-7, LR-7)

This site is located adjacent to the mouth of the Biçkiçi River, and faces directly on the beach. The remains of a substantial ancient stone wall along the west (sea-facing) edge of the site has protected it from wave damage. In addition, the whole site sits on a terrace, that is probably a cultural feature, roughly 1 m above the adjacent river alluvium, that would have provided protection from river flooding. A fortress-tower of probable Muslim construction occupies part of the site. Surface pottery is dense, but few diagnostics could be found. Field notes record a substantial number of amphora fragments and chunks of clay slag, suggesting a possible specialization in transport amphora production, although no additional evidence of specialized production was noted.

29

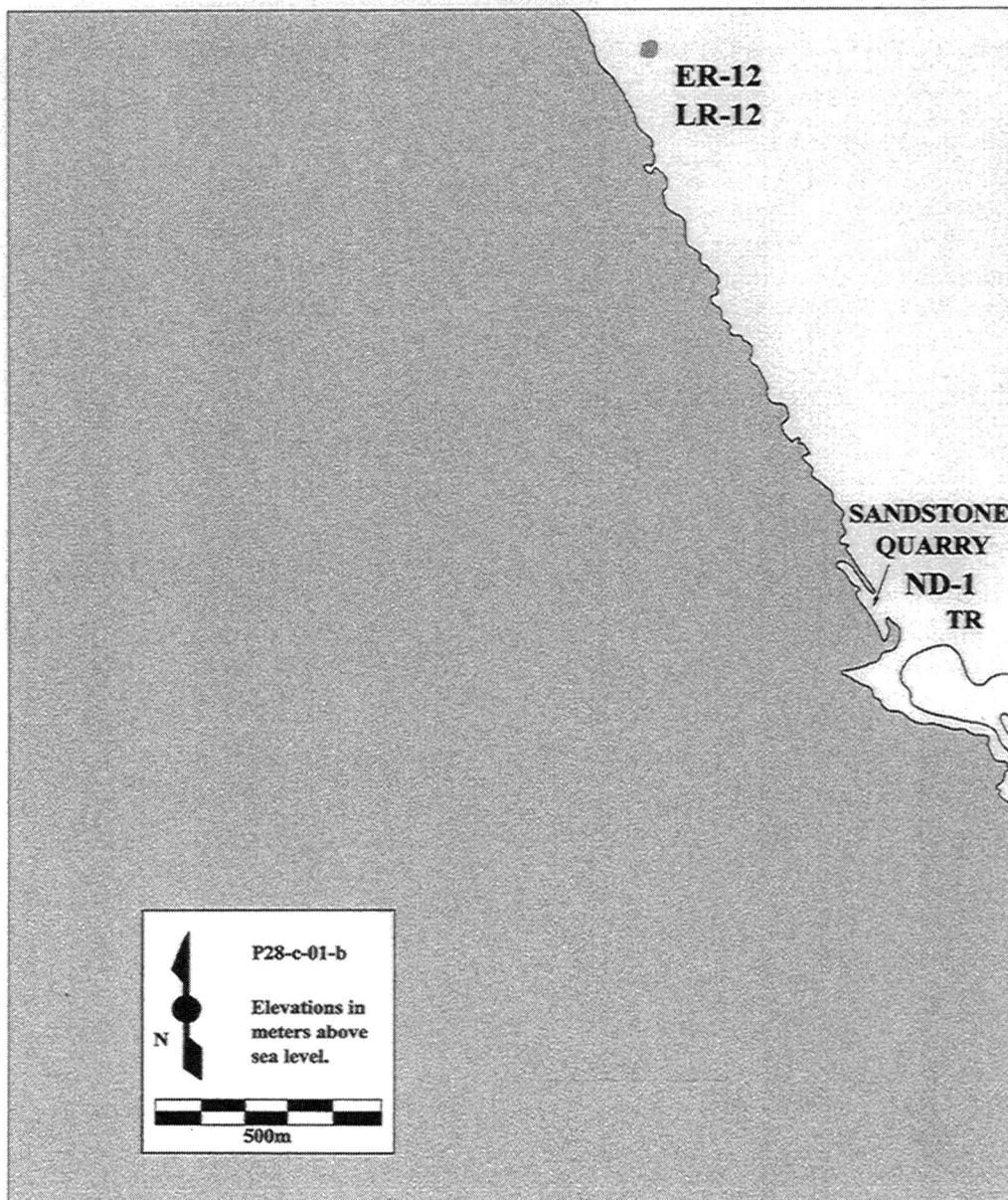

Figure 3-8. 28-c-01-b.

Caves just up slope from the site are locally famous for their chambers full of cool, fresh water. Just above the caves, at a point where a ridge of the Koças massif drops steeply to the sea, a church ruin was noted that may be the remains of the monastery called Biçkeci Kalesi (Heberdey and Wilhelm 1896: 149; Rosenbaum 1967c: 68).

28-b-21-b-6 (ER-8)

Located at the highest point of the Koças massif, at 193 masl, the site consists of several roughly cut stone wall fragments that may be the remains of an isolated farmhouse. Stone walls form an enclosure 9.5 by 12.9 m,

adjoined on its east and south edges by another enclosure or room roughly 14 m square. A few sherds were found directly adjacent to the architectural remains, including an local Antioch Zemer 41 amphora. One ER/LR cooking ware and one ER/LR fine ware were the only other diagnostics.

28-b-21-c-1 (ER-9)

This is the remains of a probable isolated farmstead, although a modern house built directly over the remains makes it difficult to interpret. It is located along the lower slopes of a small rocky knob that interrupts an otherwise flat alluvial plain north of the Haçimusa River. Pottery was not very diagnostic, but included one CL/HLN fine ware and one ER Red Ware. The other diagnostic pottery was ER or LR.

28-b-21-c-2 (ER-10, LR-8)

This is a sherd scatter roughly 130 m N-S by 100 m E-W, in the alluvial plain across the Haçimusa River from Selinus, in an area of wheat fields. The pottery collection proved disappointing. Four ER/LR sherds were the limit of diagnostic pieces (one fine ware, one transport amphora, and one Zemer 41). Thus I assigned both ER and LR site numbers. The remains of two aqueducts pass just to the east and south of the site (Features 1 and 2 in Figure 3-7). Feature 1 clearly is the main channel connecting across the river to the site of Selinus, where it can be seen as it comes into the city (Figure 3-9)(it is no longer visible in the river alluvium). Feature 2 is smaller, only approximately 1 m in height in places where it still stands (Rhys Towsend will provide drawings of the two features in his final report). It is not clear what the function of this lower aqueduct was. Perhaps it was an earlier, smaller channel that brought water to Selinus before the larger aqueduct--Feature 1--was built? Perhaps its function was only to provide water for irrigation in the vicinity of the ER-10, LR-8 site? The source of water for the two features is not clear. No obvious water-collection terraces, channels or reservoirs were noted on the nearby slopes of the Koças massif, although the beginning (or termination) point of Feature 1 does appear to be the small ridge that extends into the alluvium in the vicinity of ER-11, LR-10 (correspondingly, LR-9 is located at the probable termination/origination point of Feature 2 [Figure 3-7]).

28-b-21-c-3 (LR-9)

A small scatter of sherds located along the lower slopes of the Koças massif, adjacent to the alluvial plain. It was noted in the field notebook as the origination point for the smaller aqueduct, Feature 2. Two diagnostic amphora were noted in the collection, a Spirally Grooved and a Wheel Ridged.

28-b-21-c-4 (ER-11, LR-10)

This is a scatter of sherds 60 m in diameter on a small rocky knob near the base of the southern extension of the Koças massif. The field notebook identifies it as the origination point for the aqueduct, Feature 1. One roof tile noted.

28-b-21-c-5 (LR-11)

A sherd scatter less than 50 m in diameter on a portion of a ridge line of the Koças massif where the ridge flattens out a little. Only one diagnostic sherd was identifiable in a poor and small collection (a LR Pie Crust Rim Ware). The site area had modern sheep pens; perhaps the function of this site was as a herding community or encampment. Access to suitable agricultural land would have been problematic, as much of the adjacent land is steeply sloping, and most of the adjacent alluvium south and west of the site was probably cultivated by other communities.

28-b-21-c-6 (CL-1, HLN-2, ER-13, LR-13, BYZ-2) Selinus (formerly Selinti)(Figure 3-9)

Site Layout

The Selinus Hill faces the sea with near-vertical cliffs along its west and south face, while the slopes east and north are less steep (although no approach to the summit can be described as an easy climb, particularly given the dense cover of spiny brush). Sherds are found in varying densities over the whole area of the north and east slopes, a total area of sherd scatter of 42 ha. Sherd density drops off rapidly to the north, where the Haçimusa River runs directly by the site, but drops off rapidly also in the fields south of the river channel, possibly owing to alluviation from river flooding. The area of most dense sherd scatter extends along the lower slopes of the hill out onto a series of large terraces where public structures and spaces were built (the vicinity of our collection areas 1,6, and 14, and including Buildings 1, 2D, 3, 5, and 6 in Huber [1967: Plan 3])(Plate 3-10). These terraces elevate the public area approximately one to two meters above the river flood plain (and even higher in the vicinity of collection area 1).

Although this terraced zone may be in part a natural feature, clearly a substantial amount of construction fill was brought here, perhaps obscuring some early phases of occupation. A large concourse was built in the terraced area (H1 in Figure 3-9), with an exterior wall and colonnades (Heberdey and Wilhelm 1896: 150; Huber 1967: 29-31; Paribeni and Romanelli 1914: 144), surrounding a central structure of the Corinthian order that has a rebuilding of Islamic date. Building H3 was probably a bath, near which passed H4W, the aqueduct that crossed the river and can be seen as Feature 1 in Figure 3-7. The colonnaded square numbered H5 and H6 includes an elevated platform on its west edge. Building H2D was a theater or *odeon* (Huber 1967: 31; Heberdey and Wilhelm [1896: 151] confirm that it was once roofed), whose seats were cut into the slopes immediately above the main terraces.

West of the terraced area, overlooking the mouth of the river, is a zone of dense architectural remains, evidently both domestic and defensive in function, extending to the western tip of the hill (and including collection area 2)(Plate 3-11). A defensive wall extends from the river mouth up slope for roughly half the elevation of the hill (H8F in Huber 1967: Plan 3, and in Figure 3-9). A main road connecting the neighborhood around collection area 2 to the public area passes through the remains of a gate where the wall reaches the bottom of the slope (west of collection area 5).

Up slope from the river mouth, at the 75 m contour, a massive stone terrace extends for approximately 500 m from the cliff face east (the architects will provide a detailed description of it). The defensive wall reaches the terrace at H9 (from Huber 1967: Plan 3), but the terrace extends for another 200 m east of the defensive wall. Along the terrace, square or rectangular rooms alternate with circular features (probably cisterns), making up what was probably a substantial water collection and storage system. My crew attempted to surface collect the west end of the terrace, but few sherds were found (owing, in part, to the dense vegetation cover)(collection area 3). The remains of a church that may be Medieval in date (H10C in Huber

1967: Plan 3) are located above the defensive wall. West of the church we noted a series of terraces and rooms, perhaps residential features, that may be associated with the church (to be included in the final architectural map). The summit of the Selinus hill is dominated by a fortress dating for the most part later than the periods of occupation described here, although the area may have a lengthy history of defensive wall construction. This area had generally few sherds, although we did make it a collection area (4).

To the east and south of the main public precinct, we noted a number of smaller terraces, mostly built in a narrow strip along the very lowest slopes of the hill, that provided spaces for residential construction. The area of terrace construction is indicated by the rectangular-shaped collection areas (7, 8, 9, 10, 11, 12, and 13), and the series of parallel lines south of collection area 7 (the latter do not represent a detailed map of the terraces). Above collection areas 9-11 is the necropolis (the partial mapping of tombs in Figure 3-9 is based on Huber 1967: Plan 3). Above the necropolis, a small quarry was noted. A small rubble and mortar structure (measuring roughly 4.5 m E-W by 3.6 m N-S) with an east facing door was noted on the slopes above the southernmost extent of the site. This may have been a tomb, or might have served as a tower guarding the southern approach to the site.

Historical Background

According to Jones (1971: 194), Selinus may have a Greek origin, although the chronology of Greek migration is not clear from historical records. A Greek heritage is indicated by the coins minted here (under the rulership of Antiochus IV of Commagene, A. D. 38-72, and again in the Imperial Period from Trajan to Philip [Head 1911: 728]). Judging from the published examples, most of the site's inscriptions are in Greek (one Latin and three Greek inscriptions are reported in Bean and Mitford [1962: 206-7, 1970: 153-55]). The earliest historical record of Selinus is found in the Periplus of Scylax, done for Darius I in the late fourth century BCE (Jones 1971: 197). It is recorded as having had a Ptolemaic garrison in 197 BCE (ibid.: 198), reflecting Egyptian interest in the local forest resources, and, possibly, mercenaries (ibid.: 198). Following the rulership of Antiochus IV, the principality was divided into districts, of which Selinus was the chief town of the Selinitis district (Bean and Mitford 1962: 209; Jones 1971: 210).

Rosenbaum (1967b: 66) dates the main period of tomb construction to the 2nd and 3rd centuries AD (cf. Bean and Mitford 1962: 206-7), although some tombs were probably reused in later periods. The necropolis area also includes a chapel of Byzantine date (N4 in Huber 1967: Plan 3), and a Medieval church nearer to the summit. Huber (1967: Plan 3) noted two structures of Seljuk date (Buildings 1 and 9). Judging from these data, the main periods of occupation of the site are probably Early and Late Roman, but earlier occupation is indicated, and the site continued to be occupied into the Byzantine Period and later. The structure numbered 10C in Huber (1967: Plan 3) may be part of the Medieval sanctuary named after St. Thecla (who "restored impregnability to the fortress of Selinus" [Rosenbaum 1967c: 68]).

Collection Areas

Collection Area 1 An area of .45 ha near Huber's (1967: Plan 3) Buildings 5 and 6. Columns of a pinkish granite noted, as well as a fragment of white cut marble. This area features a comparatively high density of pottery, including numerous amphora fragments. Roof tiles noted. From the collections, the pottery is mostly ER and LR, but one Hellenistic Thickened Interior Rim Plate was collected. The high density of pottery, including amphora, and the adjacency of the space to the river inlet suggests this may have been the city's main market.

Collection Area 2 An area of .4 ha located along the lower slopes of the hill overlooking a steep cliff over the sea. Abundant terrace and house construction was noted, and an ancient road is evident connecting this residential zone with the main public area of the site. Roof tiles noted. ER and LR noted, although ER is represented by only one fine ware sherd.

Collection Area 3 An area of .25 ha extending from a small structure defining the west terminus of the water-system terrace for about 100 m of the terrace's total 500 m length. Few sherds or other evidence of residential occupation were noted. Only one diagnostic was collected, a LR CRS Form 11.

Collection Area 4 An area of .75 ha from inside the "castle" walls of the summit of Selinus hill, and along the slopes north of the castle. A few roof tiles noted. LR and BYZ noted, but few diagnostics could be found.

Collection Area 5 An area of .56 ha in a sloping field above the zone of public buildings and collection area 1. This is an area of scattered terraces and house foundations, with abundant pottery; roof tiles noted. ER, LR, and BYZ noted.

Collection Area 6 An area of .26 ha consisting of the north half of the "public square" identified by Huber (1967: Plan 3), bordered by his Buildings 1, 2D, and 3, and south of the aqueduct (his 4W). Many amphora fragments noted, and fragments of tessellated mosaic noted. Few diagnostics were found, representing only LR.

Collection Area 7 An area of .18 ha on a residential terrace east and below the necropolis. Roof tiles and amphora fragments noted. LR the only diagnostic, suggesting this southern extension of the site is LR.

Collection Area 8 An area of .15 ha in a zone of small residential terraces at the base of the hill that is now a vegetable-producing area (including some greenhouses). It also appears to be the oldest part of the ancient city; the collection included 2 Classical Black Glaze sherds, as well as diagnostic Hellenistic and CL/HLN, ER, LR, and BYZ. A loom or fishing weight was also noted.

Collection Area 9 An area of .16 ha among ancient residential terraces at the base of the slope. Roof tiles noted, as well as several fragments of hydraulic cement. Components include CL/HLN, HLN, ER, and LR.

Collection Area 10 An area of .065 ha that combines two adjacent ancient residential terraces. Fragments of tessellated mosaic noted, possibly from an elaborate tomb just uphill from the terraces. ER was noted in the tabulation.

Collection Area 11 An area of .04 ha among ancient residential terraces. Roof tiles, a fragment of a slate floor, and a marble architectural fragment were noted.

Components include CL/HLN, ER, and LR. Two possible Classical Black Glaze sherds were collected.

Collection Area 12 An area of .17 ha that was an ancient residential terrace. Roof tiles were noted. Components include CL/HLN, ER, and LR.

Collection Area 13 A long, broad terrace covering an area of .4 ha, extending east from the *odeon* (2D of Huber), above and overlooking the large colonnaded plaza. Roof tiles and amphora fragments noted. Components include CL/HLN, ER, and LR.

Collection Area 14 This is part of the "public square" identified by Huber (1967: Plan 3), bordered by his Buildings 1, 2D, and 3, south of the aqueduct fragment (his 4W), and south of collection area 6. An area of .4 ha that was densely vegetated. Roof tiles noted; components include HLN, ER, LR, and BYZ.

Summary of Population History

Selinus is identified as CL-1, even though the total number of diagnostic sherds was only four (Classical Black Glaze). No population estimate can be given for this period. Several collection areas have CL/HLN and HLN (8, 9, 11, 12, 13, and 14, and 1 has one HLN diagnostic), so HLN site number 2 was assigned to Selinus. These sherds tend to cluster in the area from about collection areas 13 and 14 to collection area 9, giving an estimated site area of 2.4 ha, or a population estimate of 300 (at 125/ha.) This estimate must be considered very provisional given the extensive later construction during ER and LR, particularly around the terraced public concourses. For ER (site number 13), the surface collections suggest a community growing in size to include our collection areas 1, 2, 5, 8, 9, 10, 11,12, 13, and 14, and an area I estimate at 10.85 ha, excluding the necropolis, which was in use by this time (Rosenbaum [1967b: 66] dates the main period of tomb construction at the site to the 2nd and 3rd centuries AD with some construction slightly earlier; cf. Bean and Mitford [1962: 206-7]). The necropolis area has very few sherds or other evidence of ancient residential occupation, and so seems to have been functionally specialized throughout the site's Roman Period history. Given this estimated area of ER occupation, the population estimate is 2,300 (at 210 per ha). All collection areas (1-14) show at least some evidence of LR, indicating this was the period of maximum population of the center. Including the possibility of some settlement in the castle area at the top of the hill, and perhaps along the narrow water-control terrace, I estimate the total area of the site for LR at 23.38 ha, giving a population estimate of 4,900 (at 210/ha). Byzantine Period diagnostics are poorly represented, consisting of only 4 fine ware sherds from four different collection areas (4, 5, 8, and 14). This scattered, faint presence is difficult to interpret, but I suggest a possible small area of settlement at the hill top (.75 ha), and a 9 ha main site area, for a total of 9.75 ha. (or a population of 2,000 at 210/ha.).

28-c-01-b-1 (ER-12, LR-12)

This is a sherd scatter 30 m in diameter on the alluvial plain south of Selinus. It is located 150 m from the beach in an area of sandy soils (although some wheat is cultivated in the vicinity of the site). An unusually high number of amphora fragments was noted (8 local W. Cilicia Zemer 41 and 2 Zemer 41 were tabulated from the collection), but we saw no evidence of amphora production. Fragments of the sandstone quarried just south of the site (Figure 3-8, ND-1, described in the next section) were noted, that perhaps had been used for house construction. One roof tile noted.

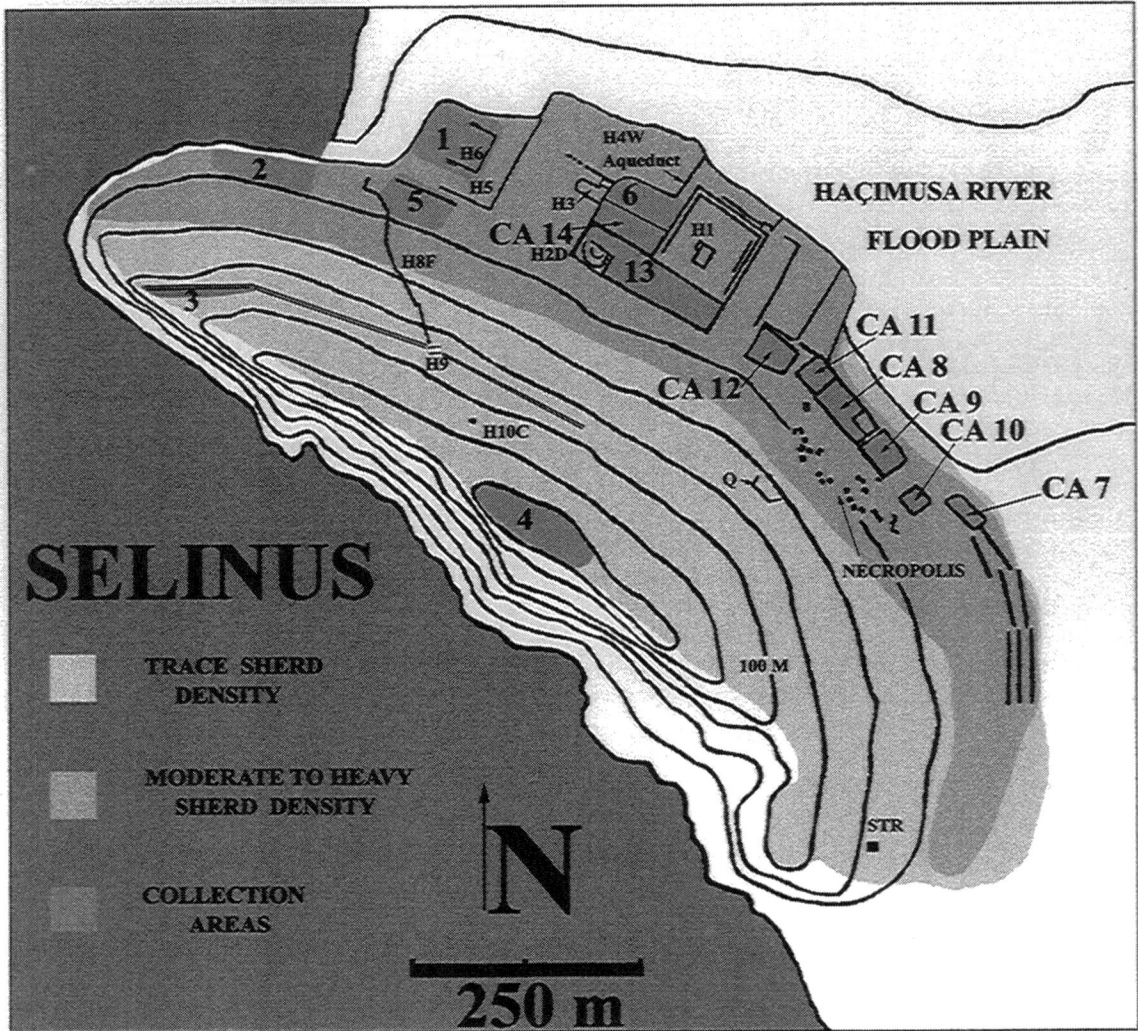

Figure 3-9. Detail of Selinus. Collection areas are indicated in the darkest fill. The highest density of pottery is indicated in the intermediate shade, and the lightest shading indicates the maximum extent of trace density pottery. Numbers preceded by 'H' are building numbers from Huber (1967: Plan 3). The feature designated as 'Q' is a quarry. The dark lines south of collection area 7 schematically indicate the locations of broad residential terraces. The flood plain of the Haçimusa is shown as it appears in the 1978 topographic maps. Today, the river flood plain has been narrowed by a dike extending east from the vicinity of H4W. This map incorporates selected parts of the Selinus plan from Huber (ibid.).

Cestrus Hinterland

The hinterland centered on the site of Cestrus (Kestroi) extends from the south edge of 28-c-01-b, and includes 28-c-02-a, 28-c-02-b and -c, and the northern part of 28-c-03-d (Figures 3-8, -10 to -13). This hinterland, of approximately 2275 ha, includes three of the highest mountain complexes in the survey area (from west to east, the Koru Dagi massif, the Macar Kalesi massif, and the Güdü massif)(Figure 2-3). Although sites throughout this area tend to be located on the mountain summits and high ridges, some alluvial soils are found west of Koru Dagi, east and north of Macar Kalesi, and north and west of Güdü, and account for an estimated 31% of the area. Steep slope occupies 30%, and moderate but arable slope makes up the final 39% of this hinterland.

The small massif labeled the Koru Dagi on the contour maps (Figure 3-10), reaches an elevation of some 375 masl (Plate 3-12). The slopes of this small massif drop steeply from its summit south to a series of cliffs over the beach line (Plate 3-13), although a natural terrace more than half-way down makes it possible to traverse east to west along this stretch of coast. Access to the sea from the massif would have been by way of a small inlet at the southwest corner of the area (near site ER-14, LR-14)(although access to the inlet here is also very steep), or by way of the beach extending north and west in grid square 28-c-01-b (Figure 3-8)(Plate 3-9).

Agriculture would have been limited on the south slopes of Koru Dagi, but a series of ridges extending northwest and north of the massif's summit are gently sloping, and become more favorable for agricultural use at the lower elevations (Plate 3-14). Several springs were noted in this same zone below about the 200 m contour line, and a number of recent houses (i.e. within the last century or two) are found near these water sources (many now abandoned). However, virtually all evidence of archaeological occupation of the massif is located at the higher elevations, including the largest site, located at the summit (ER-15, LR-17). Below the main site, but still higher than the modern occupation, two small isolated farms were recorded (LR-15 and 16), described below. Other trace deposits of Roman Period pottery (TR on the map) just below the summit were not written up as sites, owing to a comparative paucity of pottery and other artifactual or architectural remains, but some of these low-density patches could represent the remains of herding camps similar to several we noted on this hill, which appear to be in seasonal use (Plate 3-15).

East of the Koru Dagi massif is another massif of similar scale called the Macar Kalesi (named after the village of Macar located on an elevated plain east of the massif)(Figure 2-3). Cestrus (ER-17, LR-19) occupies the northern one-half of the summit ridge line, where it reaches a maximum elevation of just under 400 masl (Plate 3-16). The massif features steep, *maquis*-choked slopes south and west of the summit ridge; the south slopes drop to a series of cliffs that limit sea access (Plate 3-17). A series of more gently sloping ridge lines descend from the summit ridge to the east and north; these descend to an area of alluvial soils near the base of the massif. These lower slopes are now in cultivation or have been cultivated in the recent past. The modern village of Ekmer is located at the base of the

northern slopes. East of the massif, a high (75 to 100 masl) intermontain plateau, the site of the modern village of Macar, is a zone of intensive agricultural production making extensive use of greenhouses (Plate 3-18). Owing to this area's dense modern settlement and greenhouse construction, it could not be systematically surveyed. Where possible, however, accessible open fields and roadways were inspected. Archaeological sites were not evident, but a few trace scatters of pottery were noted.

The eastern mountain complex of the Cestrus hinterland, the Güdü massif (Plates 3-19 and 20) consists of a rugged and high ridge line (reaching 456 masl at its highest point) oriented in a NW-SE direction oblique to the coastal cliffs. Like the other mountain complexes in this hinterland, Güdü and its adjacent slopes lack convenient access to protected bays that could have served as harbors, and high cliffs separate the sea edge from upland terrain. The largest site here (ER-18, LR-21) sits at the very highest point of the massif, and faces steep slopes descending north, east, and west to the gentler slopes and alluvium far below. The massif's ridge line south of the summit is gentler and broad (Plate 3-21), but steep, and probably uncultivable, slopes drop off from this ridge on both sides.

Site Descriptions

28-c-01-b-ND (ND-1, Sandstone Quarry)

Evidence of ancient quarrying was noted in a shelf of loosely consolidated light brown sandstone that extends into the tidal zone (Plate 3-22). Several partially quarried column bases were visible at low tide (Plate 3-23). This sandstone is easily worked but not highly durable; however, stone from this quarry was noted in the public buildings at Selinus (Huber 1967: 35). In this same passage, Huber identifies the sandstone source as being near "Biçkesi Kalesi," which is north of Selinus (near ER-7 and LR-7, 28-b-21-b). We did not see any evidence of quarrying there, and suggest that ND-1 is the quarry in question. A few sherds were noted on the slopes east of the site, but no use period for the quarry can be assigned on the basis of this light scatter. The structures containing stone evidently from this quarry are ER and LR in date (e.g., at Selinus in Huber 1967: 29-35).

28-c-02-a-ND (ND-2)

This is a fragment of a substantial stone and mortar terrace located near the southeast slope of the Macar Kalesi massif, where it joins at a saddle with the Koru Dagi massif. The remaining walls of the structure form a rectangle 12 m (along the contour line) by 9 m (crossing the contour). The north corner is the highest remaining fragment, and is 2.7 m high. Construction stones are large and rough-shaped; some mortar noted. Almost no pottery was found on or around the terrace. I infer this was a traffic-control or defensive feature, located where a road passes from the area of the south slopes of Koru Dagi and ER-14, LR-14 (above a small bay), and the quarry at ND-1 (28-c-01-b-ND), going to Cestrus. A poorly preserved ramp extending from below the structure and heading NE toward Cestrus may be remains of the road in question.

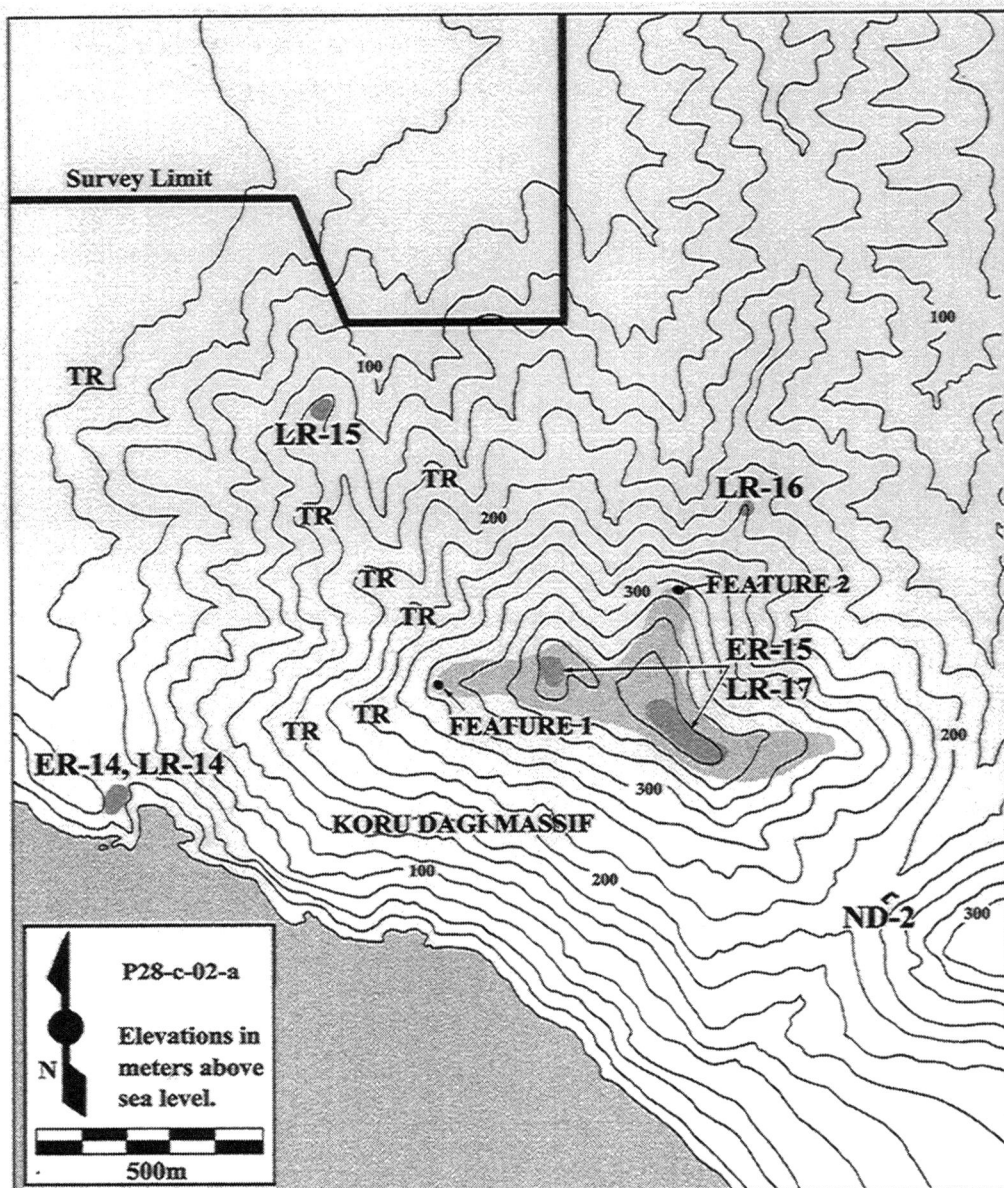

Figure 3-10. 28-c-02-a.

28-c-02-a-1 (ER-15, LR-17)

This is a hill top village consisting of two main patches of sherd scatter and construction stone. The larger patch is near the summit of the Koru Dagi massif, adjacent to a microwave tower (Plate 3-24), and a smaller area is found along the top of a rocky knob below and west of the main part of the site. The larger area has abundant remains of stone houses; a map of these will be published in the architecture report. The lower area also has structure remains, probably also houses. One measurable stone structure here is 5 m NW-SE by 3.5 m NE-SW. Terrace fragments, which may be associated with the site, were noted in the vicinity of this structure and down slope on the ridge from it west for a distance of approximately 200 m, along with a trace density of pottery. At the lowest extent of these terraces, a possible cistern was noted (Feature 1, Figure 3-10). This circular feature, 1.2 m in diameter, is constructed of cut stone with mortar plaster on the inside wall.

Additional terraces, probably also associated with the site, were noted on the ridge extending east from the larger

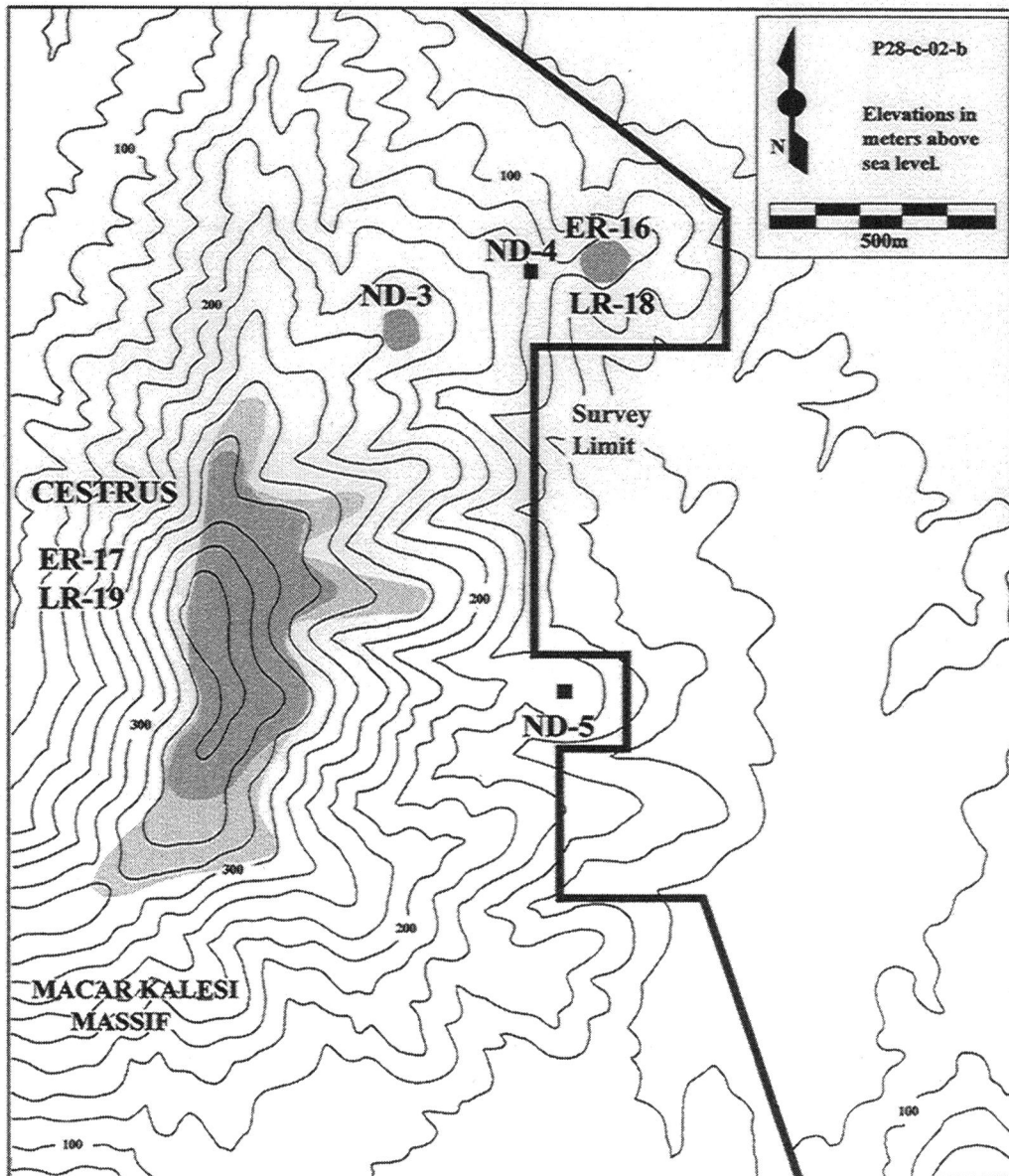

Figure 3-11. 28-c-02-b.

area of sherd scatter. This area also has a trace distribution of pottery (shown as light shading in Figure 3-10). At approximately 75 m down slope from the site, along this same ridge, the remains of a stone structure were noted, too fragmentary to measure. A cut stone box was noted near these structure walls. Terrace fragments and a trace distribution of pottery were noted also along the main ridge north from the main part of the site (and toward LR-16) for nearly 300 m. Along this ridge, at about 125 m from the main part of the site, a structure was noted consisting of two adjacent rooms made of rough-cut stone, each measuring roughly 3 by 3 m. Below this structure, a

substantial terrace wall was noted that might be a defensive feature. At the lower end of this distribution of terrace fragments and pottery, a circular feature was noted (Feature 2, Figure 3-10), 2.75 m in diameter, with smoothly cut stone walls. Judging from the solidity of construction and large size, the feature may have served as a defensive tower.

Overall, this site and its outlying terraces and features lacked very much diagnostic or decorated pottery. One definite ER Red Ware was collected, and one LR Cypriot Red Slip. Other recognizable Roman pottery was not diagnostic as to period, and the bulk of the pottery consists

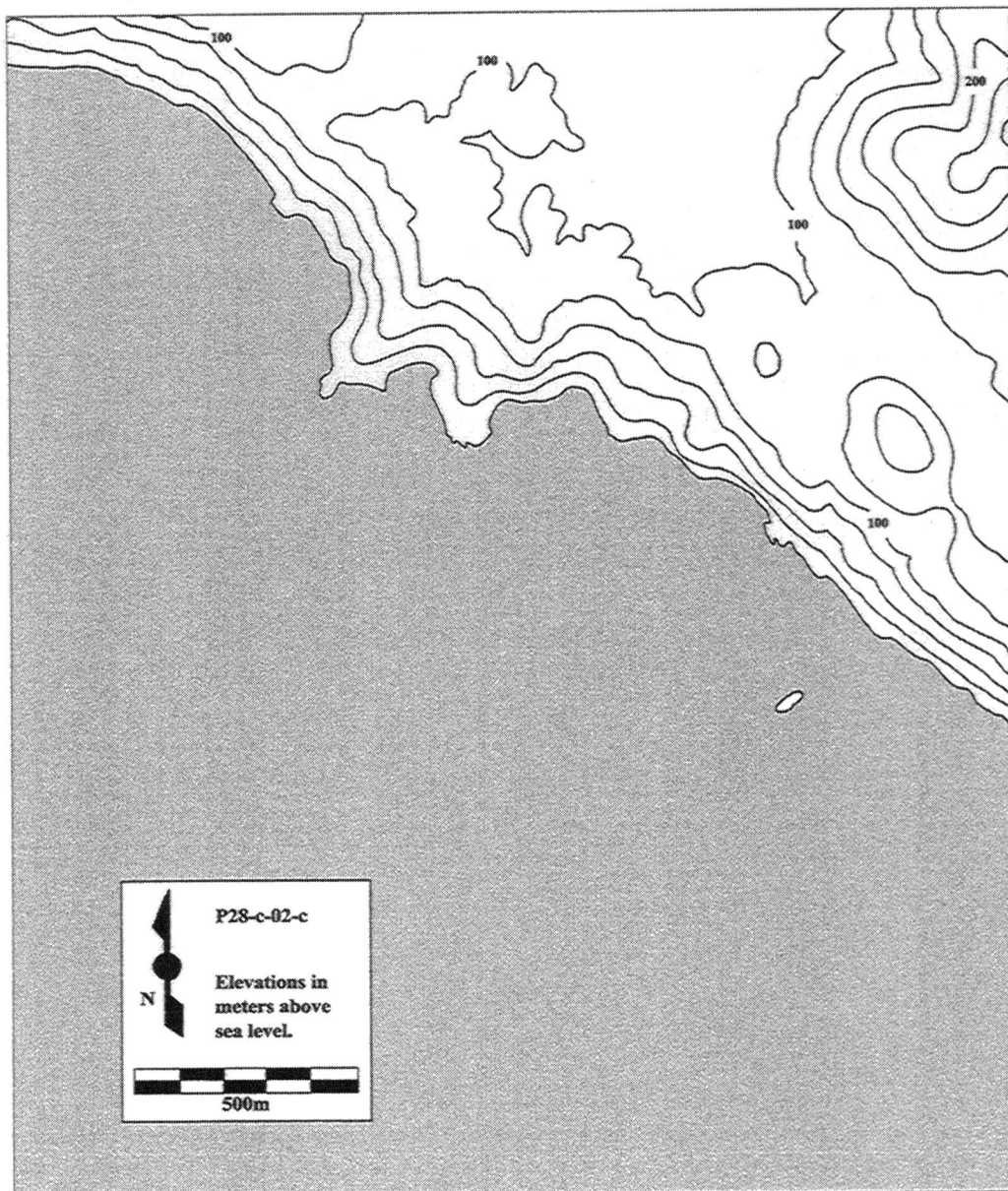

Figure 3-12. 28-c-02-c.

of various local West Cilicia types (see Appendix 2). Additionally, comparatively few roof tiles or other artifacts were noted.

28-c-02-a-2 (LR-16)

A small scatter of sherds over an area of about .1 ha, probably an isolated farm house. A well preserved stone enclosure wall measures 6.8 m (N-S) by 6.5 m (E-W). At one well-preserved point, the wall is 80 cm thick. One fragment of an olive press noted. Pottery is not abundant and could not be easily dated, but one probable LR

amphora fragment was noted, and hence the LR site number, although ER is also a possibility. No roof tiles noted.

28-c-02-a-4 (ER-14, LR-14)

This is a sherd scatter covering at most .5 ha, located in a rocky saddle between a small hill to the west and the lower slopes of the Koru Dagi massif to the east. The site overlooks a small bay, but the roughly 30 m from the site to the water's edge below is a very steep drop. In the center of the site a stone and rubble building is visible owing to a

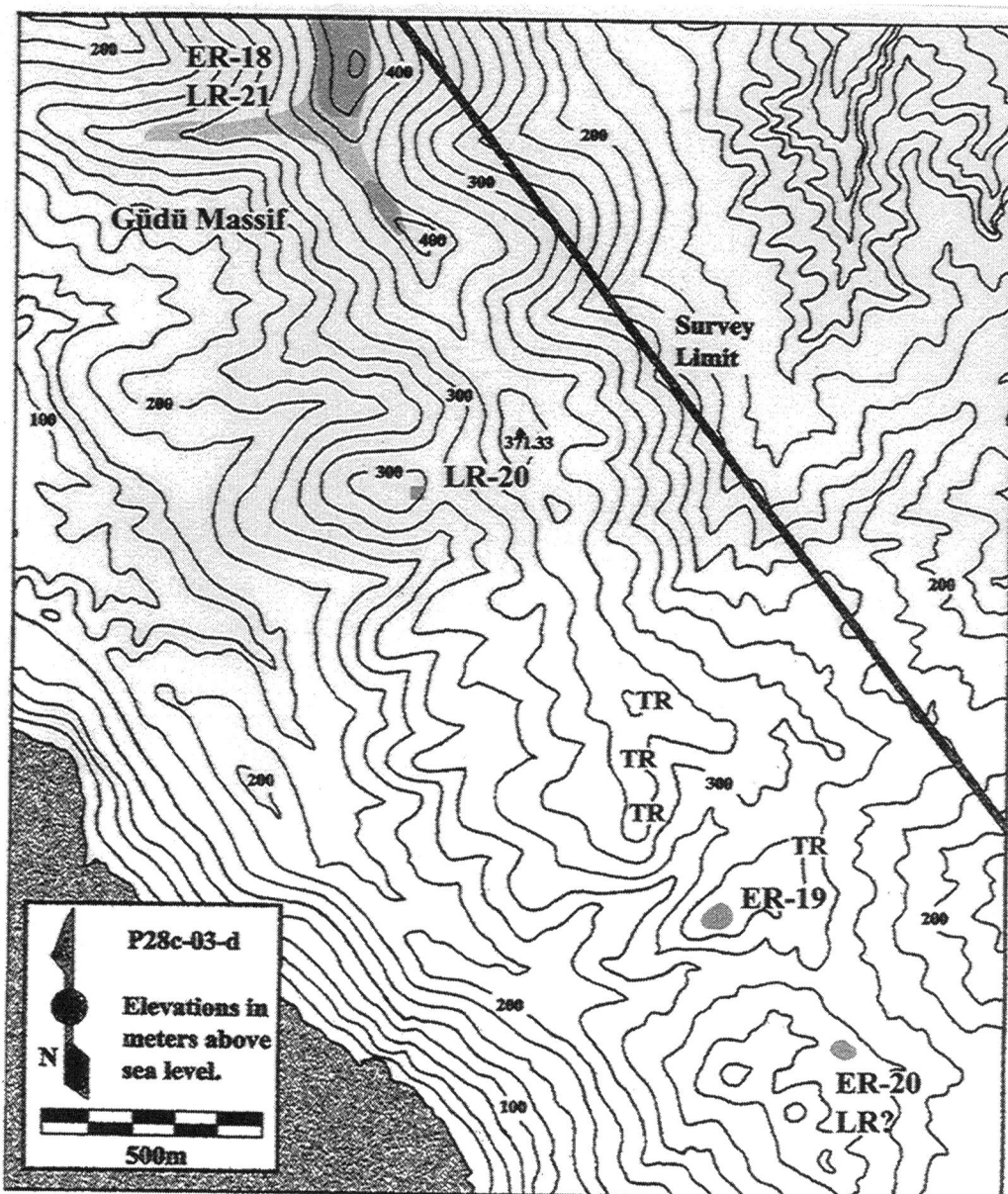

Figure 3-13. 28-c-03-d.

looter's pit that has exposed a fragment of an apse (Plate 3-25). Surrounding this structure, numerous roof tiles were noted. Fragments of glass vessels noted. One partially exposed milling or press stone was visible, but could not be measured. The stone's rough shape may indicate it was only partially completed (or was badly weathered). On a rocky knob below the site, a partially quarried circular grinding stone or press was noted. ER and LR amphora are well represented in the collection, including 1 Pseudo-Coan, 3 Zemer 41, 2 Spirally Grooved, and 4 Banded Spirally Grooved.

28-c-02-a-5 (LR-15)

This is a small scatter of mostly non-diagnostic Roman Period sherds covering approximately .1 ha. No collection was made. One possible Zemer 41 handle noted (could be ER or LR), and one Wheel Ridged Amphora (LR). Near the center of the sherd scatter there is a foundation of large rough-cut stones measuring 7 by 7 m, perhaps the remains of a house. Stone-faced terraces were noted in the area that seem to be associated with the site.

28-c-02-b-1 (ER-17, LR-19) Cestrus (Kestroi)(Figure 3-14)

Main Features

Cestrus is located along the northern half of the summit ridge of the Macar Kalesi massif (Bean and Mitford 1962: 211, 1970: 155), extending from about 275 to 390 masl (Plate 3-16). The area of most dense concentration of sherds and construction rubble extends for just under 1 km of the north-south trending ridge line. Steep slopes (even cliff faces) on the west side of the summit ridge precluded settlement growth in this direction, but several more gently sloping ridge lines extending from the summit to the east and north have evidence of residential and public use. Areas of trace sherd scatter are found extending beyond the main site, to the south, and along the ridge lines east and north of the site (Figures 3-11, 3-14). Scattered remains of terraces, house walls, and tombs could be found in these latter areas. Most of the summit ridge line appears to have been a residential zone; owing to extensive looting, this area is now a dense jumble of construction stone, with only a few structures still partially standing (Plate 3-26). Public buildings are found here as well, including an *agora* defined by temples dedicated to Vespasian, on the south, and to Antoninus Pius on the north (Figure 3-14)(the location of the temples is based on the sketch-map provided by Bean and Mitford 1970: Figure 6). One inscription at the site refers to the construction of a *stoa*, but it has not been located (Bean and Mitford 1970: 165).

A monumental terrace that served as a public area, some 60 by 15 m, has been constructed on the east side of the summit ridge line, just below its northern limit (Figure 3-14; Plate 3-27). Five inscribed statue bases line the terrace, and three niches cut into the west wall of the terrace also contained statues (Bean and Mitford 1962: 211-12). A large standing structure is located near the south limit of the terrace (at a slightly lower elevation)(Plate 3-27). Bean and Mitford (1970: Figure 6) refer to it as a "Grabhaus," but it may be a bath structure. Along this same slope, but south of the "bath," and extending for approximately 100 m, is a necropolis, now severely looted. Several other tomb fragments were noted in an area southeast of the *agora*.

A substantial reservoir is located approximately 125 m south of the probable bath, at the south limit of the necropolis (Figure 3-14, Plate 3-28). This may be what Bean and Mitford (1962: 211) interpreted as a ring-wall. The mortar and rubble wall of the reservoir is as much as 2.3 m thick; its elevation at one reasonably well preserved location is 4.5 m. I paced the basin of the reservoir with difficulty owing to dense vegetation, but was able to estimate dimensions of 35 m NS by 30 m EW.

Collection Areas

Collection Area 1 An area of .18 ha south of the bath, in the necropolis. Elaborate carved stone pieces, glass fragments, human remains, and bronze pieces were noted (as well as a few roof tiles) in this extensively looted area. The collection contained mostly ER and a little LR.

Collection Area 2 An area of .14 ha in what appears to be a residential area on the summit ridge just above the gymnasium terrace. Roof tiles noted. The collection includes ER and LR.

Collection Area 3 An area of .01 ha just south of the highest point of the summit ridge, in an area of dense construction rubble. The small collection area centered around a recently looted house. Diagnostics include ER and LR.

Collection Area 4 An area of .01 ha on and around a recently-looted house, in an area of dense construction rubble. Diagnostics included mostly ER, with some LR.

Collection Area 5 An area of .225 ha on the descending slopes south of the summit, in an area of moderate pottery and construction stone. ER and LR were collected.

Collection Area 6 An area of .125 ha close to the southern limit of the ridge summit residential zone. ER and LR noted, but fewer diagnostics were found in this area.

Historical Summary

Cestrus had been accorded full civic status (as is indicated by the mention of a council in one inscription [Bean and Mitford 1962: 216]), in spite of its short history (ibid.: 212). Jones (1971: 211) refers to it as a "hitherto unknown city" that began to issue coins after the Roman annexation. Based on their study of inscriptions (of which they record 41), Bean and Mitford (1962: 212; 1970: 157) suggest the site was occupied from the period of the annexation through the Late Roman Period, which corresponds well with the surface collected pottery. From the point of view of inscriptions, however, a "brief but intense" *floruit* is indicated, dating from the late first century AD through the second century AD (ibid. 1970: 156, 157). They mention a visit here by the emperor Hadrian in AD 129 (ibid.: 160). One inscription (#176 in Bean and Mitford 1970: 167) refers to a harbor official or someone who resides near the harbor. This is most likely in reference to the small inlet near ER-14, LR-14 (Figure 3-10).

28-c-02-b-2 (ND-3)

Located on a rocky area of ridge line down slope and NE from Cestrus. The site has only a trace density of pottery; a collection was made, but no diagnostics were found. Two structures are apparent, but wall fragments around them suggest the possibility that originally other structures or terraces were present, but these could not be measured. One structure can only be described as an extensively looted low mound, roughly 1 m in elevation, and measuring 9 m (N-S) by 14 m (E-W) at its base. Numerous roof tiles were found around this structure.

Thirty meters south of this structure is another low mound (again, roughly 1 m in elevation), measuring approximately 10 m (N-S) by 9 m (E-W). This structure has been extensively looted, exposing a circular room with an 80 cm wide entrance corridor facing SW (Plate 3-29). The inside diameter of the circular space is 3.6 m. The walls of the structure consist of small shaped stones, possibly faced with a crude mortar. The stone wall stands 80 cm at its highest remaining point. The structure wall extends below the zone of stone construction, cut into bedrock (10 cm of this bedrock cut is evident at one point, but I could not tell the total depth of the excavated portion of the wall). Little pottery was noted on or around the structure, and few roof tiles were noted.

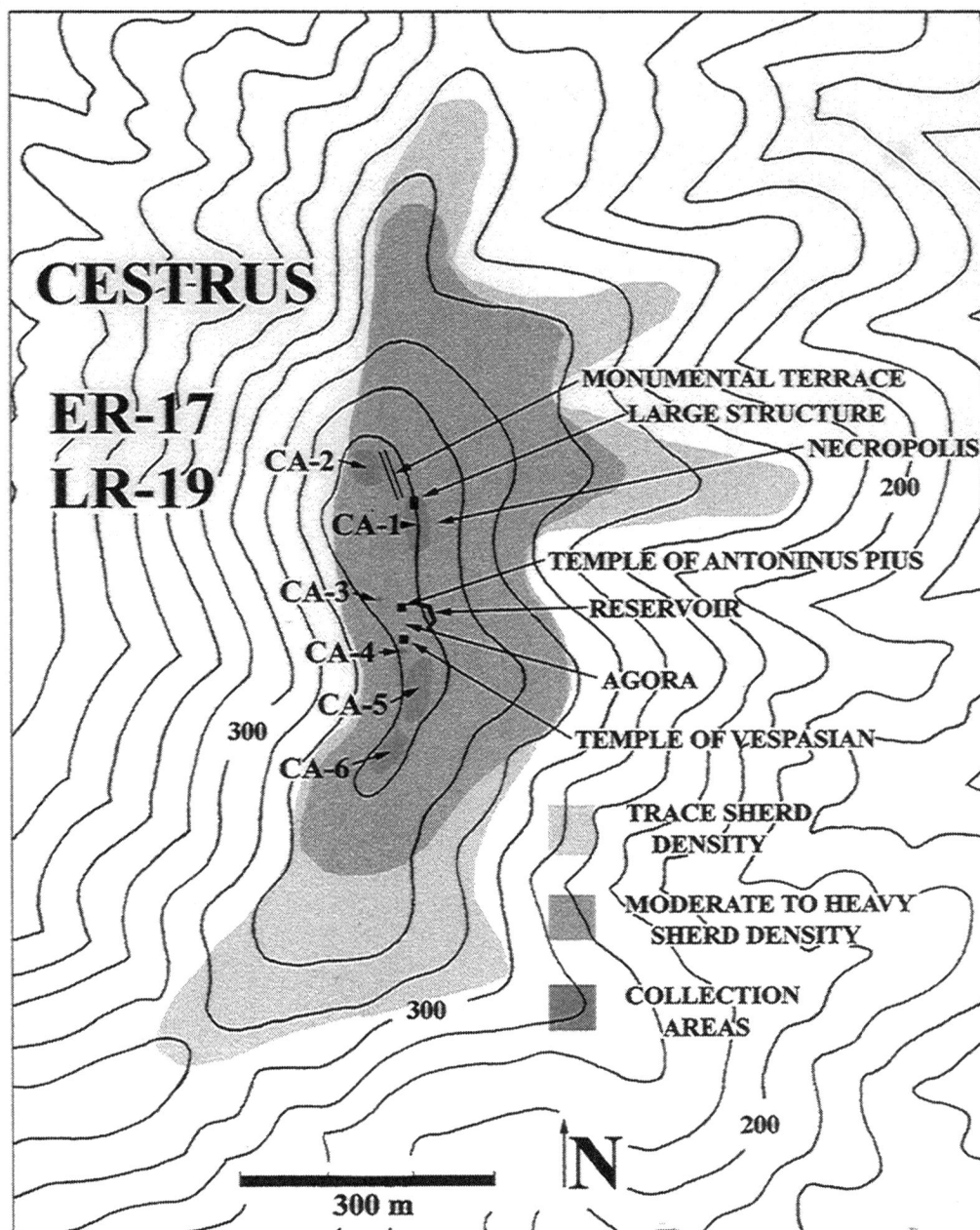

Figure 3-14. Detail of Cestrus, based in part on field notes and in part on a sketch in Bean and Mitford (1970: Figure 6)(see also their discussion in 1962: 211-12). The feature labeled Monumental Terrace is referred to as a "precinct" in their Figure 6, and is an elaborate public area with inscriptions on statue bases (a gymnasium?). The large structure south of the terrace is referred to in their Figure 6 as a tomb ("Grabhaus"), but it may plausibly be interpreted as a bath (note that it sits at approximately the same elevation as the reservoir, which could have been its water source).The locations of the Temple of Antoninus Pius, the *agora*, and the Temple of Vespasian are estimated, based on Bean and Mitford's sketch.

At first glance, I thought this circular structure might be a *tholos* tomb (e.g., Hood 1960). While the main distribution of this tomb type is in the Aegean Late Bronze Age (extending into the Early Iron Age)(ibid.), a similar tomb form is known from Cyprus (Gjerstad et al. 1934: 570, Tomb 21), also dating to the Late Bronze Age. However, several characteristics of the structure suggest it is not a *tholos* (I characterize this tomb type from Hood [ibid.], and Branigan [1970]): (1) The walls are vertical rather than the inward-leaning corbelled construction typically seen in *tholoi*; (2) no lintel was noted that would have supported the entrance portal, nor was there any evidence of a stone slab that could have served as an entrance cover; (3) the quantity of construction debris in the floor of the circular space did not seem sufficient to represent the collapsed remains of a beehive vault, although it is true that I am unable to gauge the depth of the space (perhaps more debris is hidden below the current floor level); (4) finally, the presence of at least a few roof tiles near the structure is not consistent with *tholos* construction.

On the other hand, although the structure is badly looted, it does appear to be encased in a low mound in the manner of *tholoi*. The interior dimension of the space, 3.6 m, is within the range of the smallest *tholoi* in the Aegean, which range in diameter from about 3 m to over 13 m (Branigan 1970: Figure 3); the tomb reported from Cyprus is less than 2.5 m in diameter. Unfortunately, the paucity of pottery at this site made it impossible to identify the site as to period, so the question of whether this is a *tholos* cannot be securely answered. The absence of other Late Bronze Age or Early Iron Age sites in this area also strongly suggests this is a later construction, probably related to Cestrus.

28-c-02-b-3 (ND-4)

This is a substantial stone terrace, measuring 9 m (parallel to the contour) by 5 m (crossing the contour)(Plate 3-30). The terrace is located on one of the main ridges providing access to Cestrus, and may have served as a gate-like or defensive feature for the hill-top city. Very little pottery was noted, but what was found is consistent with this structure dating to the period of occupation of Cestrus. One C. S. Rounded Everted Rim Bowl was included (ER), and one Zemer 41 amphora (ER or LR). The other diagnostic sherds were local types (an Antioch Zemer 41) and a West Cilicia Jug.

28-c-02-b-4 (ER-16, LR-18)

The site consists primarily of a sherd scatter, with little evidence of construction debris (although the site is covered with dense vegetation). Few roof tiles were noted, and the only other artifact seen was a partial grinding stone measuring 50 cm in radius.

28-c-02-b-5 (ND-5)

This is an isolated structure situated at the top of one of the main ridge lines providing access to Cestrus. Construction is of substantial shaped stones, and measures

7.5 by 7.5 m, with its orientation conforming to the ridge line (which is close to EW). The highest standing wall is approximately 2 m high. One stone roofed room in the interior of the structure is intact, exposed by a looter's pit. Almost no pottery or other artifacts were observed. This is one of three structures built on ridges below Cestrus (including ND-2 and ND-4), that may have played a role in traffic regulation and defense along the main approaches to the city.

28-c-03-d (Site not located)

Bean and Mitford (1970: 155, fn 14) describe a cliff-facing site overlooking the sea 3 km south of Macar village, previously reported by Paribeni and Romanelli, that included a dedication on a column drum, two other column drums, three Ionic capitals, part of a sarcophagus, and a tesselated pavement. From the description, the site may have been an isolated tomb. Bean revisited the site in 1963 and found little remaining evidence of it. Owing to our interest in locating residential sites, we did not inspect the cliff faces in this grid square in detail, and we did not encounter the site.

28-c-03-d-2 (LR-20)

This is an isolated walled compound located just below the top of a small rocky knob that extends west from the main ridgeline of the Güdü massif. Although measurement and surface collecting were impeded by dense vegetation, I estimate the dimensions of the compound to be 20 m (SW-NE) by 23 m (NW-SE). The stone and mortar walls measured as much as 70 cm thick. Additional wall fragments inside the east corner of the compound may be the remains of a small structure. A grinding stone (described in the field notes as a "mortar/grinder") was encountered in this corner area. The collection was very poor, but one LR Wheel Ridged amphora was tabulated. Ancient terrace fragments (not now in use) dot the slopes between the compound and the main ridge, and may be associated with this structure.

28-c-03-d-3 and 4 (ER-18, LR-21)(Figure 3-15)

This site is located along the highest ridge line of the Güdü massif (between 375 and 460 masl)(Plate 3-18). The northern site limits extend beyond our map coverage, so Figure 3-15 estimates both topography and site distribution in this direction. Two distinct patches of pottery and building stone total 4.4 ha in area, and a trace distribution of pottery was noted around these. Seven diagnostic ER fine ware sherds were collected, and LR is also present, indicated by two 2 amphora. One Rhodian Amphora (300 BCE to 50 BCE) was collected, but only one other Hellenistic sherd was present in the collection (Hellenistic Black Glaze).

A reservoir is located on the south-facing ridge of the main part of the site, near the site's southern limit. The interior dimensions of the feature are approximately 9 by 9 m. The maximum visible elevation of the reservoir wall includes 90 cm cut into bedrock and an additional 190 cm of stone and mortar construction. The construction is of large (up to 1 m long), roughly finished stones. There is some evidence of mortar. A second reservoir is located on the north-facing slope of the hill. While it has largely collapsed, I estimated the interior dimensions of approximately 10 m N-S by 5 m E-W, while its depth was at least 2 m. Northwest, and below this feature, two substantial terrace wall fragments were noted (Plate 3-31). These may be the remains of terraces constructed to create flat spaces for residential or other use, and/or may have been defensive features.

Up slope from the south reservoir we encountered a well preserved house with its door lintel still in place (Plate 3-32). The door (which is 1.2 m wide) is in the center of a front wall 5.7 m corner to corner (on the outside). The wall thickness in this front section is approximately .7 m. The structure is 6.7 m in length, again, measuring the outside, and the walls define what apparently was a single room accessible through the one door. Another room at the back of the space extends the structure by 3.1 m (and is 5.9 m wide), but is not accessible to the main chamber by way of an interior door. A large room complex is located directly above the house, and at the highest point of the hill (Figure 3-16, Plate 3-33). Construction is of roughly shaped stone, with some mortar in evidence. Wall thickness is variable, but averages approximately 50 cm. The function of this complex is unclear, but several ground stone implements in and near it suggest some kind of industrial function. The dimensions and possible functions of the stones are as follows (Figure 3-16): (1) a possible press, 90 cm in diameter; (2) function unknown; (3) estimated radius 50-60 cm, a possible press?; (4) a fragment of a possible millstone; (5) a possible press fragment located 15 m down slope and NW of the complex, with an estimated radius of 50 to 60 cm.

Overall, the site's artifact assemblage seemed poor. Diagnostic artifacts, particularly decorated pottery, are not common, and roof tiles were encountered comparatively infrequently. While most residential construction here probably was of stone, most was roughly shaped.

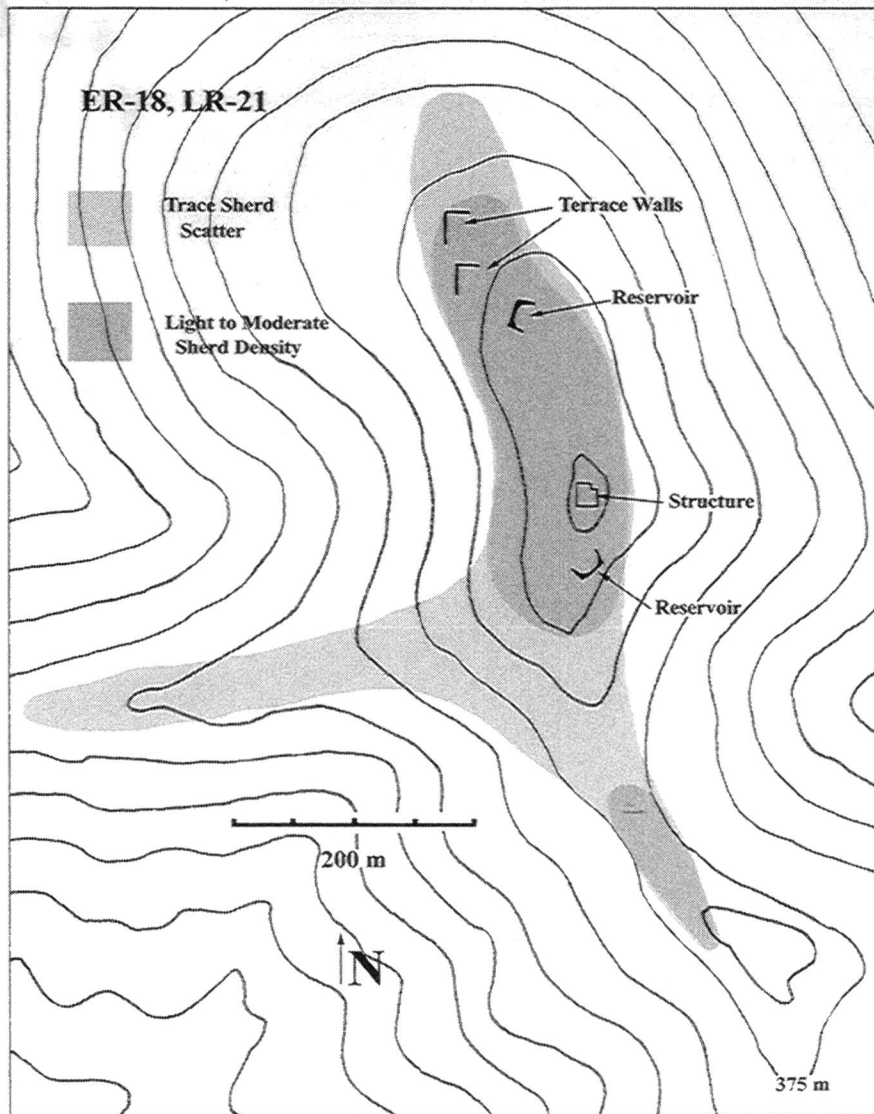

Figure 3-15. Detail of ER-18, LR-21.

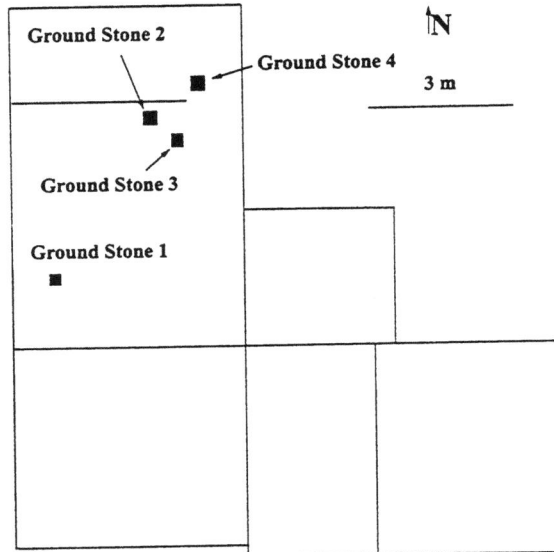

Figure 3-16. Sketch of the probable industrial structure located at the highest point of ER-18, LR-21.

Nephelion Hinterland

This hinterland consists of grid squares 28-c-08-a, b, and c and parts of 28-c-03-d and 28-c-09-d (Figures 3-13, and 3-17 to 3-20). Topographically, the area is dominated by a broad NW-SE trending ridge that I refer to as the "Muz Kent Ridge," named after the village located to northwest of Nephelion, along the north slopes below the ridge (Plates 3-34, 3-35). The ocean-facing portion of the ridge, below about 250 masl, is very steep and rugged (Plate 3-36), and is used primarily for banana terraces; little of this latter zone was investigated in detail except by way of the occasional access roads. Owing primarily to these sea-facing slopes, this hinterland contains roughly 32% steep slope. The ridge line where Nephelion is located provides the easiest access from the Muz Kent ridge to the sea in this general area. Karamut and Russell (1999: 362-3) suggest that a very small inlet located west of Nephelion was the site's harbor (Figures 3-18, 3-22). Most of the remainder of the Muz Kent ridge above the steep coastal zone, and its outlying minor ridge lines running north and northeast from the ridge, are gently sloping and have among the deepest ridge line soils in the survey area. Thus sloping but arable soils make up 60% of the hinterland area. Only 8% is alluvium, located beyond the ridge to the north, and outside of the survey area. Today the sloping but arable area is used for grazing, dry-farmed wheat, and the occasional olive grove, although modern settlement is restricted to the lower slopes beyond the north edge of the survey area. In the past, the ridge summit was probably used for agriculture, but may also have had scattered residences, as evidenced by a consistent low frequency of off-site pottery and small sherd scatters (ND-6 and ND-7). While the pottery in these latter localities was not highly diagnostic, a surface collection of the ridge line north of Nephelion included two Cypriot Sigillata Rounded Everted Rim Bowls, and another Cypriot Sigillata sherd of indefinite form (all ER in date).

Site Descriptions

28-c-03-d-1 (ER-19)

This site consists of two adjacent sherd scatters, one on the top of a small hill, and another in a field just below it to the south. One possible roof tile noted. Several stone walls in the area appear to be recent terrace construction.

28-c-03-d-5 (ER-20, LR?)

This is an area of moderate density pottery and abundant stone terrace and stone structure remains on a rocky knob overlooking the modern village of Muz Kent. While we were there it was being bulldozed for greenhouse construction. In areas of the site not yet destroyed we observed abundant remains of stone construction, with many of the stones better shaped than is seen in nearby sites (for example, ER-18, LR-21). The collection was never tabulated (the site was described on the last day of the season, and our ceramicist was already finishing up his work by this time), but field notes indicate a comparatively high density of Roman fine wares, possibly ER in date, although LR is also possible. At the highest point of the rocky knob we found a stone structure, roughly 5 by 5 m, of unknown function. Lower downhill and east of this building is another structure that appears to be a house, consisting of a four-room complex accessible by way of one door (Figure 3-21, Plate 3-37).

28-c-08-b-1 (ER-21)

A small sherd scatter on the highest point of a high, narrow, rugged ridge. This is a marginal area with little to offer in the way of cultivable soils or gentle slopes. The highest point of the ridge is the site of a rectangular structure, possibly a platform, measuring roughly 6 m NS by 7 m EW. The platform has been heavily looted. A large terrace was built below the platform along its east and south edges. Construction stone includes many large, roughly shaped pieces. The crudity of construction, lack of roof tiles, and comparative paucity of pottery suggests a short occupation or possibly a non-residential function. The collection was poor, but did include one diagnostic ER Red Ware.

28-c-08-c-1 (HLN-3, ER-22, LR-22) Nephelion (Nephelis)(Figure 3-22)

Site Area and Architecture

The site is poorly known archaeologically, but its identification as Nephelion is convincing (Karamut and Russell 1999: 364-7). It is found along three adjacent ridge lines from near sea level to 225 masl (with scattered sherd cover even higher). The highest density of pottery was found over 15 ha, while the total area, including trace sherd scatters, is 25 ha. Previous archaeological surveys by Heberdey, Wilhelm, Paribeni, Romanelli, Rosenbaum, Huber, Onurkan, Bean, and Mitford did not locate Nephelion, so published information on inscriptions and architecture is limited. Karamut and Russell (1999) visited the site several times after 1991, and provide a preliminary sketch-map and description of the major buildings and features (their Figure 5). They identify an acropolis located adjacent to a high rocky knob of the central ridge line (Plate 3-38). Two of the structures in this area are well preserved, one with standing wall fragments of multi-story height that Karamut and Russell identify as a gate tower of the acropolis ring-wall (Plate 3-39). The other is the best-preserved temple in the survey area, with the SW corner standing to the raking cornice of the rear pediment (Karamut and Russell 1999: 357-9)(Plate 3-39); several inscribed dedications are also found in this area. An olive-crushing basin was noted nearby. A well-preserved theater (*bouleuterion*) is located upslope from the acropolis (Plate 3-40), adjacent to a stone-lined water channel (Figure 3-22).

The ridge west of the acropolis served as a necropolis; very few sherds or roof tiles were noted here, but several small structures clearly are tomb remains (Karamut and Russell 1999: 362). Scattered, finely cut pieces of a marble-like white limestone are all that remains of one elaborate looted structure in this area. A stone wall that may be contemporary with one of the structures, approximately 1 m high, was constructed along the center of the ridge, dividing it into NW and SE halves.

Collection Areas

Collection Area 1 An area of .8 ha in the northern part of the acropolis area. All diagnostic pottery is LR.

Collection Area 2 An area of .03 ha located 150 m below and south of the acropolis and separated from it by a steep slope. Here, an isolated building was noted sitting on a ledge overlooking a cliff some 30 m directly above the sea (Karamut and Russell's Building E). The building is roughly rectangular, some 16 by 16 m, divided into two large rooms. Although it is covered with dense vegetation, it is still largely intact, with a well-preserved door facing north and an arched window facing the water. A collection was made from the banana terraces adjacent to the structure. All pottery is LR. The field notes suggest it may have served as a warehouse, although Karamut and Russell (ibid.: 362) suggest it may have been a coastguard station housing a small military garrison.

Collection Area 3 An area of .25 ha on the high-point of the acropolis ridge and adjacent slope to the south. Terrace construction on the slope and the comparatively dense concentration of surface pottery suggests this may have been a residential area. ER and LR are present.

Collection Area 4 An area of .18 ha near the north edge of the site, at the top of the ridge east of collection area 1, in the vicinity of Karamut and Russell's Buildings C and D. This area has

an abundance of standing stone and mortar architecture. Only LR in date.

Collection Area 5 An area of .25 ha on steep slope below and southwest of the acropolis. Here we collected a possible Classic Black Glaze sherd, and diagnostics of HLN, ER, and LR date.

Collection Area 6 An area of .6 ha along a steep slope south and east of the acropolis. Although steeply sloping, numerous terrace and retaining walls were noted, suggesting a residential function. One loom weight was noted. HLN, ER, and LR were identified.

Collection Area 7 An area of .2 ha located downhill and south of the *bouleuterion*. The only period is LR. Numerous fragments of amphora feet, handles, and rims.

Collection Area 8 An area of .27 ha northwest and down slope from the acropolis; LR only.

Historical Summary

Several scholars have identified Nephelion (or Nephelis) as the port location for the inland center of Claudiopolis at Ninica (later Juliosebaste)(Heberdey and Wilhelm 1896: 132; Jones 1971: 211; Levick 1967: 198-9); Bean and Mitford (1965: 29-30), in turn, identified inland Asar Tepe as Juliosebaste. Karamut and Russell (1999: 366-7) suggest, instead, that the Nephelion site can probably be equated with Isaurian Nephelis (cf. Ramsay 1890: 381), in part because Asar Tepe is far too small to have had *polis* status. Following their argument, the Nephelion site is the location renamed Claudiopolis at Ninica by Antiochus IV during the first century AD, and that later received a Roman Colony from Domitian (AD 81-96)(Jones 1971: 210-11). At a later date, the center was renamed Juliosebaste, or Sebaste, as it is referred to in Byzantine lists (ibid.).

I infer that Nephelion reached its maximum population size during the LR Period, given that HLN and ER diagnostics were found only in a small area near the site's acropolis (collection areas 3, 5, and 6)(Figure 3-22). Based on their review of the history of the site in late antiquity, Karamut and Russell (1999: 370-1) suggest it may have entered a period of decline in an atmosphere of endemic conflict after the mid third century. In the conclusion I evaluate their suggestions in light of the ceramic evidence.

28-c-08-c-2 (ER-23)

This site is located at the top of a rocky, steep-sided knob at the south end of a N-S trending ridge connected to the main Muz Kent ridge by a saddle (Plate 3-41). The site includes two nearby sherd scatters north of the saddle with terrace construction and a circular feature. Slopes west,

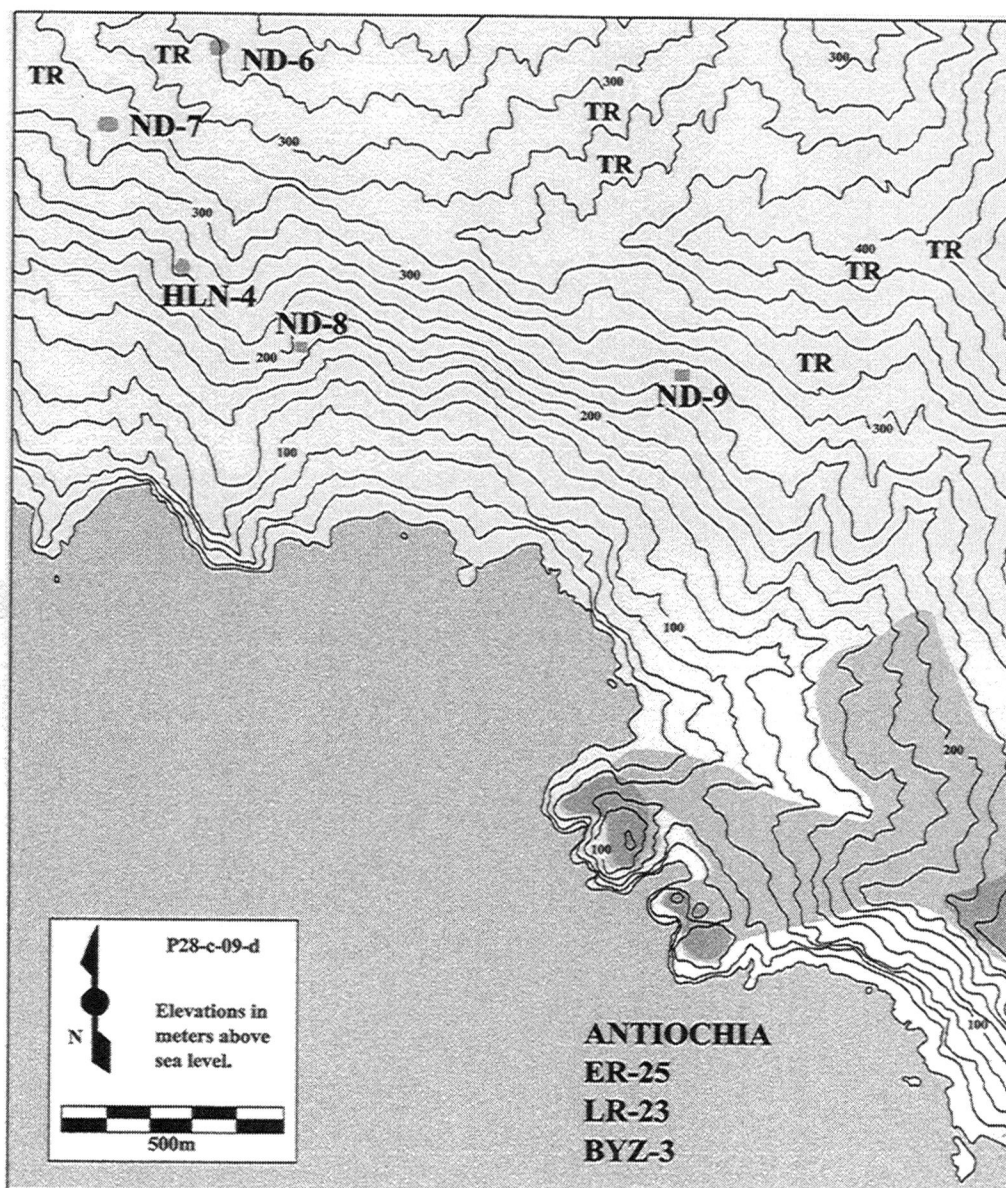

Figure 3-17. 28-c-09-d.

south, and east drop off steeply, and are now used primarily for banana terraces. Both Nephelion and Antiochia are visible from this high vantage point. The site area is steep and extensively covered with dense vegetation, and has been extensively looted. Numerous standing stone wall fragments, both of structures and terraces, can be seen, but no public buildings are in evidence. Remains of standing terrace walls are as high as 1.5 m. One of the best-preserved wall fragments runs EW just south of the saddle, at the site's north limit. It may have served as a defensive feature limiting access from the saddle. A substantial millstone, 170 cm in diameter and

55 cm thick, is located just north of this same wall, near the saddle. Near the stone there is a partially visible circular feature, perhaps a cistern. One loom weight noted. Comparatively few roof tiles were noted.

28-c-09-d-4 (ND-6)

Small scatter of Roman sherds, but no period diagnostics noted.

28-c-09-d-5 (ND-7)

Small sherd scatter. No Roman Period diagnostics evident.

28-c-09-d-6 (HLN-4)

A small area of sherd scatter of less than .1 ha, but whose pottery included two diagnostic Hellenistic types, a Corinth Type VII Lamp and one sherd of Hellenistic Fine Ware. A mortar and rubble wall fragment is part of what appears to be a platform measuring 9 m EW by 7 m NS (Plate 3-42). Some looting. Function unknown.

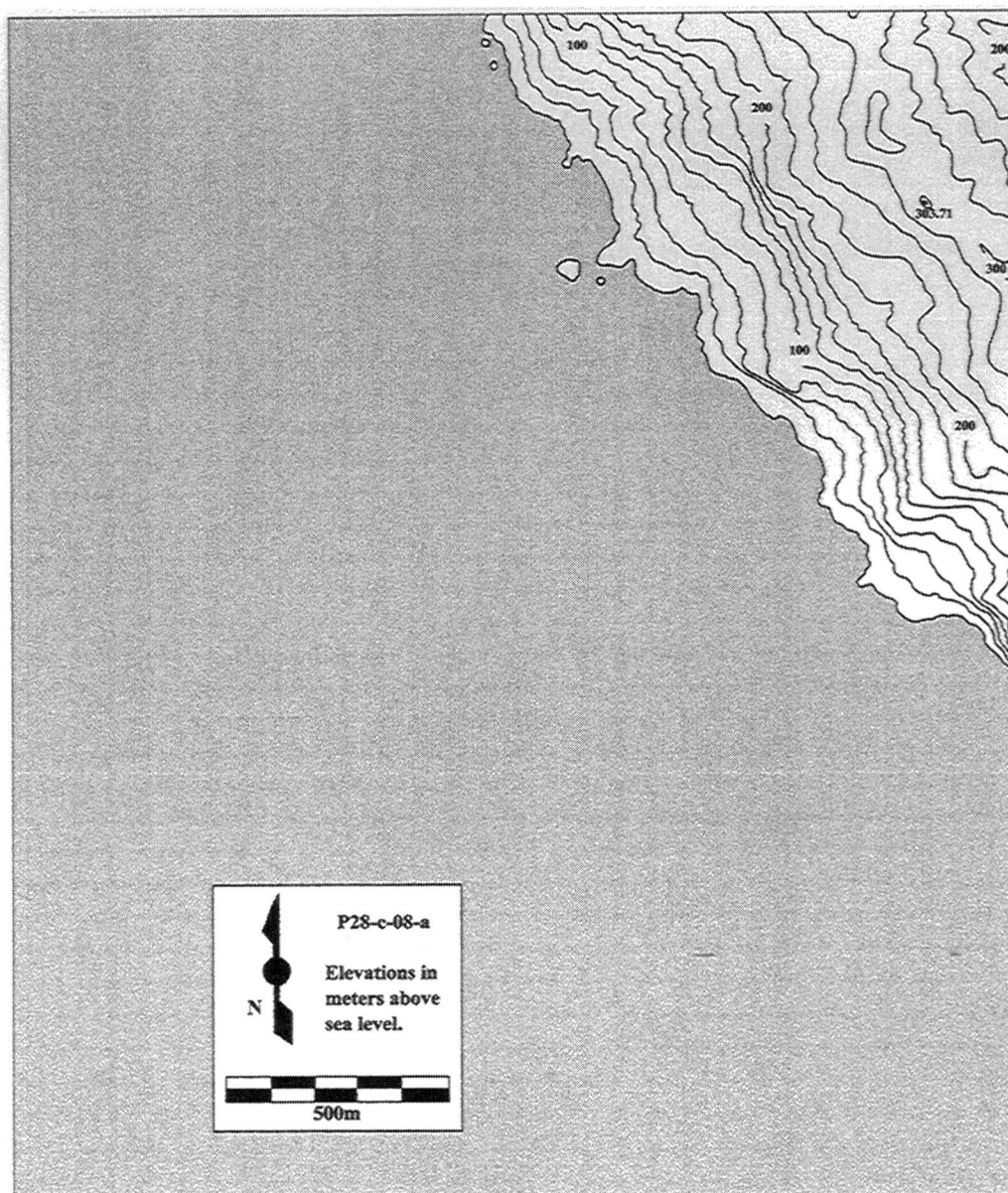

Figure 3-18. 28-c-08-a.

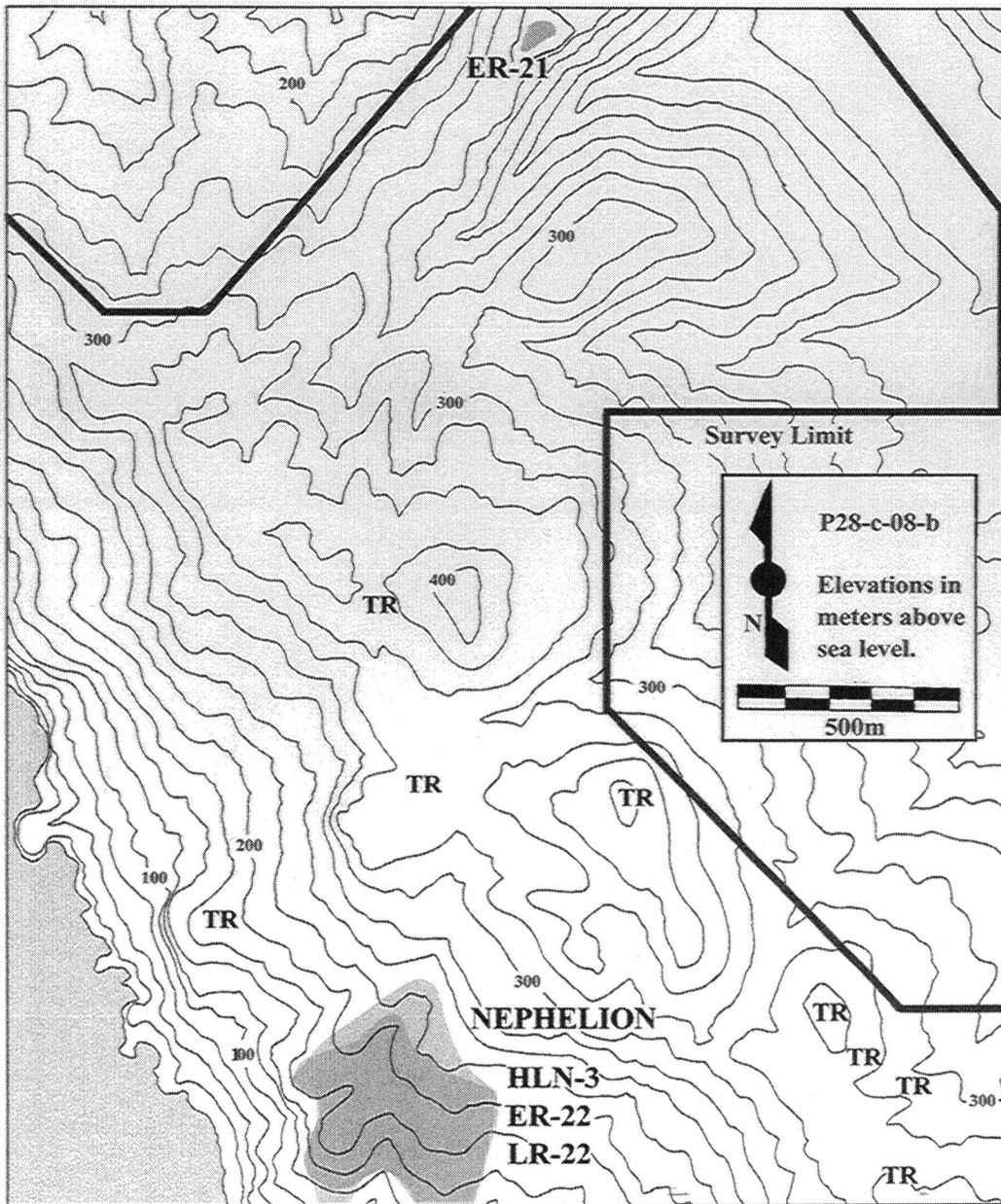

Figure 3-19. 28-c-08-b.

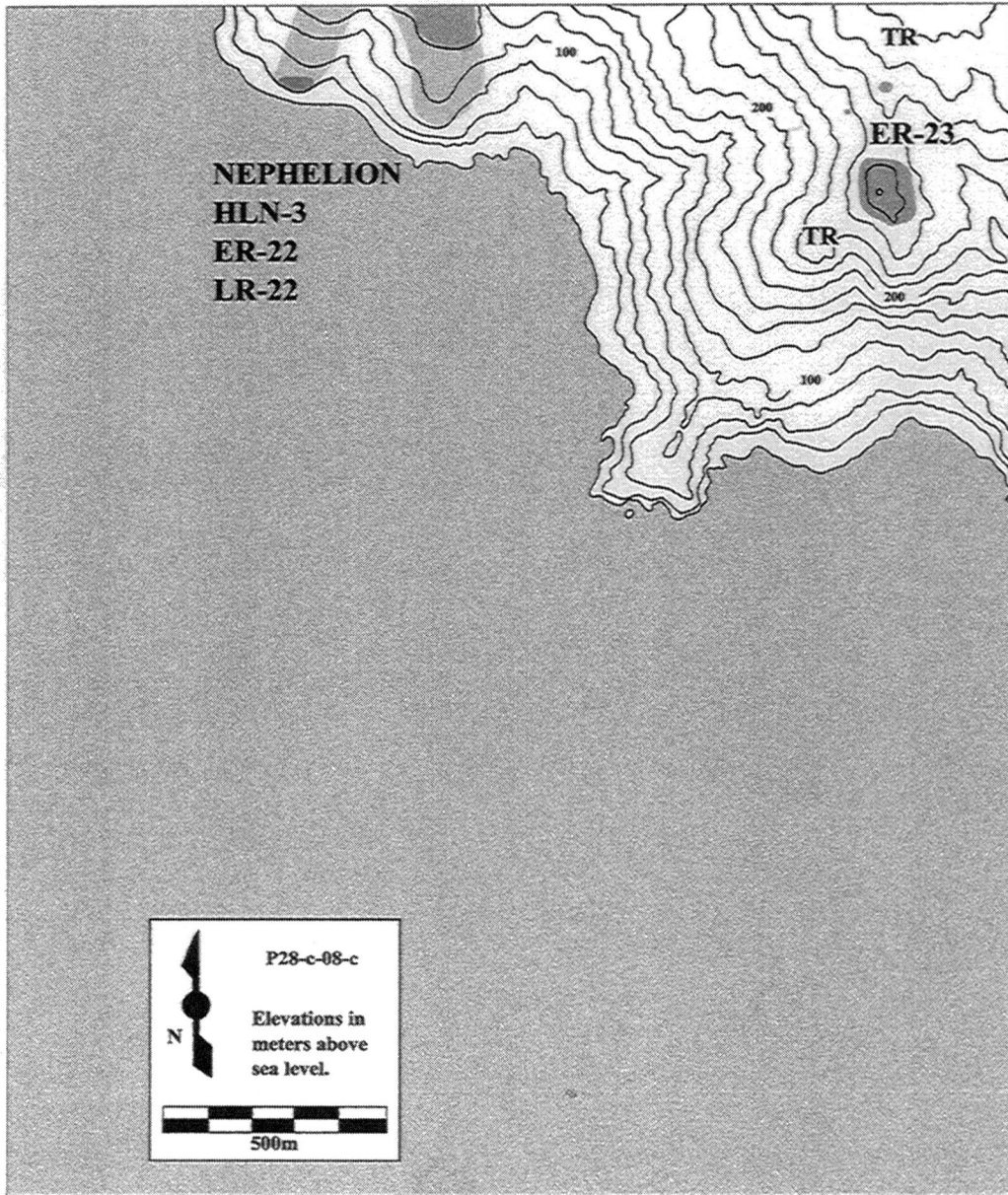

NEPHELION
HLN-3
ER-22
LR-22

P28-c-08-c

Elevations in
meters above
sea level.

500m

Figure 3-20. 28-c-08-c.

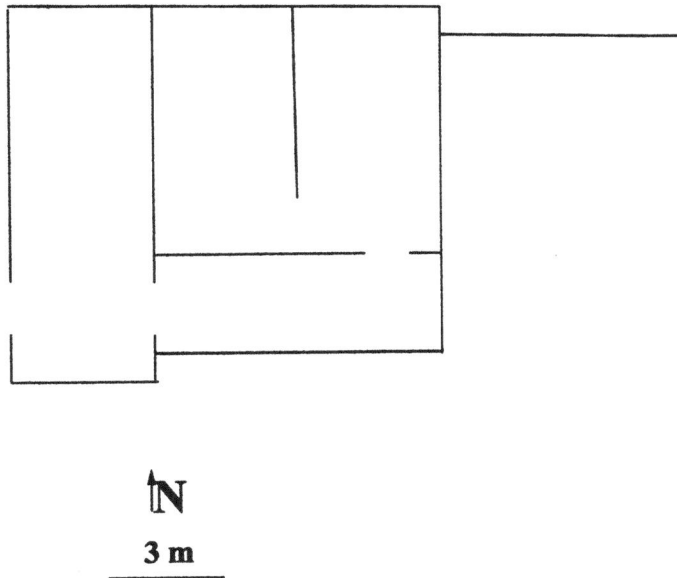

Figure 3-21. Sketch of house at ER-20.

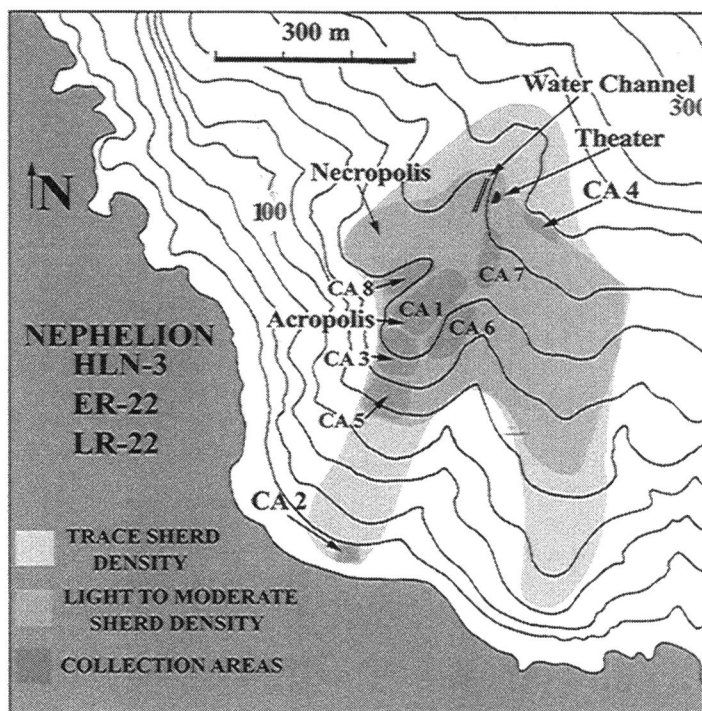

Figure 3-22. Detail of Nephelion.

Antiochia Hinterland

The hinterland of Antiochia is a rugged zone dominated by the Karadag massif (reaching an elevation of 600 masl) and its ridges running southwest (eventually joining the Muz Kent ridge) and southeast (Figure 2-3, Plates 3-43, 3-44). Relevant grid squares are 28-c-09-d, 28-c-09-c, and 2c-14-b (Figures 3-20, 3-23, 3-24). While the upper slopes of the Karadag are steep, both ridge systems below it are gently sloping along their summits and along their north facing slopes. In this direction, multiple ridge lines connect the high ridges to a small, narrow valley defining the north edge of the hinterland, and that separates the massif from the much higher and more rugged system of ridge lines farther inland. The small stream draining this valley (the Beyrebucak Dere) appears to have only a seasonal flow, and very little flat alluvial soil is found here.

This zone of ridge lines and adjacent gentle slopes east of Karadag massif are all now under cultivation, consisting mostly of dry-farmed wheat, but some greenhouses are to be found as well. Little evidence of pre-modern settlement was found in this valley or along this gently sloping area, except for a few trace scatters along the top of the ridge directly above and east of the Antiochia site (Figure 3-23). The modern community of Güney Koy extends from the valley bottom up to the latter ridge, with its most distant outlying houses nearly at the top of the ridge. An extension of Güney Koy called Nohut Yeri Mahallesi is located on the sea-facing side of the ridge, and overlaps with part of the Antiochia site.

Slopes south and west of the Karadag massif face the sea, and drop much more precipitously than those below it to the east. The upper part of the Antiochia site occupies the only comparatively flat terrain in this sea-facing zone, at an elevation of about 300 masl (Figure 3-25). South of this civic and residential area, steep cliffs drop off precipitously to the sea edge below (Plate 3-45). West of the main site area is a zone of moderate sloping ridge lines, divided by a wadi, that lead down to the lower site area (Plate 3-46). Both ridges show a trace density of pottery, the southernmost one all the way to the sea edge. Both ridges have scattered structures, including tombs (Huber 1967: Plan 2), but otherwise these lower ridges do not appear to have had ancient residential occupation. Northwest of these ridges is an even steeper and more rugged area forming a bowl-shaped inlet. Occasional sherd scatters and two isolated structures, probably tombs (ND-8, 9, Figure 3-20) are all that was found in the bowl-shaped area, now intensively used for banana terracing.

Two very steeply-sloped rocky promontories are located at the base of the ridge leading down from the main site area; this was also an area of settlement that is regarded here as a lower division of the Antiochia site as a whole (Plate 3-46). The northernmost promontory reaches an elevation of 125 masl, and is capped with a double line of fortifications (Huber 1967: Plan 2)(Plate 3-47). The abundance of Byzantine fine ware pottery here, combined with the fact that Huber (1967: 21) found a church built into the lower wall line, suggests a primarily Byzantine date for this construction, but we also collected ER, LR here, and one Greek Black Glaze sherd.

The smaller promontory projects some 50 to 75 masl. It is divided into northern and southern sections that are connected by a natural bridge over an opening providing access to a small enclosed bay (Plate 3-48). The bay is only about 50 by 75 m, but is one of the few protected moorings to be found along this rugged section of coast. A spring adjacent to the bay is still used today as a source of fresh water for boat crews (small tourist and fishing boats are able to pass through the narrow entrance). Some construction is found on this promontory, including six tombs and a church (Huber ibid.: 24).

The Antiochia hinterland was problematic to define, as it is not clear what its southeastern boundary should be. The next known site of substantial size, Charadrus, is located approximately 13 km down the coast (Bean and Mitford 1965: 42-43; 1970: Map B)(Figure 2-6), well beyond the limits of our survey. I placed the southeastern limit of the subregion arbitrarily at approximately 2500 m from the center, a distance equal to the city's estimated boundary with Nephelion. To the northeast, the boundary was arbitrarily placed along the base of the high ridge line north and east of the Karadag massif. Beyond the boundary line in this direction the high ridges vastly exceed those of the survey area in elevation, and the steep slopes inhibit agriculture. The Antiochia hinterland is generally hilly, with very little alluvial soil, even in the small valley northeast of the Karadag, and includes 41% steep slopes, 57% arable slopes, and only 2% alluvial soils.

Site Descriptions

28-c-09-d-2 (ND-8)

Fragment of a probable isolated tomb on a steep slope facing Antiochia.

28-c-09-d-3 (ND-9)

Isolated structure, possibly a tomb, on a steep slope facing Antiochia. Very little pottery. Mortar and rubble structure roughly 7 by 10 m, with two barrel-vaulted chambers evident.

28-c-09-c-1 (ER-24)

Village site located at the summit of the Karadag massif (Plate 3-44). At 600 masl, this is the highest site in the survey region. Here we found two discrete patches of pottery and construction stone, with only scattered sherds between them. The larger area looks directly over the steep northern slopes of the mountain. A large stone platform was located at the north edge of this area, measuring roughly 15 m (NW-SE) by 14 m (NE-SW)(Plate 3-49). Some roof tiles were observed. Pottery is not highly diagnostic.

28-c-09-d-1 (ER-25, LR-23, BYZ-3) Antiochia (also known as Antiocheia ad Cragum, Antioch on Sea, Antiocheia on the Kragos)(Figure 3-25)

Main Features

Huber (1967: Plan 2) describes the major architecture of Antiochia (cf. Erdemgil and Ozoral 1975). The upper site area contains the most construction and also has the most evidence for domestic settlement based on the high density of surface pottery. The main construction includes an acropolis on a high ridge over the sea-facing cliffs (our

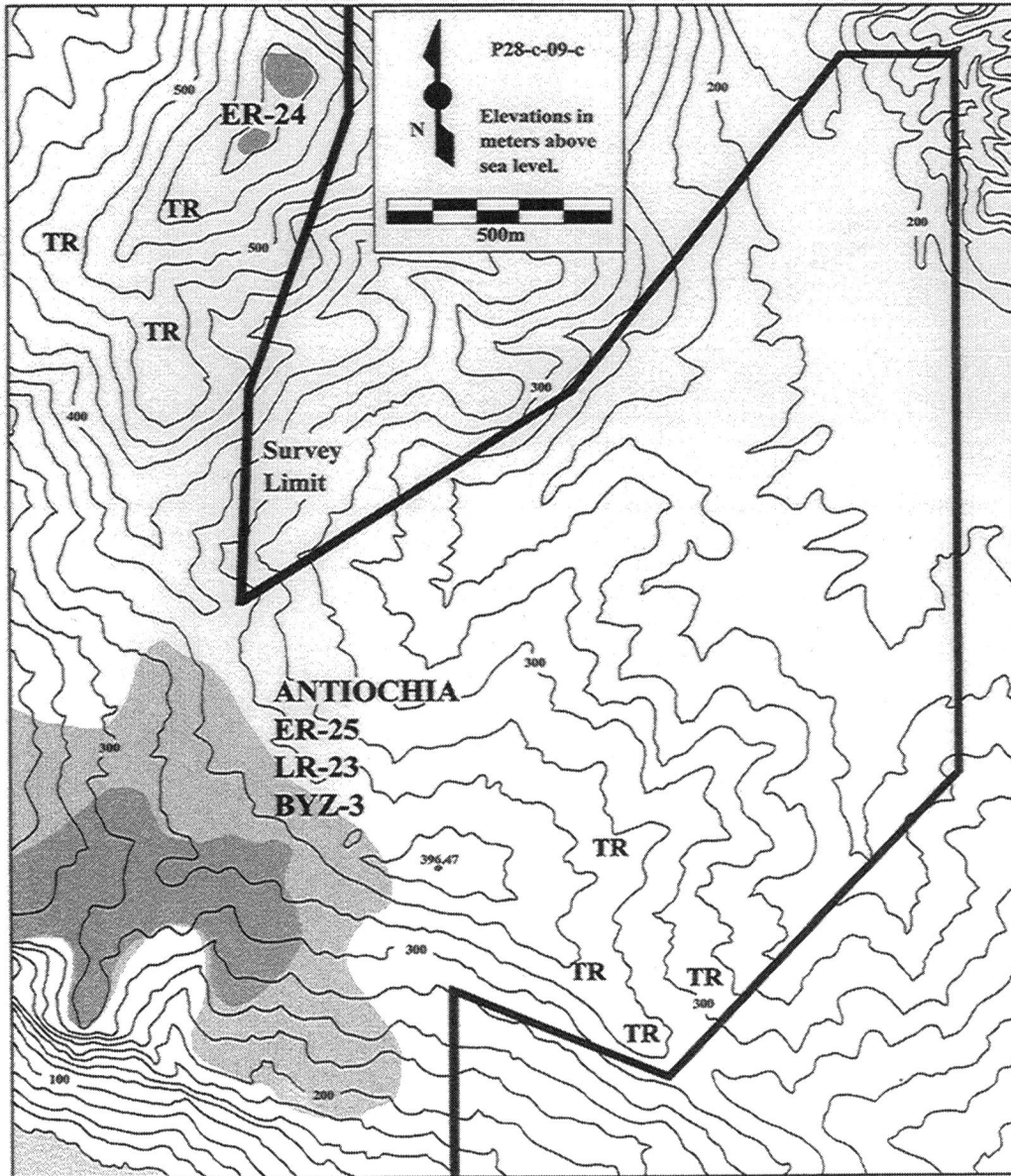

Figure 3-23. 28-c-09-c.

collection area 6), a large colonnaded square, measuring 40 by 60 m, that fronts a massive multi-storied building (including our collection area 2). This square is connected to a colonnaded terrace, our collection area 1, 150 m EW by 15 m NS, leading to a massive gate facing a wadi to the east where a bath structure was constructed (I. 12A in Huber, ibid.) Other substantial buildings in this area include a church on the ridge southeast of the bath (our collection area 16), and a marble building, north of the bath, constructed in the Corinthian Order, that was probably a temple dedicated to Zeus Lamotes (Bean and Mitford 1965: 36-41). A necropolis is located north of the large colonnaded terrace, near the edge of the site limit. Here, two "monumental tombs" were studied (Rosenbaum 1967b: 52). Heberdey and Wilhelm (1896: 152) mention seeing fragments of a water conduit leading to the ancient city along the ridge above the temple and our collection area 8 (Figure 3-25), but we were unable to locate it.

Collection Areas

Sixteen collection areas were identified, but two of these were not tabulated owing to a lack of suitable diagnostic pottery. I summarize the remaining areas as follows:

Collection Area 1 An area of .46 ha in the vicinity of the long terrace and massive gate. Mostly LR in date.

Collection Area 2 An area of .14 ha, in the northern portion of the large colonnaded terrace. Most pottery is LR and BYZ. Tile mosaic fragments noted in comparatively large quantities.

Collection Area 3 An area of .06 ha along a road-cut, and just above the long terrace. Most of the diagnostics are LR.

Collection Area 4 Extends over .3 ha, in an area of public construction southwest of the colonnaded terrace. Many roof tiles and mosaic tile pieces. One piece of iron slag noted. Pottery is mostly ER and LR, but one non-diagnostic CL/HLN Fine Ware was found.

Collection Area 5 An area of .36 ha along part of a ridge extending west from the civic center and above collection area 4. ER and LR noted.

Collection Area 6 An area of .4 ha along the west slope of the acropolis ridge, just below the summit. Although this area is densely vegetated, we were able to collect ER, LR and one Classical Transport Amphora.

Collection Area 7 This area north of the large terrace is densely vegetated and lacked sufficient diagnostics, so the collection was not kept. This appears to have been a residential zone; although the pottery collection was poor, we noted numerous roof tiles, two loom weights, and two small ground stone press fragments.

Collection Area 8 An area of .32 ha along the northern edge of the main residential zone. Includes ER and LR pottery. Here we noted numerous transport amphora fragments, clay slag, and one misfired transport amphora fragment. We infer a amphora production in this area.

Collection Area 9 We attempted to collect in this area that is part of the modern village, but found it very difficult to locate diagnostic sherds, so we did not keep this collection. LR appears to be the main period, based on our field assessment. Several Roman glass fragments and a loom weight were noted.

Collection Areas 10 and 11 (combined) This is an area totaling .7 ha along the ridge line near the west edge of the upper residential zone. Only LR was noted. One loom weight was noted.

Collection Areas 12 and 13 (combined) An area totaling 1.13 ha, on the top surface of the large promontory and along the north slopes of the promontory outside the defensive walls where Huber (1967: Plan 2) identified 3 chapels with cisterns (II. 3C, II. 4C, II.5C). BYZ was comparatively frequent in the upper zone, and some ER and LR noted. One sherd of Greek Black Glaze was also collected.

Collection Area 14 An area of .42 ha on the top surface of the lower promontory. ER, LR, and BYZ noted, along with a diagnostic HLN Strap Handle Cookpot.

Collection Area 15 An area of .45 ha just outside and below the large city gates, facing the wadi. LR noted.

Collection Area 16 An area of .3 ha in the vicinity of a church (I.15 in Huber 1967: 27, 28), and close to the eastern limit of the site's upper residential and public area. ER, LR, and BYZ noted.

Notes on Population History

Late Roman was found in every collection, and two collections (10/11 and 9) are LR only. I infer the site reached its largest population size during this period. Based on the more limited distribution of ER in the collection areas, I assume this period was approximately 15% smaller than LR in area. Byzantine pottery was found in both the upper and lower site areas, but is restricted in the upper site to the area adjacent to the main public buildings (collection areas 2 and 16). I put forward a rough estimate of 6 ha for this period, while realizing that it is difficult to estimate the size of the site based on so few diagnostic sherds. Hellenistic pottery is not well represented at Antiochia; far more was found at Iotape, Selinus, and Nephelion. The presence of a well-dated Hellenistic diagnostic in collection area 14, as well as a Greek Black Glaze and a Classical Transport Amphora, suggest the possibility of a small settlement here prior to the ER period, but no site number was assigned due to the paucity of diagnostics.

Historical Summary

"Antiocheia Upon Cragus" (or "Antiocheia ad Cragum" in Bean and Mitford [1965: 34], Antiochia ad Cragum in Huber [1967: 18], and Antioch on Sea in Jones [1971: 211]) was a namesake founding of Antiochus IV sometime between the time he was reinstated to rulership in AD 41 and the end of his reign in AD 72 (Jones 1971: 211; Magie 1975: 549). Although evidence for Hellenistic Period occupation may have been largely overwhelmed by the ER and LR occupations, our ceramic collections indicate very little Classical or Hellenistic presence. After its foundation, Antiochia appears to have rapidly increased in importance; by the middle of the second century, it had a city council and public officials (Magie 1975: 550). The city issued coins in the Roman Imperial Period, from Antoninus Pius to Valerian (Head 1911: 717). Later, Antiochia was listed as a see of bishops in lists like the *notitia episcopatuum*, belonging to Isauria and the metropolis of Seleucia (Rosenbaum 1967a: viii). There is no subsequent record of a community here until the recent period (ibid.), although Rosenbaum (1967c: 68) suggests that two structures located on the slopes below the upper fortified citadel were Medieval pilgrimage churches.

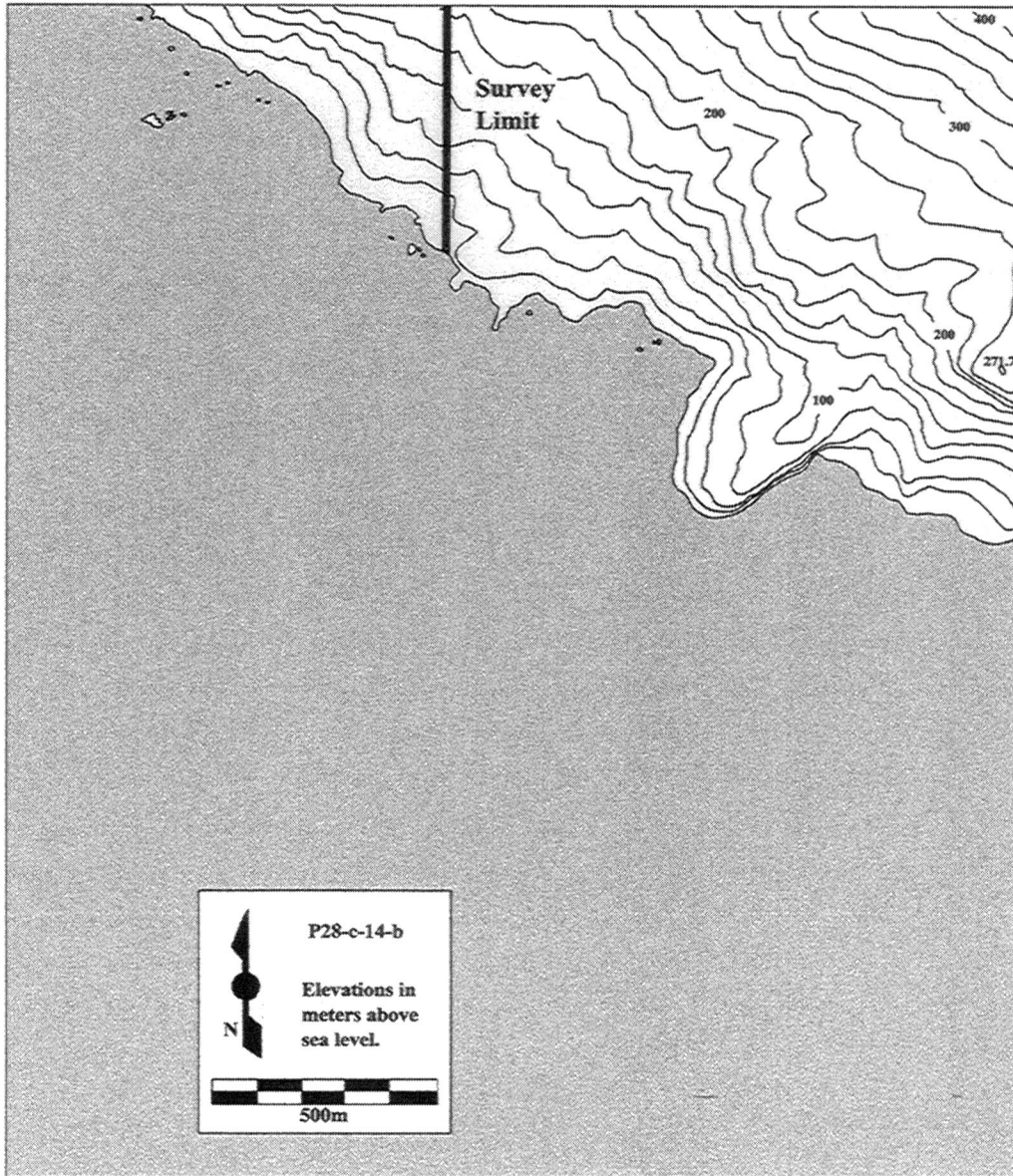

Figure 3-24. 28-c-14-b.

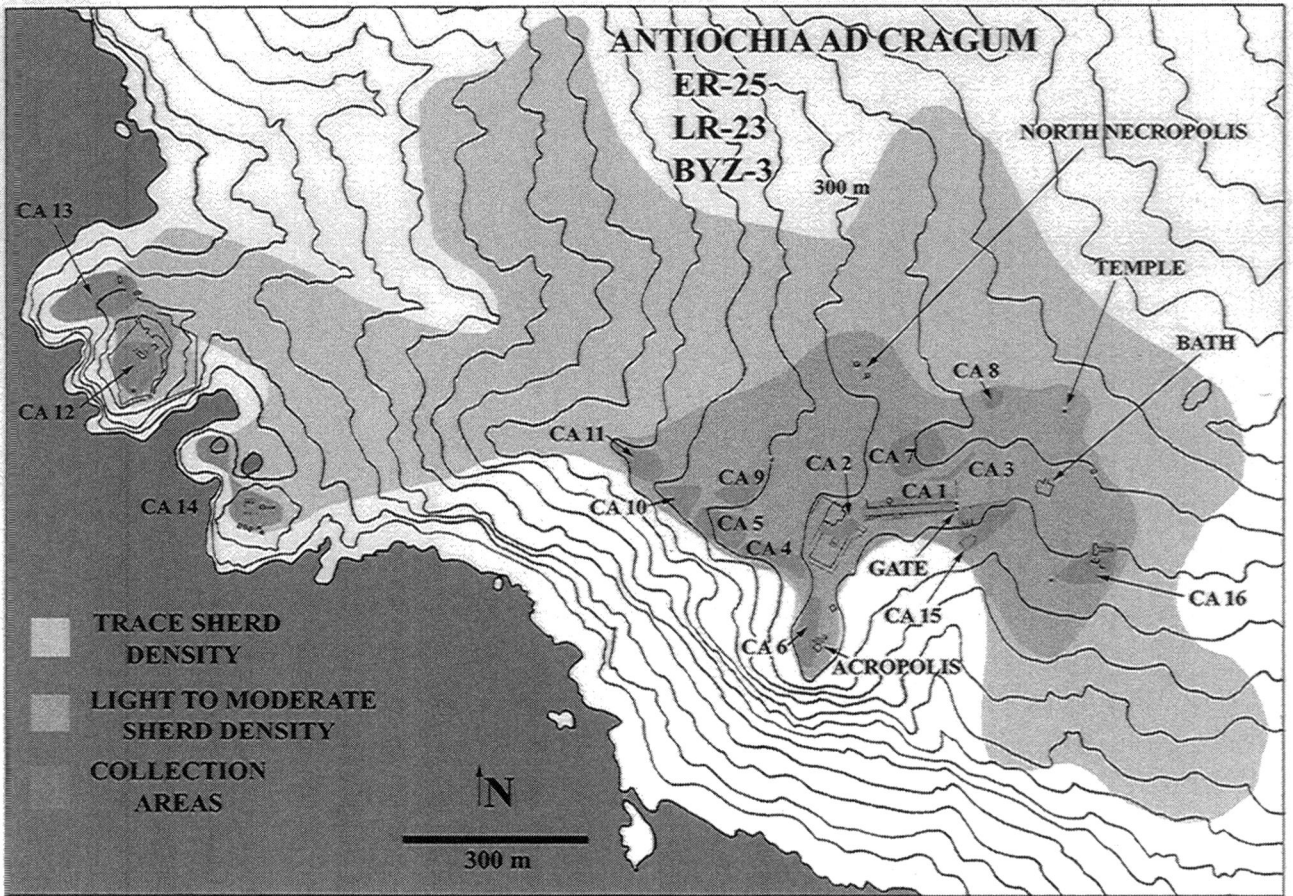

Figure 3-25. Antiochia, showing limits of sherd scatter, collection areas, and main features of public architecture and public spaces.

Chapter 4

Conclusions

Authors including Shaw (1990), Hopwood (1983, 1986) and Braun (1982: 14, 15) describe the persistent military conflict, banditry, and piracy characteristic of Cilicia Tracheia. The endemic conflict and insecurity evidently made human settlement problematic in the survey area, but the intervention of strong states could create conditions more conducive to community life. But under what conditions would states intervene? Coastal Rough Cilicia (along with adjacent upland Isauria), was beyond the limits of effective state control until quite late, including Assyrian, Hittite, Babylonian, and Persian states (mid second millennium to mid fourth century BCE). According to Shaw (1990: 203-11), what power was exercised episodically took the form of weak personal ties between rulers and local mountain-based chiefs, leaving the area without any real administrative presence (ibid.: 210). It was not until after 300 BCE that Seleucid Syria and Ptolemaic Egypt established settlements with an eye toward regulating coastal traffic and exploiting local forest resources, but even then Cilicia was a "debatable ground" disputed between these two powers (Jones 1971: 197-8), and these outposts were abandoned after 200 BCE (Shaw 1990: 218). After 67 BCE, the Roman state intervened far more directly and powerfully than had any prior polity.

The willingness of a state to establish effective control has to be seen in light of what advantages might accrue through the exercise of power. Only when resources are deemed worth exploiting, or when there is a strategic advantage, is it likely that a state will expend the resources necessary to invest administratively and militarily in a marginal area. I suggest it was not until the Hellenistic Period that the region's potential for the production of forest resources became sufficiently of economic interest that military and administrative actions were initiated; Rostovtzeff (1941: 1168-70) documents the intensification of forest exploitation under the Hellenistic kingdoms. For the Romans, in addition, the coastal settlements became part of a ring of defenses circling the lawless and rebellious Isaurians (Hopwood 1986: 344; Jones 1971: 212), and provided a staging area for the passage of Roman troops and officials to the east (Onurkan 1967: 74). For example, Trajan appears to have used Iotape as his last port of call before sailing to Cyprus on his way to Syrian Antioch (Bean and Mitford 1965: 29), and an inscription at Antiochia (Bean and Mitford 1965: 41, their number 44) honors a Roman official passing through on a mission to the emperor, who was in the eastern frontier.

Hellenistic Period Population Growth

I suggest that these changing political, strategic, and economic conditions account for the near absence of settlement prior to the Classical Period, while for the Hellenistic Period we found four sites (and a few other areas of scattered sherds), with an estimated total population of about 1400 (Table 4-1, Figures 4-1, 4-2).

This was no profound demographic transition, but it does appear to signal a changing international scene in which a little used area was finally undergoing the process of marginal periphery incorporation into larger political and economic domains.

The modest increase documented by the survey for the Hellenistic Period largely confirms the conclusions of prior researchers who studied public architecture, tombs, and inscriptions, namely, that there is only a small pre-Roman presence in the survey area and elsewhere along the coast lands of Rough Cilicia. In the whole coastal area from Side to Seleucia on the Calycadnus, Bean and Mitford (1970: 109) count only 5 pre-Roman inscriptions. Of course, Luwian-speaking groups living here could have used local diagnostic pottery types that we are unable to recognize, but this seems unlikely, at least for the coast, where aboriginal populations are known to have readily adopted Hellenistic and Roman cultural elements (Hopwood 1986: 345). Ptolemaic interest in the timber resources of coastal Rough Cilicia (Bean and Mitford 1962: 187) would have favored the growth of communities with easy access to higher elevation forests, including Iotape and Nephelion. A Ptolemaic garrison was placed at what must have been the longest established community in this area, at Selinus (Bagnall 1976: 115).

A Piracy Hypothesis

In the scenario just presented, only strong states make settlement of the coast feasible. An alternative hypothesis has been offered by Rauh (n.d.). He describes a substantial growth of fortified centers extending from the gulf of Pamphylia to coastal Rough Cilicia during the period of Cilician piracy, between 139 and 67 BCE. Based on a vague reference to a pirate base at the "Kragos mountain," Rauh concludes that Antiochia of the survey area can be included as one of the sites in question (ibid.: 4). Rauh's argument is that in the absence of a strong state, population growth and economic development will occur in a location such as coastal Rough Cilicia. Weak control provides a suitable environment for immigrant dissident elements from diverse quarters who organize illicit but profitable enterprises. This is similar to Rostovtzeff (1941: 781-5), who suggests that weak Seleucid control of the Rough Cilician coast and adjacent mountains, combined with the emergence of an Asia Minor slave trade, created conditions favoring the growth of Cilician piracy in the Late Hellenistic Period (cf. Jones 1971: 201; Ormerod 1978: 201-7).

Would piracy have been a highly profitable economic strategy for groups in the survey area during the Late Hellenistic Period? The extremely small population size inferred from the survey data suggests this process did not, in fact, play out here to any great degree. However, it would be impossible to give a definite answer to this question, given that the current ceramic chronology does

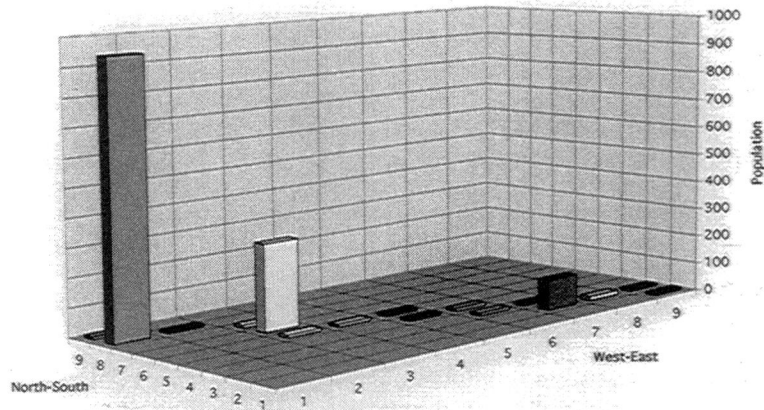

Figure 4-1. Hellenistic Period population totals by grid square (from Figure 2-4).

Table 4-1. Population estimates by period, hinterland, and community type. The category Res/Hamlet refers to isolated farmsteads.

Sum of Population		Comm Type			
Period	Subregion	Res/Hamlet	Urban	Village	Grand Total
1 HLN	1 IOT		945		945
	2 SEL			300	300
	4 NEPH	5		106	111
1 HLN Total		5	945	406	1356
2 ER	1 IOT		2184	194	2378
	2 SEL	128	2300	638	3066
	3 CES	60	3360	831	4251
	4 NEPH		140	348	488
	5 ANT		7665	125	7790
2 ER Total		188	15649	2136	17973
3 LR	1 IOT		2184	194	2378
	2 SEL	163	4900	638	5701
	3 CES	75	3360	831	4266
	4 NEPH		3150		3150
	5 ANT		9030		9030
3 LR Total		238	22624	1663	24525
4 BYZ	1 IOT		1575		1575
	2 SEL		2000		2000
	5 ANT		1260		1260
4 BYZ Total			4835		4835
Grand Total		431	44053	4205	48689

58

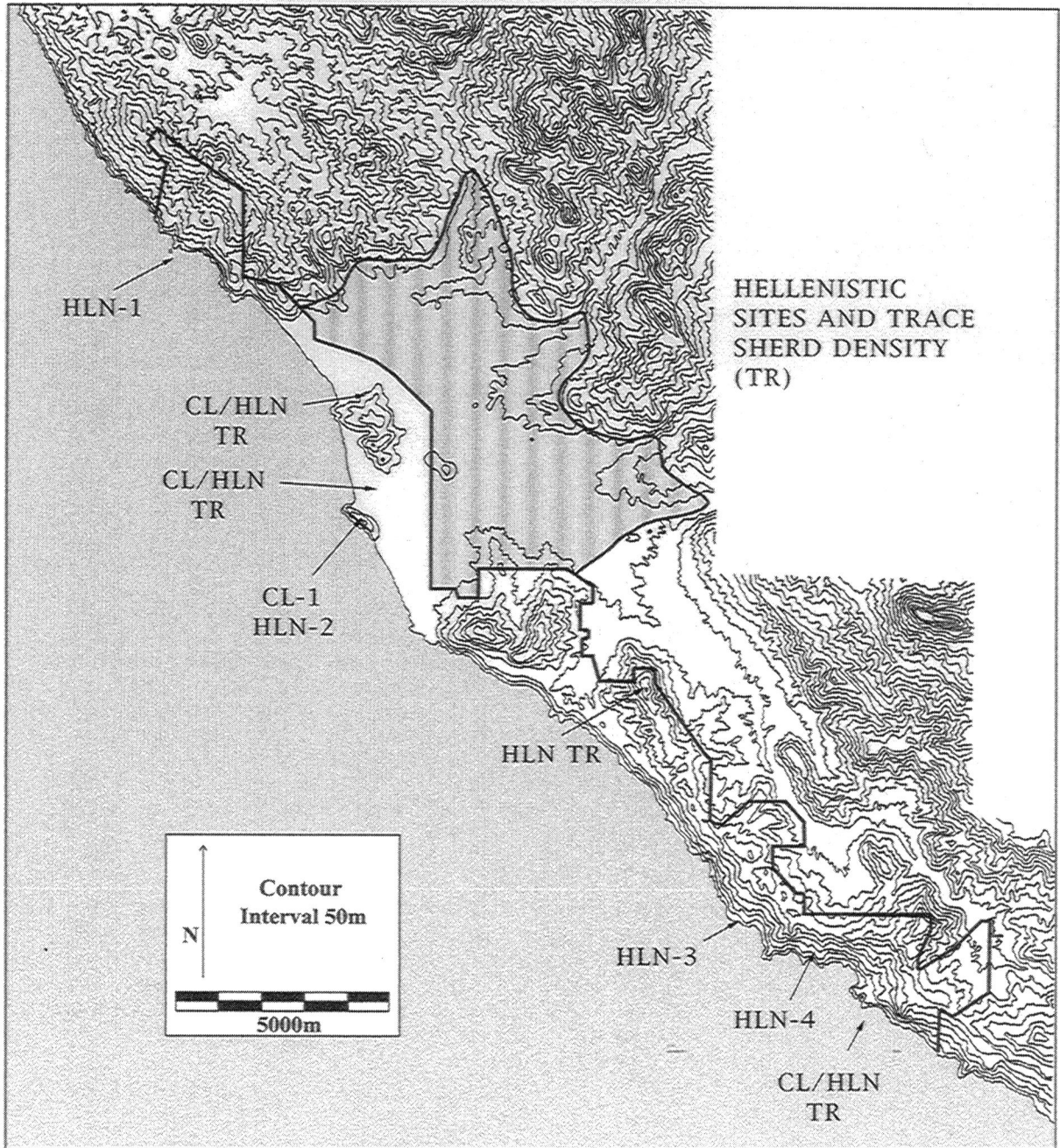

Figure 4-2. Hellenistic Period sites

not allow us to distinguish the specific time span of the period of piracy, 139 to 67 BCE. It is telling, however, that one of the pirate bases identified by Rauh, Antiochia, has so little Hellenistic pottery it was not even assigned a site number. Clearly, during the Hellenistic Period, the population of the survey area was not involved in a wine for slave trade on a scale similar to that between Italy and Gaul in the 2nd and 3rd centuries BCE (Tchernia 1983). If this had been the case, we would have found a large number of diagnostic amphora of the Late Hellenistic Period, but we did not. For the Classic and Hellenistic Periods combined, we surface-collected only 18 imported amphora out of a total of 650 collected, and 15 of these (Pseudo Coan) may date to Early Roman as well.

Also counter to Rauh's hypothesis is evidence suggesting that piracy could actually have inhibited economic activity for some coastal settlements. In one of the Hellenistic Period inscriptions studied by Bean and Mitford (1965: 22, their 26), from Syedra (the next large coastal site north of Iotape), a complaint is registered concerning how the city had been harassed by pirates. And later inscriptions support the contention that settlement growth can be attributed significantly to state intervention, and that an important function of local polities in this area was policing against the endemic banditry of the hill peoples. At Iotape, a type of policing official is mentioned, the *paraphulax,* rarely seen in inscriptions from other parts of the Roman Empire (Hopwood 1983: 176-7). This was an official "...whose duties included the patrolling of civic boundaries and the control of remoter villages" (Bean and Mitford 1965: fn. 19). At Iotape and other sites of the survey region, an unusually large proportion of inscriptions name Roman officials, reflecting both gratitude for imperial beneficence (for example to Trajan at Iotape [Bean and Mitford 1965: 29]) and local approval of imperial involvement. Such texts are found, for example, in two temples at Cestrus devoted to the Imperial cult (Bean and Mitford 1962: 211-12; 1970: 156), and in texts honoring other imperial officials at Iotape, Cestrus, and Antiochia (Bean and Mitford 1970: 70, 161)(for Nephelion, see Karamut and Russell 1999: 364, 368-9). A monument at Cestrus declares loyalty to the Flavian dynasty following the abolition of the kingdom of Antiochus in AD 72 (Bean and Mitford 1970: 157). Bean and Mitford 1970: 157) describe the Early Roman *floruit* at Cestrus as "...a testimony to the value of Roman provincial administration." At Direvli (in the hills above Gazipasa), Bean and Mitford (1970: 178) identified a tomb of immigrant Selgian masons, who, they conjecture, following the pacification by Antiochus had found work in "...a country previously both remote and backward." I conclude that the extension of imperial administration, not piracy, explains the origins of social and economic complexity in the survey region.

Early and Late Roman Population Growth

The Early Roman Period (65 BCE to AD 250) saw substantial population growth in every city and hinterland of the survey area, but was particularly pronounced at Selinus, Cestrus, and Antiochia (the latter two were new foundations at this time)(Table 4-1, Figures 4-3, 4-4). The total estimated Early Roman population of about 18,000 implies an increase of over 16,000 within a period of 300 years, and represents the largest relative increase in site numbers of all the coded surveys (Table 4-2, Column A).

It is not clear whether this growth resulted from a steady addition of population over the whole period or was more episodic. The historical records suggest a rapid growth during AD 38-74, when a new community foundation was made at Antiochia during the principality rule of Antiochus IV of Commagene (Jones 1971: 211). Iotape and possibly Nephelion (assuming the identification of this site with Claudiopolis at Ninica) also benefited from his efforts to "civilize" the kingdom (ibid.) According to Jones (1971: 212) it "...is possible that some of Antiochus IV's cities were military colonies peopled by his mercenaries." Roman troops were sent to Rough Cilicia in AD 52 and 62 to suppress revolts of local tribal peoples, and some troops may have stayed in the area to provide security (Onurkan 1967: 74). Claudiopolis at Ninica received a Roman colony from Domitian (Jones 1971: 211-12). As the architecture, tombs, and inscriptions of Iotape, Selinus, Cestrus, and Antiochia indicate (summarized in the site descriptions), the period of the first through the third centuries was a *floruit* attributable to the playing out of Roman imperial interests, particularly in relation to their geopolitical strategies in Rough Cilicia and beyond (cf. Patterson 1991, regarding Lycia).

Population growth continued, but at a slower rate, into the Late Roman Period (AD 250 to 700), with an increase over Early Roman of an estimated 6500 (Table 4-1, Figures 4-5, 4-6). Two centers and their hinterlands, in particular, experienced substantial growth into the latter part of the Roman Period, Selinus and Nephelion. Although our data for the Byzantine Period (AD 700 to 1071) are scanty, I estimate a decline in population of approximately 20,000, nearly back to pre-Roman levels (Table 4-1, Figures 4-7, 4-8).

The continued population growth during the Late Roman Period is surprising in light of the almost exclusively Early Roman date for new public construction, tomb building, and erection of inscriptions (summarized in the preceding chapter)(although Huber [1967] and Rosenbaum [1967b] point out that many structures and tombs likely were in use later, some into the Byzantine Period). Only scattered textual references imply Late Roman construction, including at Selinus, where St. Thecla "...restored impregnability to the fortress..." (Rosenbaum 1967c: 68), and in an inscription at Nephelion, expressing gratitude to Zeno for restoring the *polis* (Karamut and Russell 1999: 370). Karamut and Russell (1999: 370-1) posit a period of decline in the area after the early 3rd century following the Persian advance (which extended to Antiochia and Selinus), repeated Isaurian rebellions, and other military disturbances. Why did population growth continue?

The Nature of Periphery Incorporation

I suggest that the incorporation of the western coast lands of Rough Cilicia into the Roman world-system occurred in two somewhat distinct phases, the first reflecting primarily Early Roman imperial strategy. The second, during Late Roman Period, was based on a greater degree on the growth of commercial activities. In this connection, it is of interest to note that one of the local wares, Cilicia White Ware (Appendix 2) has a strong association with Nephelion (Figure 4-9), and, I assume, the Late Roman Period, when Nephelion reached its maximum population size (Williams's [1989: 71] similar White Kitchen Ware dates to Late Roman). Since there is no known ceramic production site at Nephelion, I

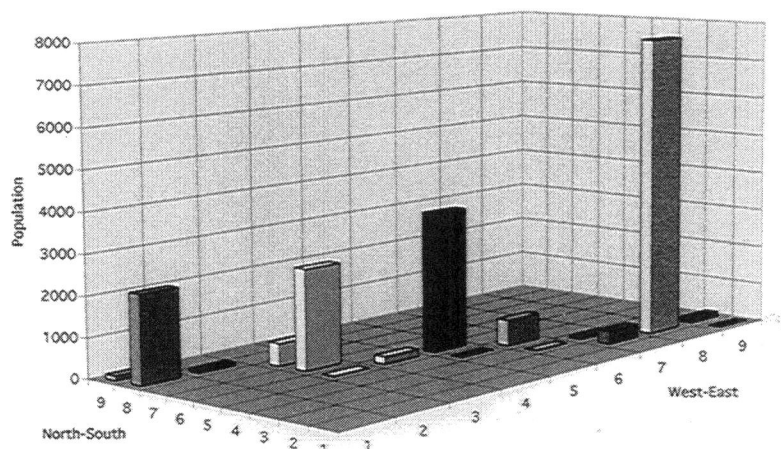

Figure 4-3. Early Roman population estimate totals by grid square.

preliminarily conclude that Cilicia White Ware is an imported type whose abundance there reflects a growing external trade. Two capacious, two-story buildings at Nephelion (Karamut and Russell's Buildings D and E), located in areas where only Late Roman pottery was collected (collection areas 2 and 4), may have served as warehouses. Building D (collection area 7), also dating to Late Roman, had an exceptional density of amphora fragments, suggesting a commercial function for this quarter of the city.

Other data support the proposed intensification of external commercial linkages in the Late Roman Period. Figures 4-10 and 4-11 illustrate the increased frequency of imported transport amphora in the Late Roman Period as compared with Early Roman. Perhaps more of the local transport amphora were in use in the Early Roman Period, reflecting primarily a local economy of production and exchange, while by the Late Roman Period more goods were being imported in foreign amphora. Interestingly, at Nephelion, which experienced substantial Late Roman population growth, we found by far the highest densities of both imported Late Roman Fine Wares and transport amphora.

The statistics summarized in Table 4-2, drawn from my comparative coding (Appendix 3), allow me to throw additional light on Late Roman Period population growth by seeing it in relation to the population dynamics of other regions of the Mediterranean. The figures in column B of the table are the ratios of Late Roman to Early Roman site numbers (LR divided by ER). Obviously this is only a proxy for population change, but I use it because population estimates based on site area are provided in only a few of the survey reports. While Late Roman site numbers declined in Italy (Capenas, Sutri, Faliscus, Veientanus, Cosanus, Rieti), areas more marginal to what

had been the core of the empire remained roughly constant or even show increased numbers, particularly in the eastern empire (Melos, Lasithi, Kavousi, northern Keos, and southern Argolid, in addition to the survey area). I suggest that the Early Roman to Late Roman transition of the survey region reflects a general process in which an increased intensity of economic activity and population growth occurred in regions east of Rome. Jameson et al. (1994: 404) point out that as the eastern empire separated from west, opportunities for economic activity increased from the Aegean to as far east as Syria; as described by Bintliff and Snodgrass (1988: 179) this produced a "...flourishing of settlement in the eastern Mediterranean following the sack of Rome" (Alcock 1993: 37-48, summarizes the data from Greece; cf. Bintliff 1991: 128-31 on Boeotia; Tchalenko 1953, on northern Syria).

The Evolution of a Periphery in Comparative Perspective

The coastal lands of western Rough Cilicia were both like and unlike other regions of the Roman Empire. One important aspect of similarity and difference pertains to the proportion of population in each survey area living in cities and towns versus farmsteads, villas, and villages (Tables 4-1, and 4-2, columns D and E). The survey area, like other regions of the eastern Mediterranean, is clearly more urbanized than the Italian Peninsula's rural hinterland of Rome. This cross-regional difference would be even more obvious if population estimates had been available for the cities of south Etruria (surveys 1-4 of Table 4-2), a region that is recognized as having been strongly rural (Potter 1979: Figure 35; Lloyd 1991: 234). As I coded the various surveys, it became evident that considerable

61

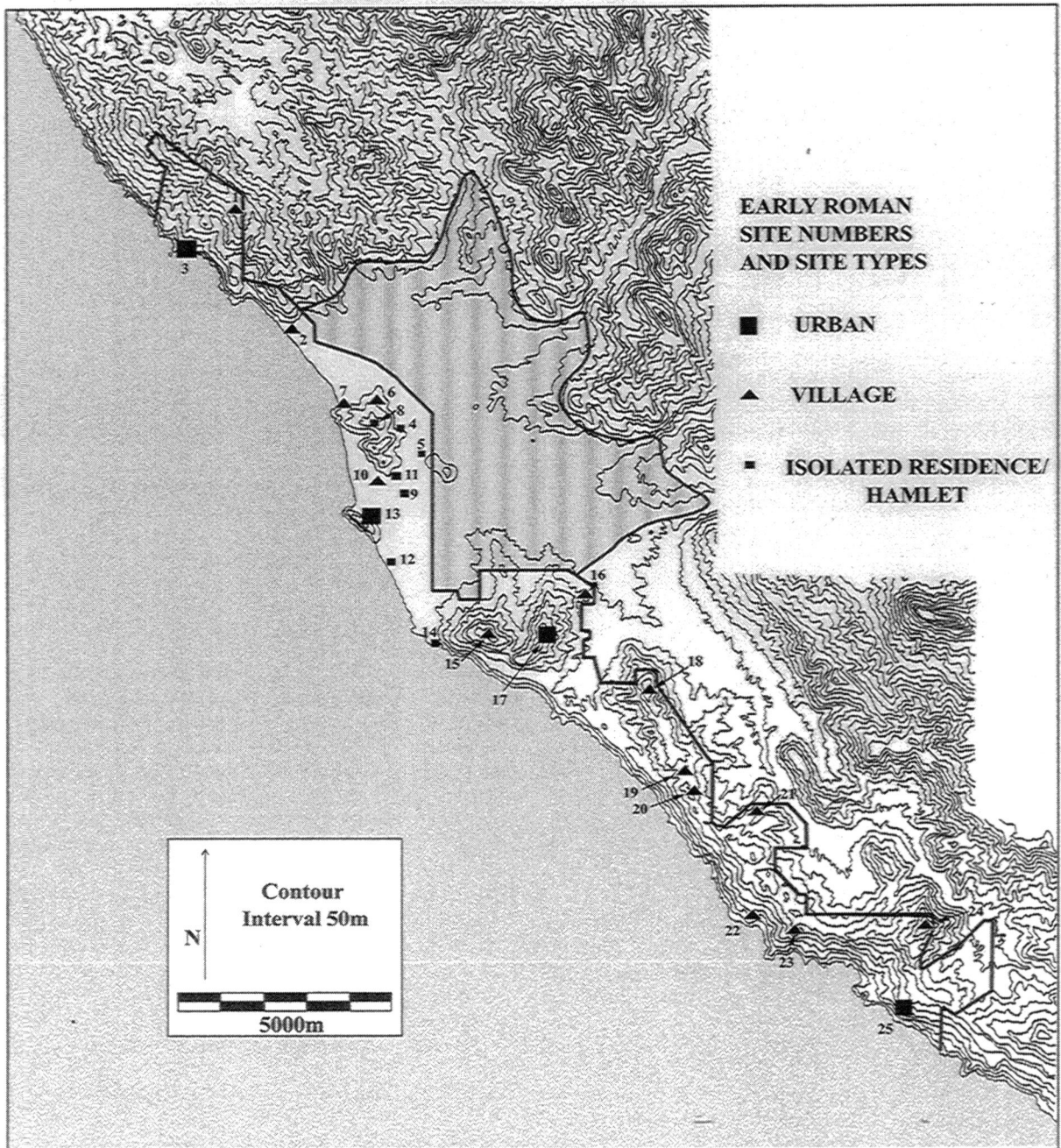

Figure 4-4. Early Roman site numbers and site types.

Table 4-2. Summary statistics from the comparative data (from Appendix 3).

	A	B	C	D	E	F	G
1. CAPENAS	1.1	.01	70	-	-	-	-
2. SUTRI	1.6	.02	200	-	-	-	-
3. FALISCUS	.9	.11	120	-	-	-	-
4. VEIENTANUS	1.4	.2	250	-	-	-	-
5. GUADALQUIVIR	-	-	99	-	-	-	-
6. COSANUS	.8	.7	550	-	-	-	-
7. RIETI	.9	.5	-	32	48	151	100
8. MELOS	2.	3.4	-	95	90	172	443
9. LASITHI	1.	13.	66	98	-	8.4	-
10. KAVOUSI	-	1.	-	-	-	-	-
11. W MESARA	1.	.22	-	-	-	-	-
12. VROKASTRO	-	-	-	-	-	-	-
13. S EUBOEA	1.2	.35	14	94	98	163	133
14. AYIOFARANGO	1.7	.3	-	-	-	-	-
15. N KEOS	.23	2.8	-	0	0	43	112
16. S ARGOLID	.15	3.4	-	70	53	77	249
17. PYLOS	-	-	-	-	-	-	-
18. PALAIPAPHOS	1.8	.4	-	89	89	129	97
19. C R CILICIA	6.3	.9	21	86	92	225	307

Key: Column A: ER site numbers/HLN site numbers

Column B: LR site numbers/ER site numbers

Column C: Estimated territory sizes for ER centers

Column D: Estimated % urban, ER

Column E: Estimated % urban, LR

Column F: ER population density per square kilometer

Column G: LR population density per square kilometer

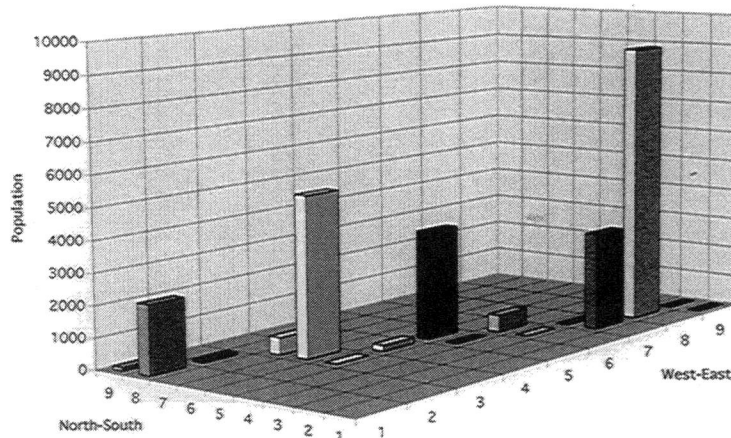

Figure 4-5. Late Roman population estimate totals by grid square.

variation existed across regions in the comparative frequencies of farms, villas, villages, and towns and cities. My purpose in this section is to preliminarily identify the nature of frequency variation in settlement types, with the primary aim of developing a deeper knowledge of settlement patterns of the survey area.

Given the variation found in survey methodology, in describing and reporting of survey data, and in the social formations represented by the survey data, it is sometimes difficult to differentiate the categories farmstead, villa, village, and town/city in a manner that makes comparison feasible (e.g., Jameson et al. 1994: 248-52). For purposes of this analysis, I established a system of site categorization of settlement types that is, by necessity, somewhat arbitrary, but that is highly consistent with definitions used by many of the settlement pattern researchers themselves. Very small artifact scatters, but that I judged to represent isolated residential sites, were coded as farmsteads (usually, they are described as such in the survey reports). In cases where site areas are provided, I followed Potter (1979: 122) in using an upper size limit of .2 ha for farmsteads, slightly smaller than Alcock's cutoff value of .3 ha (1993: 60), or Whitelaw's .5 ha (1994: 172). However, only minor differences in my comparative statistics would have resulted had I used either of these larger values. Cherry, Davis, and Mantzourani (eds., 1991:336) include in their rural farmstead category sites of considerably larger size (up to 2 ha). However, I would argue that sites this large, even when they are missing evidence of closely packed houses, are likely to represent the remains of small communities rather than isolated single-family farms (e.g., Whitelaw 1994: 172).

Villas were family farms, although their labor force typically included more extra-family workers, including slaves, than would normally be found in the case of a farm (White 1970: Ch. 12). For this reason, and because they

often had more kinds of agricultural outbuildings and other structures, such as baths, they were larger in area and more architecturally and artifactually elaborate than farmsteads. For South Etruria, Potter [1979: 122] suggests an average size of farmsteads of between .1 and .14 ha, while villas averaged around .35 ha. The survey projects I coded used somewhat variant criteria to distinguish villas based on surface evidence, but generally after the 2nd century BCE they were "rich country houses" (McKay 1975: 101; Potter 1979: 122) readily identifiable by the presence of decorative stone, multi-colored painted plaster, marble veneer, stucco decoration, and glass tesserae (Alcock 1993: 64-5; Dyson 1978: 257; Potter 1979: 122; but cf. Small 1991: 208). Villas were often equipped for large-scale pressing and storage of oil and wine (Potter ibid.), making use of equipment and facilities too costly for ordinary farm families.

Villages were multi-household residential settlements, but smaller and less architecturally complex than towns and cities (centers). Centers are presumed to have had a greater degree of regional scale significance than villages, providing administrative, ritual, and commercial functions for their adjoining territories and beyond. Centers included sites identified as *municipia* that were centers of regional governance and the enactment of imperial policies and tax collection, semi-autonomously governing a surrounding fixed territory (e.g., Garnsey and Saller 1987: 27). Other centers provided regional-scale industrial or market services but did not necessarily have *municipium* status. The published survey data didn't always distinguish centers from villages in a consistent manner, so for the comparative analysis I arbitrarily identified villages as settlements larger than .2 ha, but smaller than 3 ha. In Vallat (1991: 12) some "village" sites in North Africa and Syria are reported to be much larger in area, and probably represent dispersed farmsteads sharing a cooperative

64

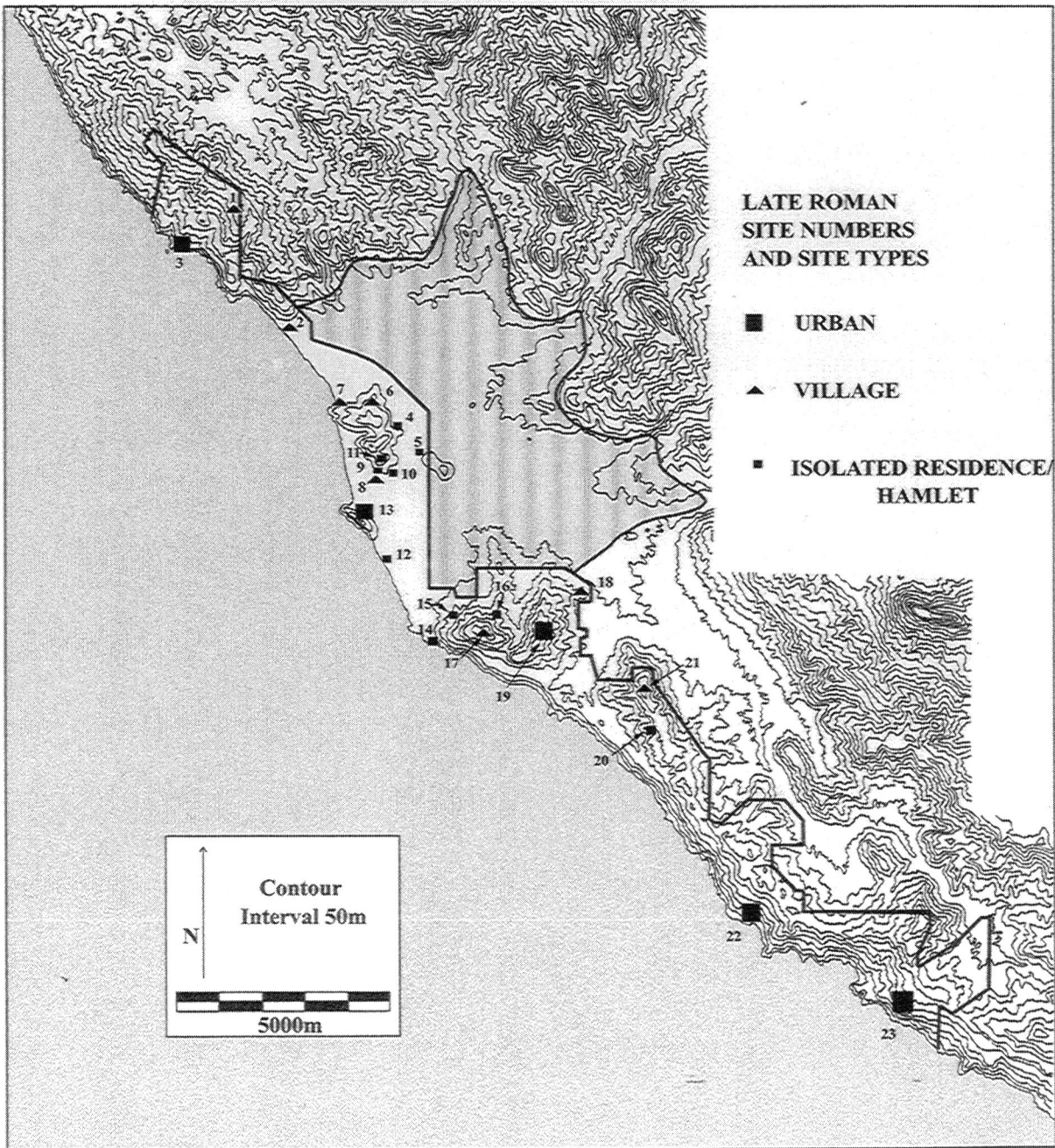

Figure 4-6. Late Roman site numbers and site types.

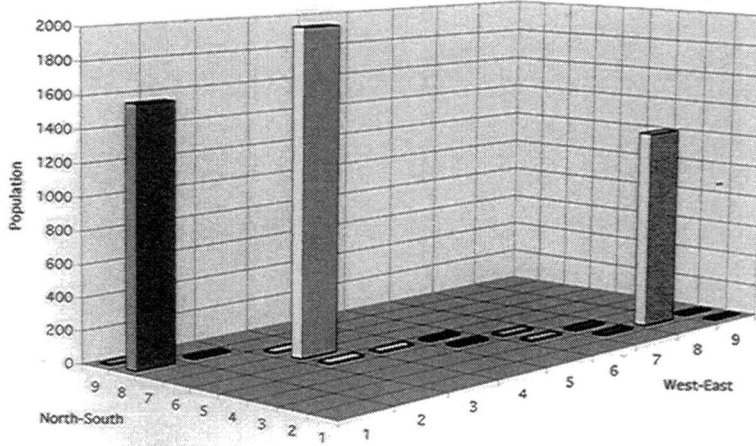

Figure 4-7. Byzantine Period population estimate totals by grid square.

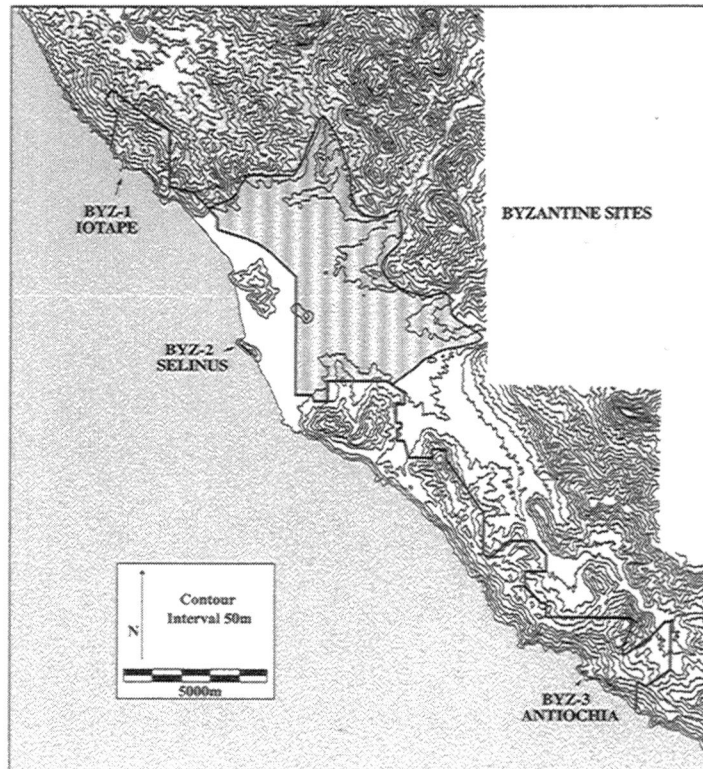

Figure 4-8. Byzantine Period site numbers.

LOCAL POTTERY CATEGORIES

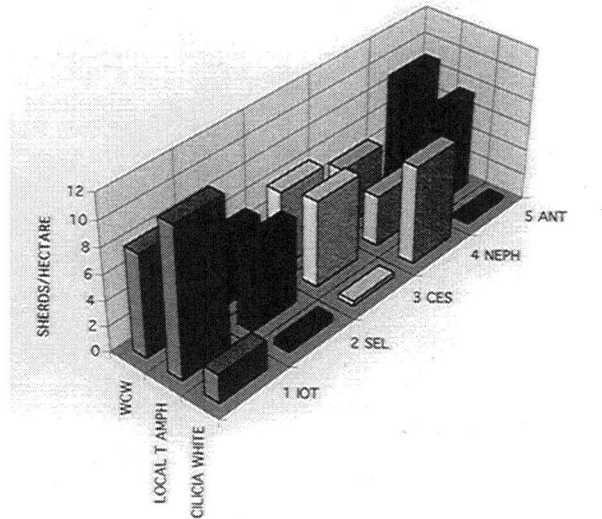

Figure 4-9. Density in sherds per ha of collected area of local pottery categories, by hinterland. The categories are West Cilicia Ware (WCW), local transport amphora, and Cilicia White Ware. From Appendix 2.

economy such as the Tripolitanian *gasr* (a typical example covers 50 ha and has a population of 250)(Burns and Mattingly 1980-81). In the coded surveys, villages were more nucleated.

I identify as centers sites that are 3 ha or more in area, implying a minimum population size of 600 (at 210/ha for urban sites, in Jameson et al [1994: Appendix B]). Some of the sites I coded as centers are less than 3 ha, in cases where the field researcher specifically identified a site as a town or city based on the presence of substantial civic architecture or other evidence of central-place functions. Obviously, the 3 ha cutoff point for centers is largely arbitrary, and will be subject to evaluation in future comparative studies, but it does seem to have some comparative validity. In Roman Britain, the smallest sites identified as towns had enclosed areas in the vicinity of 2.1 ha (Burnham and Wacher 1990: 22) or total areas of about 2.5 to 3 ha (Millett 1995: Table 4.1).

By now it is well known that an earlier literature, based primarily on elite-biased textual sources, had overemphasized the importance of the community, and especially urban life, in the structure and function of the Roman Empire (cf., Lloyd 1991: 233, who calls this earlier view the "Central-Place Model"). Surveys in South Etruria and elsewhere in Italy showed unexpectedly high frequencies of farmsteads and villas, but comparatively few urban centers and urban dwellers (Potter 1979: Chapter 5). The combined data from the coded surveys illustrates this pattern (Figure 4-12), with farmsteads the most frequently occurring Early Roman settlement type overall. By Late Roman, villages are the most frequent category (Fig. 4-12), with farmsteads still the second most frequent category.

When coded data from the surveys are summarized by sector (as I did previously, into east, Crete, Greece and the Aegean, and west sectors; Table 2-5), obvious differences are apparent in the relative frequencies of the main settlement types across the Mediterranean; change between the Early and Late Roman Periods is also detectable (Figures 4-13, 4-14). For the Early Roman Period, Italy and the Guadalquivir region of Spain show a higher density of farmsteads per square kilometer of surveyed area than any of the other sectors; by Late Roman, Greece and the Aegean and even Crete had higher density values of farmsteads than the west sector, although in the west sector, farmsteads remained the most frequent settlement type. Villas also occur in higher densities in the Early Roman west sector, and remained a comparatively important type there into the Late Roman Period in spite of overall declines in settlement density. Conversely, centers and villages occur less frequently in the west sector than elsewhere, excepting Crete.

The differential distribution of settlement types suggests two broadly alternative forms of regional organization in the Roman Empire. A western rural pattern featured a high density of farmsteads and villas, while a community-based eastern pattern had both villages and centers as major forms of settlement formation. In the areas where community life was emphasized, centers were found in relatively greater density. To find the estimated territory sizes of centers, I simply divided total survey area size by the number of centers to get an average value of territory size for a region (for the Rough Cilicia survey area, I used the center hinterland values). As expected, these data illustrate the larger territory sizes of the more rural survey areas (Table 4-2, column C). The mean value for Early Roman west sector is 215 km^2 (minimum=70 km^2, maximum=550 km^2, for 6 cases). For the sectors

67

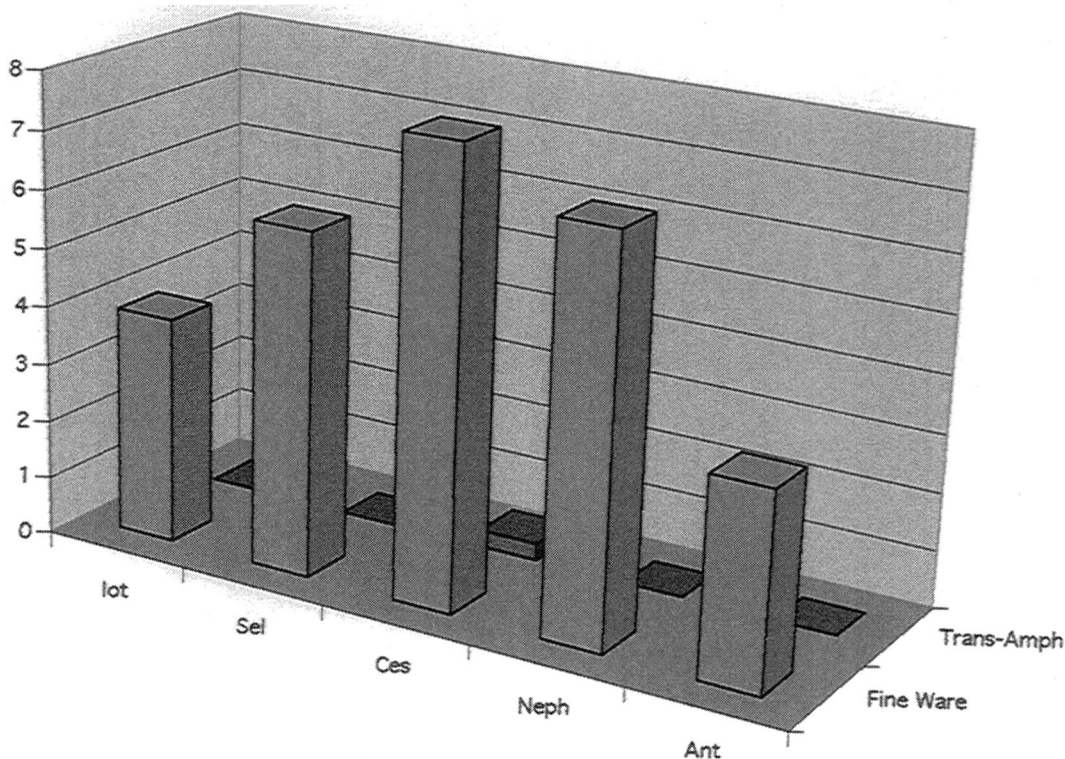

Figure 4-10. Average density in sherds/ha of collected area, Early Roman Fine Ware and Transport Amphora, by hinterland.

An Excess of Population

with the dominance of a community pattern, the mean value is 36 km² (minimum=14 km², maximum=66 km², for 3 cases).

The Roman Period settlement pattern of the survey region is in many respects similar to other regions of the eastern Mediterranean. It had few farmsteads (7 in ER, 10 in LR), and no sites that look at all like the architecturally elaborate villas of the Italian peninsula or elsewhere in the western sector. Most rural dwellers lived in villages, but overall the population was predominantly urban (Table 4-1). Estimated city hinterland territories were comparatively small, averaging 21 kms².

Although the settlement pattern of the survey area is similar to other regions of the eastern Mediterranean, in one respect it is unique, namely in its significant excess of population in relation to local agricultural resources. This is an important datum that is relevant to understanding the nature of this region as a type of periphery in the Roman Empire. Clearly, during both the Early and Late Roman Periods, the population of the coast lands of western Rough Cilicia exceeded its estimated agricultural carrying capacity. Even if we use just the population estimates for the intensively surveyed area (Table 4-1) in relation to the total estimated carrying capacity of each center's hinterland (Table 2-2), an excess of population is indicated, by an estimated 11,500 (ER) and 18,000 (LR). Some of the population of these two periods must have been supported by imported food. This import economy reflects the area's

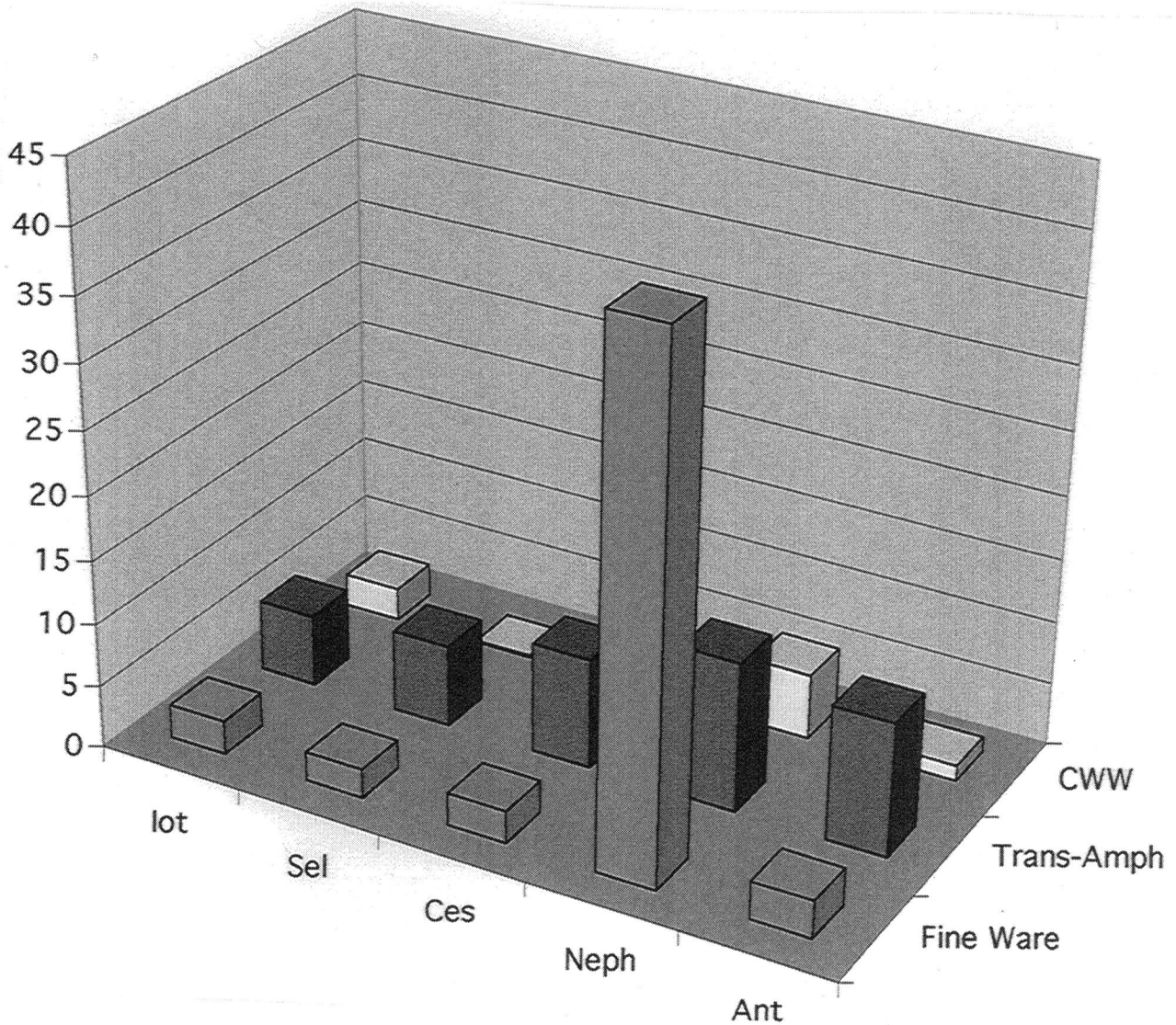

Figure 4-11. Average density in sherds/ha of collected area, Late Roman Fine Ware and Transport Amphora, by hinterland. The density of Cilicia White Ware is also shown.

geopolitical significance to the Roman Empire as well as its potential to export forest products.

The agricultural deficit of the survey area was a product not only of overall high population densities, but also the tendency for population to concentrate inefficiently in centers and in defensible, but agriculturally marginal locations (Table 4-3). The preferred setting for communities in the survey area, with the partial exception of sites in the hinterland of Selinus, included the more marginal ridge lines and hill summits. The major zones of alluvial soils in the vicinity of the Delice, Biçkiçi, and Haçimusa Rivers, and in the vicinity of modern Gazipasa and Macar Village were not extensively settled. Large villages that I suspect were cultivating these and other zones of alluvial soils were often placed in high locations adjacent to, but at some distance above, nearby agricultural resources (e.g., ER-6,

LR-6; ER-15, LR-17; ER-21; ER-18, LR-21; ER-24). All of the sites in this list have substantial terrace construction or other features that may have been defensive in nature (of the urban centers, Iotape, Selinus, Nephelion, and Antiochia have defensive walls, although their construction phases are not well dated). Several farmsteads feature enclosed areas bounded by substantial stone walls (ER-2, LR-2, ER-8, LR-16, LR-20). Three sites situated in the alluvium (ER-2, LR-2, ER-7, LR-7, and ER-12, LR-12) have evidence of ceramic production, indicating that access to nearby clayey soils was more important than defensive location for these specific sites. The militarily unsettled conditions that evidently limited pre-Greek settlement of the survey area obviously continued to some degree in spite of the Roman imperial presence, and reduced the potential

69

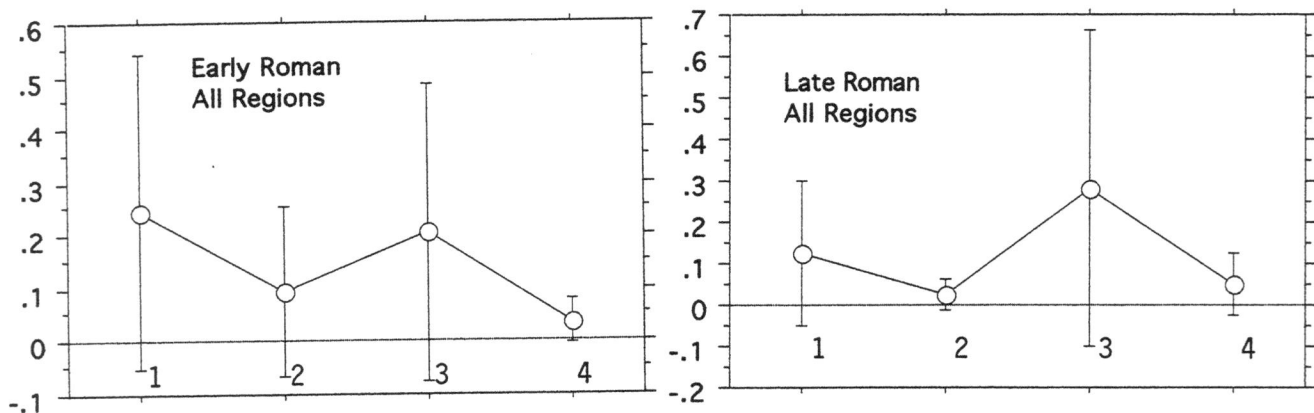

Figure 4-12. Average density per km² of settlement types, Early and Late Roman Periods; 1=farmsteads, 2=villas, 3=villages, 4=centers. From Appendix 3.

agricultural productivity.

For each site, by period, I estimated the longest distance to agricultural fields, based on the availability of arable soils, estimated population of the community, and the presence of nearby communities that would also have been using land (Appendix 1). Sea edge communities are at a disadvantage in terms of distance to fields, because the zone of cultivation around the community is truncated. Given these variables, the relationship of population size and estimated distance to most distant fields is not linear (Figure 4-15). Generally, a field distance of greater than about 2 km is considered inefficient by preindustrial farmers (Chisholm 1968; cf Engels 1990: 29). Given the nature of local conditions in the survey area, especially a high proportion of steep slopes, all communities with populations of over 1000, and some with less than 1000 (Figure 4-16), would have been forced to cultivate at least some inefficiently distant fields (up to a maximum of the approximately 10 kms estimated for Antiochia). These data lend support to the idea that agricultural surplus production, or even local agricultural self-sufficiency, were not major goals in the periphery development of coastal Rough Cilicia.

A Scenario for Explaining the Patterns of Settlement in the Coast Lands of Western Rough Cilicia

Based on the survey and other data, I arrive at several conclusions about the settlement history of the survey area and propose several hypotheses to explain it. By necessity, I would argue, any such summing up is most productively based on a causal model built around processes operative at large spatial scales of region and world-system. Settlement development was retarded, owing to a lack of effective state control, until changing geopolitical and economic conditions of the Hellenistic Period resulted in an initial

phase of population growth and the foundation of several new settlements, but a radical social and demographic transformation was contingent on establishment of an endurable provincial administration by Rome. Given the small scale of the Hellenistic Period demographic transition, the Hellenistic to Early Roman increase in site numbers is the largest of the survey areas in the comparative sample (Table 4-2, column A); in the Early Roman period, most existing communities experienced growth, while many new settlements were established. While population growth was primarily urban, a rural component of the settlement system increased markedly as well (only two of the Roman Period villages, ER-6, -18, have evidence of pre-Roman pottery). Most rural population resided in nucleated villages as opposed to isolated residences (Table 4-1). An ideal location for a village was near a center (ER-1, 10, 15, 16, 24), or in a location allowing access to two adjacent centers (discussed below). Defensible location was also desirable for villagers (ER-1, 6, 15, 18, 23, 24). Cities, as well, grew in naturally defensible positions (Cestrus, Nephelion, Antiochia), while Iotape and Selinus probably depended in part on fortifications built on adjacent high ground.

Production for Export?

According to my estimates, assuming each rural household can support, on average, one other household, rural wheat production could have supplied at maximum only about 12% of local urban demand for Early Roman, and 8% for Late Roman. Some additional proportion of urban demand would have been met by farm families living within city limits, but trips to distant fields would render this component of production inefficient. While the nature of rural-urban relations in the area is not evident from inscriptions or other sources, clearly the survey area was not a periphery like the Bagradas Valley of northern Tunisia where numerous rural *coloni* (small-holders)

70

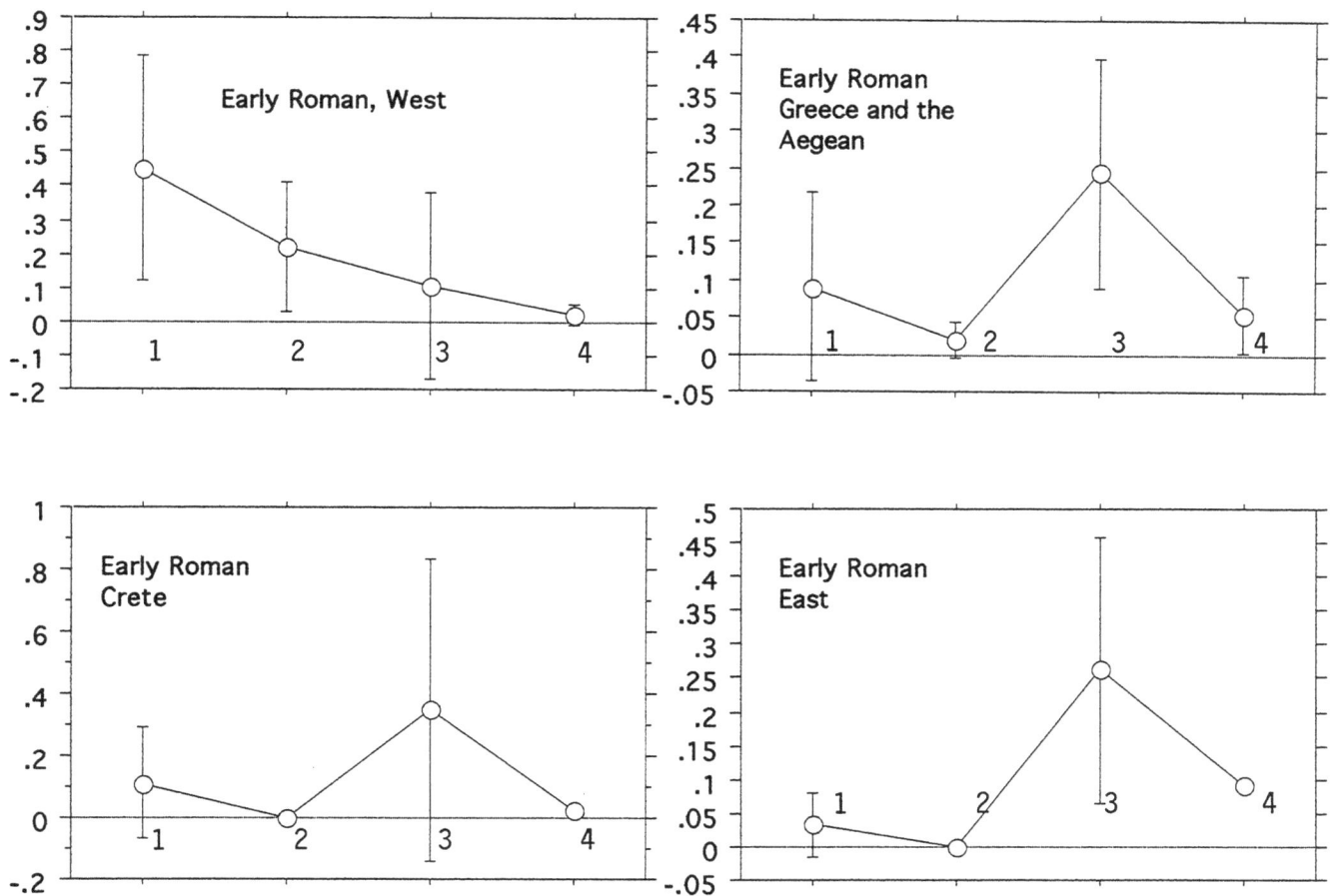

Figure 4-13. Average density per km² of settlement types, Early Roman Period, by sector; 1=farmsteads, 2=villas, 3=villages, 4=centers.

produced significant grain surpluses for export to Rome (Kehoe 1988). Nor was the survey area one of a category of periphery formations based on an industrial-scale export industry of oil and/or pottery, such as Southern Spain, Tunisia, Libya, and Syria (cf. Mattingly 1988). While it is not possible to date the use of oil production implements we located on survey as to Early or Late Roman, for purposes of comparison I assume that all sites with implements were in production at one time. At a total of ten sites we located a press bed or *trapete* (sometimes more than one) implying a density of pressing operations of about 1 per 4.5 kms² of intensively surveyed area (or 1 per 8 kms² for the entire survey area). By comparison, in the less systematically surveyed Fergian region of Libya (Mattingly 1988: 35), one pressing operation was found for every 2 kms² (and all were likely to have been in operation by the 2nd century AD). The pressing operations in Tunisia and Libya appear to have been far more materially elaborate and larger than those in the survey area, but even if we use Mattingly's value for the capacity of a Libyan producer of about 5-10,000 liters/year, the total production of the survey area would have been 50-

100,000 liters per year (a perhaps more plausible production value is that given by Forbes and Foxhall [1978: 46], for smaller operations, of 2,500 to 3,000 liters/year). Using Mattingly's production value and an estimate of 20 liters/year of oil consumption per person for the Roman Period (ibid.: 34), the entire local industry is estimated to have provided oil for (at most) between 2500 and 5000 persons, or about 28% of the Early Roman population, and 20% of Late Roman. While the local oil industry might have provided a low-cost alternative product suitable for some consumer uses, it is likely that imported oil would have provided most of the population's needs.

Other industries evidently were similarly of small scale, although it is difficult to estimate the parameters of production in relation to local consumption. Four sites (ER-2, -7, -12, and -25, LR-2, -7, -12, and -23) have at least some evidence for ceramic production, including amphora (which would have complemented the local oil industry). Other evidence of specialized production is scanty. Loom weights were noted at Nephelion (1),

71

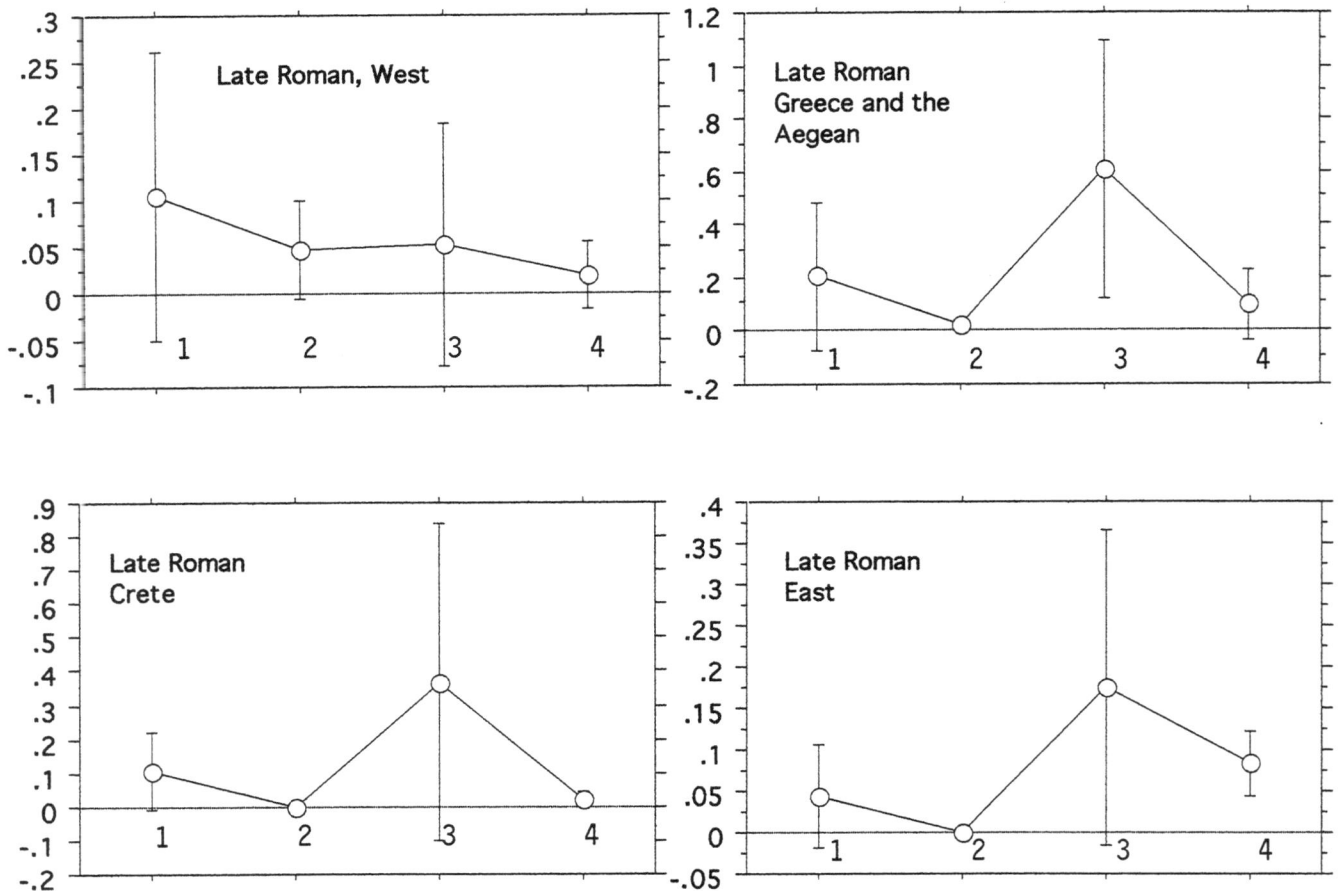

Figure 4-14. Average density per km² of settlement types, Late Roman Period, by sector; 1=farmsteads, 2=villas, 3=villages, 4=centers.

Antiochia (4), Selinus (1), and ER-6 (1) and ER-23 (1), but this spotty distribution might reflect no more than normal household production. The kind of regional division of labor between mountain-based animal herders and coastal farmers (e.g., Whittaker 1978, regarding North Africa) is not detectable. Local farming and oil processing could not have produced significant surpluses for exchange, and the small scale of local farming would not have required seasonal labor subsidies from herding families as was true in parts of North Africa. Local oil production was not of a sufficient volume to have been the basis of an oil for slave trade with inland groups of Asia Minor. While forest product exports are assumed to have been a major component of the economic system, no artifacts are in evidence that would indicate how this industry was materialized.

Urban-Rural Relations

The nature of Roman Period urban-rural relations in the survey area is uncertain. The absence of villas is consistent with a comparative lack of "villa culture" found elsewhere in Asia Minor, and would probably also indicate a relative

unimportance of rural slave labor (Broughton 1975: 690). Assuming villagers were free, were they then independent landowners? Or were they communities of free tenant farmers working land owned by state, temple, or wealthy families? Tenancy and non-tenancy forms of rural production were found in Roman Asia Minor (Broughton 1975: 691), but inscriptions from the survey area do not address urban-rural relations in detail. On several of the sites classified as villages (ER-6, -18, -20, LR-6, -21, and possibly ER-21, -24), we found what were variously referred to in the field notebooks as "platforms," "towers," or "industrial buildings" consisting of square or rectangular stone structures that appear to have had public functions. Oil-processing or other large grinding implements were found in association with these structures at ER-6 and -18, LR-6, and -21. These meager but interesting data suggest the development of forms of cooperative rural production and/or commodity storage associations (cf., de Ligt 1993: 166; Kehoe 1988: 197). Such communal facilities may reflect a situation in which the large-scale processing and storage of commodities such as oil are too costly for ordinary rural farm families (Jameson et al. 1994: 391;

72

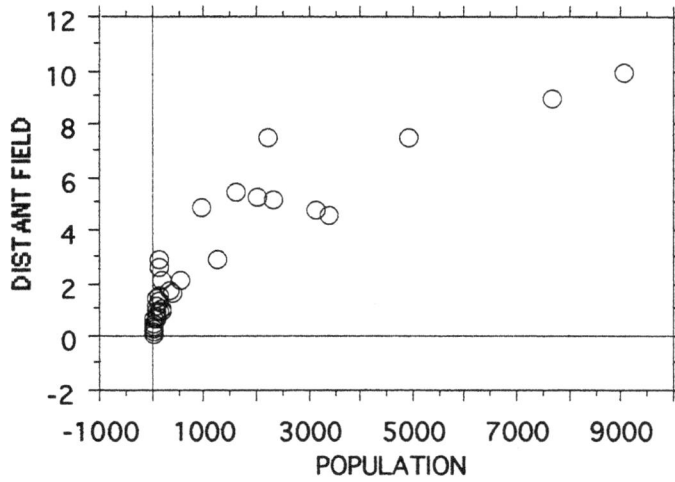

Figure 4-15. Scattergram showing the relationship between site estimated population size and estimated distance to most distant fields, all Early Roman sites. From Appendix 1.

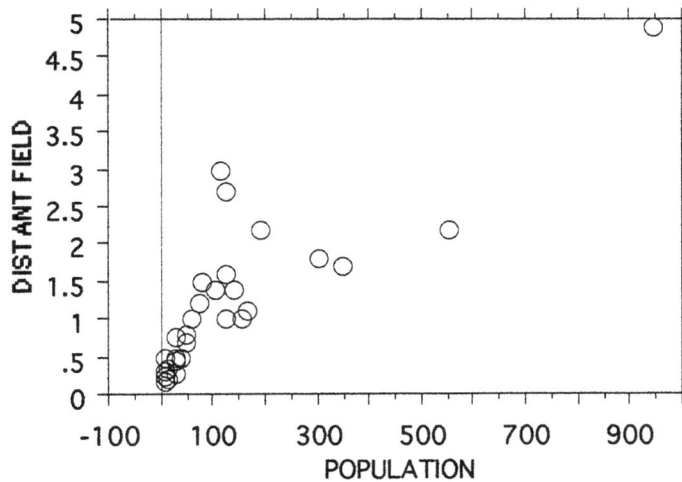

Figure 4-16. Scattergram showing the relationship between site estimated population size and estimated distance to most distant fields, Early Roman sites less than 1000 population.

Table 4-3. Sum of estimated population by period, hinterland, and environmental setting, where 1=alluvial or other very gentle slopie; 2=moderate slope; 3=ridge line; 4=mountain summit.

Sum of Population	Subregion						
Period	Setting	1 IOT	2 SEL	3 CES	4 NEPH	5 ANT	Grand Total
1 HLN	1	0	300	0	0	0	300
	2	945	0	0	111	0	1056
1 HLN Total		945	300	0	111	0	1356
2 ER	1	79	2656	60	0	0	2795
	2	2184	50	156	215	7665	10270
	3	115	350	0	273	0	738
	4	0	10	4035	0	125	4170
2 ER Total		2378	3066	4251	488	7790	17973
3 LR	1	79	5276	60	0	0	5415
	2	2184	50	166	3150	9030	14580
	3	115	375	5	0	0	495
	4	0	0	4035	0	0	4035
3 LR Total		2378	5701	4266	3150	9030	24525
4 BYZ	1	0	2000	0	0	0	2000
	2	1575	0	0	0	1260	2835
4 BYZ Total		1575	2000	0	0	1260	4835

Mee et al. 1991: 226-7). A possible analog for this kind of rural cooperative economy is the *gasr* of the Romano-Libyan Period of North Africa that linked several adjacent farm households. According to Burns and Mattingly (1980-81: 35), the "...*gasr* served as a storehouse for olives, oil, possibly wine, grain, and above all fodder. It served as a distribution point for grain, olive oil, and cereal as well as being a focal point for water supply and manpower."

Several village sites grew in locations facilitating access to more than one adjacent center. The following village sites are easily within a one-day round trip to two centers: ER-2, -7, -6, -15, -16, -18, -19, -20, and -23 (LR-2, -7, -6, -17, -18, -21). One average, these optimally located settlements are larger in population (ER mean=187) than their more poorly located counterparts (ER mean=113), and they show marginally more evidence for affluence as indicated by stone architecture, roof tiles, imported amphora and fine-ware pottery (excepting ER fine ware, which is more frequent in collections from sites lacking multiple center access)(Table 4-4). These data suggest that rural households were able to make locational decisions that maximized economic choice in a regional economy that integrated multiple center hinterland territories.

The growth of centers in the coast lands of Rough Cilicia did stimulate a degree of economic development of rural hinterlands, but this rural economy was not adequate to meet most consumer demand. Continuing uncertain military conditions that favored an inefficient nucleation of population, often in marginal but defensible locations, coupled with generally poor environmental potential for agricultural development, restricted rural population growth and agricultural intensification; the near-absence of off-site pottery in most of the survey area is consistent with this interpretation. The comparative efficiency of dispersed farms, that minimizes travel distance to fields, is widely recognized in the literature on the agricultural economics of the Mediterranean (Cherry, Davis, and Mantzourani eds., 1991: 463, Table 22.1).

The regional economy that developed in the survey area is unlike that described in many sources on Roman Period economics. Numerous sources depict an economic system in which wealthy urban families maximize profit and earn most of their income by investing in farming enterprises (Duncan Jones 1978: 6, Ch. 2; Hopkins 1978b, 1983: xii; de Ligt 1993: 240), but this arrangement would not have applied in an area that had so little rural development and that would have been so strongly dependent on staple goods imports. The comparative lack of military security would have been a factor limiting such investment in rural enterprises (White 1975: 217). The idea that regions of the empire were locally self-sufficient in staple goods (and, correspondingly, that each Roman city had an autonomous market hinterland)(e.g., Bekker-Nielsen 1989: 9; de Ligt 1993: 230, 236-7), also does not apply in a situation where the bulk of economic transactions would have involved both the state and an urban elite whose interests would have been in commerce and shipping, linking the region to distant consumers and suppliers (cf. Pleket 1983). These activities concentrated most of the wealth of the region in the hands of urban interests. The surface densities of imported fine ware pottery and imported transport amphora are strongly skewed toward the urban settlements (Figure 4-17). But this need not imply that the centers of the survey area were "consumer cities" dominating local rural populations. City growth appears to have stimulated a minor degree of rural development, but city economies were based largely on interregional exchange, not on the exploitation of local rural populations.

Table 4-4. Values of statistical significance comparing the frequency of stone construction, roof tiles, fine ware, and transport amphora, by sites with access to two centers versus sites lacking access to two centers. From Appendix 1. For stone construction and roof tiles, the value given is the Chi Square p-value; for fine ware and transport amphora, the value given is the t-test p-value of difference of means.

	Stone Construction	Roof Tiles	Fine Ware	Transport Amphora
ER	.9	.03	.2	-
LR	.35	.09	.34	.59

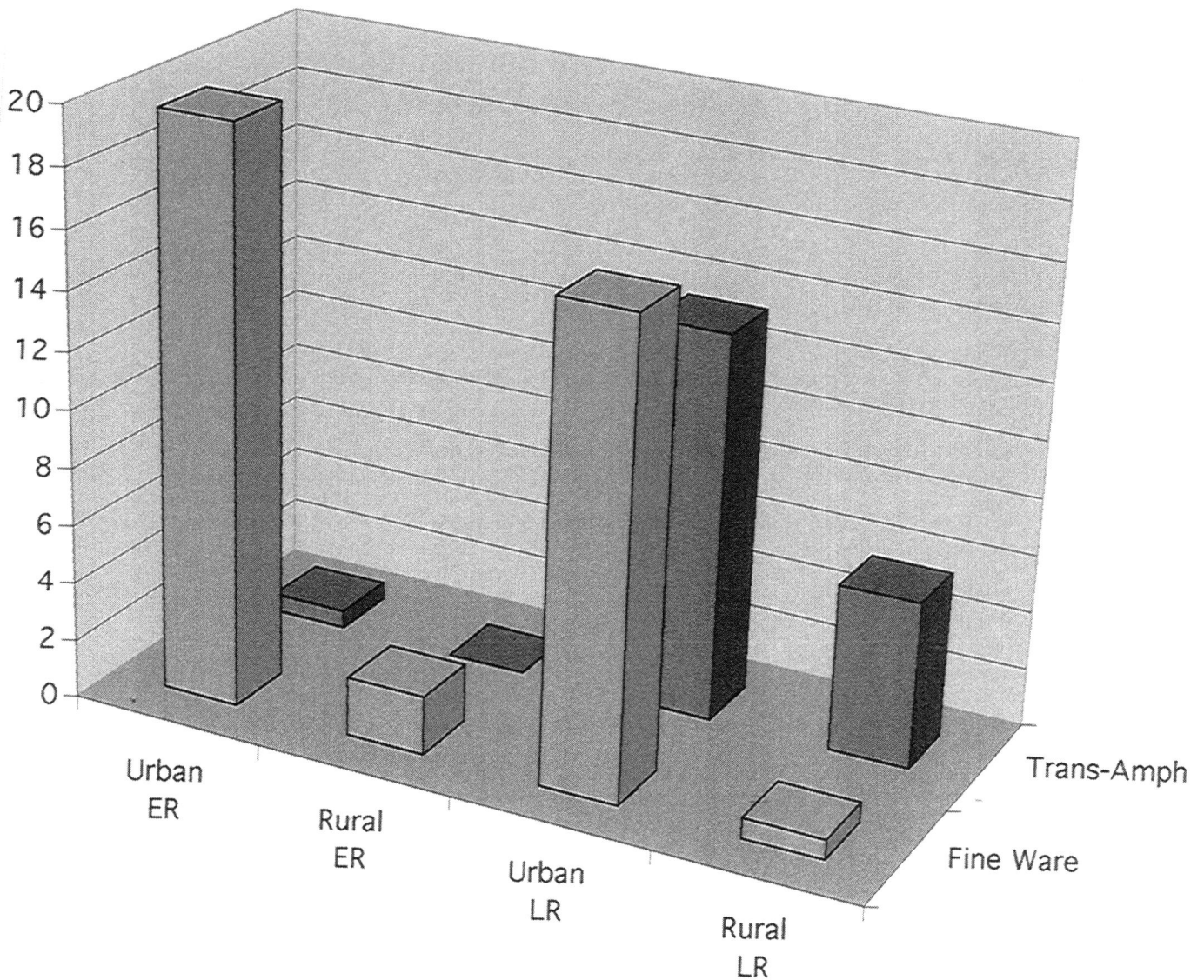

Figure 4-17. Average density in sherds per ha of collected area, Early and Late Roman fine wares and transport amphora, by community type. From Appendix 2.

75

Appendix 1

Coded Site Data

Section 1 Key

Period	HLN=Hellenistic, ER=Early Roman, LR=Late Roman, BYZ=Byzantine
Number	Site number for that period
Hinterland	IOT=Iotape, SEL=Selinus, CES=Cestrus, NEPH=Nephelion, ANT=Antiochia
CA Size (ha)	Total area collected in hectares
Elevation	Elevation in meters above sea level of the main site area
Setting	1=alluvial or adjacent to alluvial plain, 2=moderate slope, 3=ridge line, 4=mountain summit
Population	Site population estimate, based on 125 persons/ ha of site area for farmsteads and villages, and 210 persons/ha of site area for centers (Cherry et al 1991: 280; Jameson, Runnels, and Van Andel 1994: 542-550)
% Ridge Soil	Percent arable ridge or other sloping soil within the site's estimated agricultural catchment (the area that would have been required for agricultural production, assuming 2 ha of arable land per person, counting surplus production, from Table 2-1)
% Alluv Soil	Percent of alluvial soil within the site's estimated agricultural catchment (the area that would have been required for agricultural production, assuming 2 ha of arable land per person, counting surplus production, from Table 2-1)
Distant Field	Estimate of distance to the most distant fields, considering population size, availability of arable land, and the presence of neighboring sites and their catchment areas
Roof Tiles	0=no roof tiles noted on the surface, 1=present but infrequent, 2=well represented (blank indicates uncertain for that period)
Stone Archit	0=site lacks evidence of stone construction, 1=stone construction, but generally roughly shaped, 2=finely shaped architectural stone well represented
Comm Type	Res/Hamlet=isolated residence or small cluster of residences, Village= community of densely-packed residences with minimal evidence public buildings or spaces (such as terraces or defensive walls), Urban=larger population size (usually 600 or more) and/or other evidence of city status, including large public buildings and inscriptions

Appendix 1, Section 2   Data

Period	Number	Hinterland	CA Size (ha)	Elevation	Setting	Population	%Ridge Soil	%Alluv Soil	Distant Field	Roof Tiles	Stone Archit	Comm Type
HLN	1	IOT	2.07	0	2	945	36	10	4.9			Urban
HLN	2	SEL	4.24	0	1	300	5	95	1.8	2	2	Village
HLN	3	NEPH	2.6	175	2	106	20	0	1.4			Village
HLN	4	NEPH	0.1	275	2	5	0	0	0.5	0	1	Res/Hamlet
ER	1	IOT	0.92	375	3	115	100	0	3	1	1	Village
ER	2	IOT	0.63	0	1	79	0	100	1.5	2	2	Village
ER	3	IOT	2.07	0	2	2184	36	0	7.5	2	2	Urban
ER	4	SEL	0.4	25	2	50	25	30	0.7	1	0	Res/Hamlet
ER	5	SEL	0.2	25	1	25	35	65	0.28	0	0	Res/Hamlet
ER	6	SEL	2.8	100	3	350	25	65	1.7	1	2	Village
ER	7	SEL	1.05	0	1	125	20	55	2.7		1	Village
ER	8	SEL	0.1	194	4	10	55	0	0.2	0	1	Res/Hamlet
ER	9	SEL	0.1	0	1	5	35	65	0.18		0	Res/Hamlet
ER	10	SEL	1.3	0	1	163	20	80	1.1	0	0	Village
ER	11	SEL	0.2	15	1	25	0	60	0.5	1	0	Res/Hamlet
ER	12	SEL	0.1	0	1	13	0	100	0.35	1	1	Res/Hamlet
ER	13	SEL	4.24	0	1	2300	5	95	5.2	2	2	Urban
ER	14	CES	0.5	30	1	60	45	30	1	2	2	Res/Hamlet
ER	15	CES	1	375	4	125	60	0	1.6	1	2	Village
ER	16	CES	1.25	125	2	156	60	20	1	1	0	Village
ER	17	CES	0.69	395	4	3360	39	31	4.6	2	2	Urban
ER	18	CES	4.4	450	4	550	35	30	2.2	1	1	Village
ER	19	NEPH	0.28	300	3	35	90	0	0.5	1	0	Village
ER	20	NEPH		275	2	75	60	0	1.2	1	2	Village
ER	21	NEPH	0.4	300	3	50	25	0	0.8	0	1	Village
ER	22	NEPH	2.6	175	2	140	20	0	1.4	2	2	Urban
ER	23	NEPH	1.5	300	3	188	50	0	2.2	1	1	Village
ER	24	ANT	1	600	4	125	25	0	1	1	1	Village
ER	25	ANT	5.42	300	2	7665	57	2	9	2	2	Urban
LR	1	IOT	0.92	375	3	115	100	0	3	1	1	Village
LR	2	IOT	0.63	0	1	79	0	100	1.5	2	2	Village
LR	3	IOT	2.07	0	2	2184	36	0	7.5	2	2	Urban
LR	4	SEL	0.4	25	2	50	25	30	0.7	1	0	Res/Hamlet
LR	5	SEL	0.2	25	1	25	35	65	0.28	0	0	Res/Hamlet
LR	6	SEL	2.8	100	3	350	25	65	1.7	1	2	Village
LR	7	SEL	1.05	0	1	125	20	55	2.7		1	Village
LR	8	SEL	1.3	0	1	163	20	80	1.1	0	0	Village
LR	9	SEL	0.2	25	1	25	15	55	0.45	0	0	Res/Hamlet
LR	10	SEL	0.2	15	1	25	0	60	0.5	1	0	Res/Hamlet
LR	11	SEL	0.2	150	3	25	50	25	0.75	0	0	Res/Hamlet
LR	12	SEL	0.1	0	1	13	0	100	0.35	1	1	Res/Hamlet
LR	13	SEL	4.24	0	1	4900	25	75	7.5	2	2	Urban
LR	14	CES	0.5	30	1	60	45	30	1	2	2	Res/Hamlet
LR	15	CES		150	2	5	50	0	0.3	0	1	Res/Hamlet
LR	16	CES		225	2	5	50	0	0.3	0	1	Res/Hamlet
LR	17	CES	1	375	4	125	60	0	1.6	1	2	Village
LR	18	CES	1.25	125	2	156	60	20	1	1	0	Village
LR	19	CES	0.69	395	4	3360	39	31	4.6	2	2	Urban
LR	20	CES	0.1	300	3	5	70	0	0.25	0	2	Res/Hamlet
LR	21	CES	4.4	450	4	550	35	30	2.2	1	1	Village
LR	22	NEPH	2.6	175	2	3150	60	8	4.8	2	2	Urban
LR	23	ANT	5.42	300	2	9030	57	2	10	2	2	Urban
BYZ	1	IOT	2.07	0	2	1575	36	0	5.5	1	2	Urban
BYZ	2	SEL	4.24	0	1	2000	5	95	5.3	2	2	Urban
BYZ	3	ANT	5.42	300	2	1260	57	2	3	2	2	Urban

Appendix 2

Ceramic Tabulations

Dr. Richard Rothaus completed a ceramic tabulation of surface collections during a 20 day period in August of 1997 (Rothaus n.d.). In addition to tabulating known ceramic types, Dr. Rothaus developed a provisional typology of local wares (Antioch ad Cragum Ware, West Cilicia Ware, local transport amphora, and Cilicia White Ware), and assembled a study collection that will be stored in the Alanya Archaeological Museum. In his report, Dr. Rothaus emphasizes that this study was done quickly in anticipation that the bulk of the collection would have to be discarded at the end of the 1997 season, and thus it must be considered as a preliminary effort that can be refined with further study. This work could not have been completed without the diligent assistance of Paige Rothaus and Jason DeBlock.

Section 1 of this appendix includes the ceramic type master list. Preceding each type is a number corresponding to a column number in Section 2 where the counts are found by site field number, site period number, and collection area, where applicable. The collection area tabulation indicates only presence-absence of the type, and was used to establish collection area periodization. Total counts for each type are tabulated under the site number. The numbers following the type listing indicate the estimated chronological range of the type. Section 2 indicates hinterland (1=Iotape, 2=Selinus, 3=Cestrus, 4=Nephelion, 5=Antiochia), grid square, site field number, collection area number, collection area in ha, site period number(s) and counts of types 1 to 163.

Section 1

Classical/Hellenistic

Coarse and Cooking Wares

1	Classical/Hellenistic Coarse and Cooking Wares, Misc.	-498	-66
2	Hellenistic Everted Rim Bowl	-332	-66
3	Hellenistic Grooved Rolled Rim Bowl	-332	-66
4	Hellenistic Strap Handle Cookpot	-332	-66

Fine Ware

5	Classical/Hellenistic Fine Ware, Misc.	-498	-66
6	Classical Black Glaze	-498	-333
7	Hellenistic Dribble Ware	-332	-66
8	Hellenistic Black Glaze	-332	-66
9	Hellenistic Black Glaze Cup	-332	-66
10	Hellenistic Black Glaze Fish Plate	-350	-200
11	Hellenistic Black Glaze Flat Rim Plate	-300	-100
12	Hellenistic Black Glaze Kantharos	-399	-300
13	Hellenistic Black Glaze Large Echinus Bowl	-399	-300
14	Hellenistic Black Glaze Rolled Rim Plate	-300	-100
15	Hellenistic Black Glaze Thickened Interior Rim Plate	-300	-175
16	Hellenistic Black Glaze Knobbed Rim Plate	-300	-175
17	Hellenistic Lamp	-332	-66
18	Greek Black Glaze	-498	-66

Plain Ware

19	Classical/Hellenistic Plain Ware	-498	-66

Transport Amphora

20	Classical/Hellenistic Transport Amphora	-498	-66
21	Hellenistic Transport Amphora Rhodian	-300	-50

Early Roman

Coarse and Cooking Wares

22	Early Roman Coarse and Cooking Wares, Misc.	-65	249
23	Early Roman Pedestal Krater	150	299
24	Early Roman Carinated Cookpot	1	299
25	Early Roman Stamnos	-65	250
26	Early Roman Flanged Vertical Neck Cookpot	-65	249
27	Early Roman Frying Pan	-65	249
28	Early Roman Slipped Coarse Red Ware	-65	250

Fine Ware

29	Early Roman Fine Ware, Misc.		-65	249
30	Early Roman Arretine		60	100
31	Early Roman Cypriot Sigillata		1	199
32	Early Roman Cypriot Sigillata Dish		1	150
33	Early Roman Cypriot Sigillata Roulleted Rim Bowl		1	50
34	Early Roman Cypriot Sigillata Inturned Dish		1	99
35	Early Roman Cypriot Sigillata Krater		100	150
36	Early Roman Cypriot Sigillata Offset Neck Jar		50	150
37	Early Roman Cypriot Sigillata Rounded Everted Rim Bowl		1	99
38	Early Roman Lamp		-65	250
39	Early Roman Red Ware		-65	250
40	Early Roman ESA		100	150
41	Early Roman ESB I		1	100
42	Early Roman ESB II		50	199
43	Early Roman Lead Glaze Ware		-65	250
44	Early Roman Moulded Bowl		-199	199

Plain Ware

45	Early Roman Plain Ware, Misc.		-65	249
46	Early Roman Globular Cup		1	299
47	Early Roman Trefoil Jug		1	199

Transport Amphora

48	Early Roman Transport Amphora, Misc.		-65	249
49	Early Roman Italian Transport Amphora		-100	100

Late Roman

Coarse and Cooking Wares

50	Late Roman Coarse and Cooking Wares, Misc.		250	699
51	Late Roman Decorated Basin		250	699
52	Late Roman Decorated Jug		250	699
53	Late Roman Carinated Casserole		500	699
54	Late Roman Small Amphora		600	699
55	Late Roman Pie Crust Rim Ware		550	699

Fine Ware

56	Late Roman Fine Ware, Misc.		250	699
57	Late Roman African Red Slip		250	699
58	Late Roman Cypriot Red Slip		400	699
59	Late Roman Cypriot Red Slip Form 1		350	475
60	Late Roman Cypriot Red Slip Form 2		500	550
61	Late Roman Cypriot Red Slip Form 7		550	625
62	Late Roman Cypriot Red Slip Form 8		500	599
63	Late Roman Cypriot Red Slip Form 9		550	660
64	Late Roman Cypriot Red Slip Form 10		600	700
65	Late Roman Cypriot Red Slip Form 11		550	650
66	Late Roman Cypriot Red Slip Saucer		550	650
67	Late Roman Red Ware		250	699
68	Late Roman Phocaean Ware		350	600

Plain Ware

69	Late Roman Plain Ware, Misc.		250	699

Transport Amphora

70	Late Roman Transport Amphora, Misc.		250	699
71	Late Roman Aegean Transport Amphora		200	399
72	Late Roman Banded Spirally Grooved		600	699
73	Late Roman Banded Combed		600	699
74	Late Roman Combed Transport Amphora		500	699
75	Late Roman Decorated Amphora		500	699
76	Late Roman Gaza Type Amphora		400	599
77	Late Roman Amphora Type B		400	699
78	Late Roman Pale Gritty Amphora Type B		400	699
79	Late Roman Small Combed Amphora		500	699
80	Late Roman Small Spirally Grooved Amphora		500	699
81	Late Roman Spirally Grooved Amphora		300	599
82	Late Roman Wheel Ridged Amphora		300	599

Non-Diagnostic Roman

Coarse and Cooking Wares

83	Roman Coarse and Cooking Wares, Misc.	-65	699
84	Roman Micaceous Water Jar	100	699
85	Roman Coarse Inturned Rim Basin	-65	699
86	Roman Decorated Table Amphora	-65	699
87	Roman Painted Basin	-65	699
88	Roman Slipped Folded Rim Basin	-65	699
89	Roman Stepped Coarse Rim Basin	-65	699

Fine Ware

90	Roman Fine Ware, Misc.	-65	699
91	Roman Candarli	100	300
92	Roman Cypriot Red Ware Offset Concave Jug	1	700
93	Roman Cypriot Red Ware Offset Neck Jar	1	700
94	Roman Grey Ware	-65	699
95	Roman Lamp	-65	699
96	Roman Red Ware	-65	699

Transport Amphora

97	Roman Transport Amphora	-65	699
98	Zemer 41	1	399

Local Wares

99	Antioch ad Cragum Ware
100	West Cilicia Ware
101	West Cilicia Ware Basin
102	West Cilicia Ware Carinated Cookpot
103	West Cilicia Ware Channeled Rim Stewpot
104	West Cilicia Ware Concave Lip Stewpot
105	West Cilicia Ware Drooping Everted Rim Bowl
106	West Cilicia Ware Decorated Triangular Rim Bowl
107	West Cilicia Ware Everted Rim Bowl
108	West Cilicia Ware Folded Rim Bowl
109	West Cilicia Ware Everted Rim Stewpot
110	West Cilicia Ware External Flange Basin
111	West Cilicia Ware External Flange Jug
112	West Cilicia Ware Folded Rim Storage Jar
113	West Cilicia Ware Frying Pan
114	West Cilicia Ware Hanging Concave Rim Basin
115	West Cilicia Ware Hooked Rim Basin
116	West Cilicia Ware Internal Ridge Basin
117	West Cilicia Ware Inturned Rim Fine Bowl
118	West Cilicia Ware Jug
119	West Cilicia Ware Large Storage Jar
120	West Cilicia Ware Lid
121	West Cilicia Ware Lipped Storage Jar
122	West Cilicia Ware Ridged Stewpot
123	West Cilicia Ware Ring Foot Plate
124	West Cilicia Ware Rolled Rim Jug
125	West Cilicia Ware Round Cookpot
126	West Cilicia Ware Rounded Rim Basin
127	West Cilicia Ware Stewpot
128	West Cilicia Ware Strainer Jug
129	West Cilicia Ware Triangular Rim Bowl
130	West Cilicia Ware Concave Rim Basin
131	West Cilicia Ware Upturned Rim Basin
132	West Cilicia Ware Upturned Sharp Rim Basin
133	West Cilicia Ware Vertical Grooved Lip Basin
134	West Cilicia Ware Vertical Neck Cookpot
135	Cilicia White Ware
136	Cilicia White Ware Carinated Caserole
137	Cilicia White Ware Everted Rim Stewpot
138	Cilicia White Ware Frying Pan
139	Cilicia White Ware Miniature Jug
140	Cilicia White Ware Stepped Rim Basin
141	Cilicia White Ware Upturned Everted Rim Stewpot

Transport Amphora
142	Antioch Zemer 41		
143	West Cilicia Transport Amphora		
144	West Cilicia Aegean Transport Amphora		
145	West Cilicia Zemer 41		
146	Cilicia White Ware Amphora		
147	Zemer 41 Pseudo Coan White Ware		
148	Zemer 41 White Ware		

Byzantine

Coarse and Cooking Wares
149	Early Byzantine Coarse and Cooking Wares	700	969
150	Late Byzantine Coarse and Cooking Wares	970	1071
151	Early/Late Byzantine Coarse and Cooking Wares	700	1071

Fine Ware
152	Early Byzantine Fine Ware	700	969
153	Late Byzantine Fine Ware	970	1071
154	Early/Late Byzantine Fine Ware	700	1071

Plain Ware
155	Early Byzantine Plain Ware	700	969
156	Late Byzantine Plain Ware	970	1071
157	Early/Late Byzantine Plain Ware	700	1071

Transport Amphora
158	Early Byzantine Transport Amphora	700	969
159	Late Byzantine Transport Amphora	970	1071
160	Early/Late Byzantine Transport Amphora	700	1071

Non-Diagnostic

161	Non-diagnostic Coarse Ware
162	Non-diagnostic Plain Ware
163	Non-diagnostic Transport Amphora (includes Pseudo-Coan Amphora)

Appendix 2 Section 2

Hinterland	Gridsquare	FLD#	CA#	CA HA	HLN#	ER#	LR#	BYZ#	1	2	3	4	5	6	7	8	9	10	11	12	13	14	15
1	28-a-20-b	1	0	0.92	.	1	1	.	0	0	0	0	0	0	0	0	0	0	0	0	0	0	0
1	28-a-20-c	1	0	2.07	1	3	3	1	0	1	1	0	4	0	0	0	0	0	0	1	2	0	0
1	28-a-20-c	1	1	0.6	1	3	3	1	0	0	0	0	1	0	0	0	0	0	0	0	0	0	0
1	28-a-20-c	1	2	0.7	1	3	3	1	0	1	1	0	1	0	0	0	0	0	0	1	1	0	0
1	28-a-20-c	1	3	0.27	1	3	3	1	0	0	0	0	0	0	0	0	0	0	0	0	0	0	0
1	28-a-20-c	1	4	0.5	1	3	3	1	0	0	0	0	1	0	0	0	0	0	0	0	0	0	0
1	28-b-16-d	1	0	0.63	.	2	2	.	0	0	0	0	0	0	0	0	0	0	0	0	0	0	0
2	28-b-21-b	5	0	2.8	.	6	6	.	0	0	0	0	1	0	0	0	0	0	0	0	0	0	0
2	28-b-21-b	5	1	0.1	.	6	6	.	0	0	0	0	1	0	0	0	0	0	0	0	0	0	0
2	28-b-21-b	5	2	2.7	.	6	6	.	0	0	0	0	0	0	0	0	0	0	0	0	0	0	0
2	28-b-21-b	4	0	1.05	.	7	7	.	0	0	0	0	0	0	0	0	0	0	0	0	0	0	0
2	28-b-21-b	6	0	0.1	.	8	.	.	0	0	0	0	0	0	0	0	0	0	0	0	0	0	0
2	28-b-21-b	1	0	0.4	.	4	4	.	0	0	0	0	0	0	0	0	0	0	0	0	0	0	0
2	28-b-21-b	2	0	0.2	.	5	5	.	0	0	0	0	0	0	0	0	0	0	0	0	0	0	0
2	28-b-21-c	2	0	1.3	.	10	8	.	0	0	0	0	0	0	0	0	0	0	0	0	0	0	0
2	28-b-21-c	5	0	0.2	.	.	11	.	0	0	0	0	0	0	0	0	0	0	0	0	0	0	0
2	28-b-21-c	3	0	0.2	.	.	9	.	0	0	0	0	0	0	0	0	0	0	0	0	0	0	0
2	28-b-21-c	4	0	0.2	.	11	10	.	0	0	0	0	0	0	0	0	0	0	0	0	0	0	0
2	28-b-21-c	1	0	0.1	.	9	.	.	0	0	0	0	1	0	0	0	0	0	0	0	0	0	0
2	28-b-21-c	6	0	4.24	2	13	13	2	1	0	0	0	41	4	2	1	0	0	0	1	4	0	2
2	28-b-21-c	6	1	0.45	2	13	13	2	0	0	0	0	0	0	0	0	0	0	0	0	0	0	1
2	28-b-21-c	6	2	0.4	2	13	13	2	0	0	0	0	0	0	0	0	0	0	0	0	0	0	0
2	28-b-21-c	6	3	0.25	2	13	13	2	0	0	0	0	0	0	0	0	0	0	0	0	0	0	0
2	28-b-21-c	6	4	0.75	2	13	13	2	0	0	0	0	0	0	0	0	0	0	0	0	0	0	0
2	28-b-21-c	6	5	0.56	2	13	13	2	0	0	0	0	0	0	0	0	0	0	0	0	0	0	0
2	28-b-21-c	6	6	0.26	2	13	13	2	0	0	0	0	0	0	0	0	0	0	0	0	0	0	0
2	28-b-21-c	6	7	0.18	2	13	13	2	0	0	0	0	0	0	0	0	0	0	0	0	0	0	0
2	28-b-21-c	6	8	0.15	2	13	13	2	0	0	0	0	1	1	0	0	0	0	0	1	1	0	0
2	28-b-21-c	6	9	0.16	2	13	13	2	0	0	0	0	0	0	0	1	0	0	0	0	0	0	1
2	28-b-21-c	6	10	0.07	2	13	13	2	0	0	0	0	0	0	0	0	0	0	0	0	0	0	0
2	28-b-21-c	6	11	0.04	2	13	13	2	0	0	0	0	1	1	0	0	0	0	0	0	0	0	0
2	28-b-21-c	6	12	0.17	2	13	13	2	0	0	0	0	1	0	0	0	0	0	0	0	0	0	0
2	28-b-21-c	6	13	0.4	2	13	13	2	0	0	0	0	1	0	1	0	0	0	0	0	0	0	0
2	28-b-21-c	6	14	0.4	2	13	13	2	0	0	0	0	1	0	0	0	0	0	0	0	1	0	0
2	28-c-01-b	1	0	0.1	.	12	12	.	0	0	0	0	0	0	0	0	0	0	0	0	0	0	0
3	28-c-02-a	1	0	1	.	15	17	.	0	0	0	0	0	0	0	0	0	0	0	0	0	0	0
3	28-c-02-a	4	0	0.5	.	14	14	.	0	0	0	0	0	0	0	0	0	0	0	0	0	0	0
3	28-c-02-b	4	0	1.25	.	16	18	.	0	0	0	0	0	0	0	0	0	0	0	0	0	0	0
3	28-c-02-b	1	0	0.69	.	17	19	.	0	0	0	0	0	0	0	0	0	0	0	0	0	0	0
3	28-c-02-b	1	1	0.18	.	17	19	.	0	0	0	0	0	0	0	0	0	0	0	0	0	0	0
3	28-c-02-b	1	2	0.14	.	17	19	.	0	0	0	0	0	0	0	0	0	0	0	0	0	0	0
3	28-c-02-b	1	3	0.01	.	17	19	.	0	0	0	0	0	0	0	0	0	0	0	0	0	0	0
3	28-c-02-b	1	4	0.01	.	17	19	.	0	0	0	0	0	0	0	0	0	0	0	0	0	0	0
3	28-c-02-b	1	5	0.225	.	17	19	.	0	0	0	0	0	0	0	0	0	0	0	0	0	0	0
3	28-c-02-b	1	6	0.125	.	17	19	.	0	0	0	0	0	0	0	0	0	0	0	0	0	0	0
3	28-c-03-d	4	0	4.4	.	18	21	.	0	0	0	0	0	0	0	1	0	0	0	0	0	0	0
3	28-c-03-d	2	0	0.1	.	.	20	.	0	0	0	0	0	0	0	0	0	0	0	0	0	0	0
4	28-c-03-d	1	0	0.28	.	19	.	.	0	0	0	0	0	0	0	0	0	0	0	0	0	0	0
4	28-c-08-b	1	0	0.4	.	21	.	.	0	0	0	0	0	0	0	0	0	0	0	0	0	0	0
4	28-c-08-c	1	0	2.6	3	22	22	.	0	0	0	0	10	1	2	0	0	0	0	0	0	0	1
4	28-c-08-c	1	1	0.8	3	22	22	.	0	0	0	0	0	0	0	0	0	0	0	0	0	0	0
4	28-c-08-c	1	2	0.03	3	22	22	.	0	0	0	0	0	0	0	0	0	0	0	0	0	0	0
4	28-c-08-c	1	3	0.25	3	22	22	.	0	0	0	0	0	0	1	0	0	0	0	0	0	0	0
4	28-c-08-c	1	4	0.18	3	22	22	.	0	0	0	0	0	0	0	0	0	0	0	0	0	0	0
4	28-c-08-c	1	5	0.25	3	22	22	.	0	0	0	0	1	1	1	0	0	0	0	0	0	0	0
4	28-c-08-c	1	6	0.6	3	22	22	.	0	0	0	0	1	0	0	0	0	0	0	0	0	0	1
4	28-c-08-c	1	7	0.2	3	22	22	.	0	0	0	0	0	0	0	0	0	0	0	0	0	0	0
4	28-c-08-c	1	8	0.27	3	22	22	.	0	0	0	0	0	0	0	0	0	0	0	0	0	0	0
4	28-c-08-c	2	0	1.5	.	23	.	.	0	0	0	0	0	0	0	0	0	0	0	0	0	0	0
5	28-c-09-d	6	0	0.1	4	.	.	.	0	0	0	0	1	0	0	0	0	0	0	0	0	0	0
5	28-c-09-c	1	0	1	.	24	.	.	0	0	0	0	0	0	0	0	0	0	0	0	0	0	0
5	28-c-09-d	1	0	5.42	.	25	23	3	2	0	0	1	1	0	0	0	0	0	0	0	0	0	0
5	28-c-09-d	1	1	0.46	.	25	23	3	0	0	0	0	0	0	0	0	0	0	0	0	0	0	0
5	28-c-09-d	1	2	0.14	.	25	23	3	0	0	0	0	0	0	0	0	0	0	0	0	0	0	0
5	28-c-09-d	1	3	0.06	.	25	23	3	0	0	0	0	0	0	0	0	0	0	0	0	0	0	0
5	28-c-09-d	1	4	0.3	.	25	23	3	0	0	0	0	1	0	0	0	0	0	0	0	0	0	0
5	28-c-09-d	1	5	0.36	.	25	23	3	0	0	0	0	0	0	0	0	0	0	0	0	0	0	0
5	28-c-09-d	1	6	0.4	.	25	23	3	0	0	0	0	0	0	0	0	0	0	0	0	0	0	0
5	28-c-09-d	1	8	0.32	.	25	23	3	0	0	0	0	0	0	0	0	0	0	0	0	0	0	0
5	28-c-09-d	1	9	0.38	.	25	23	3	0	0	0	0	0	0	0	0	0	0	0	0	0	0	0
5	28-c-09-d	1	10	0.7	.	25	23	3	0	0	0	0	0	0	0	0	0	0	0	0	0	0	0
5	28-c-09-d	1	12	1.13	.	25	23	3	0	0	0	0	0	0	0	0	0	0	0	0	0	0	0
5	28-c-09-d	1	14	0.42	.	25	23	3	0	0	0	1	0	0	0	0	0	0	0	0	0	0	0
5	28-c-09-d	1	15	0.49	.	25	23	3	0	0	0	0	0	0	0	0	0	0	0	0	0	0	0
5	28-c-09-d	1	16	0.3	.	25	23	3	0	0	0	0	0	0	0	0	0	0	0	0	0	0	0

Appendix 2, Section 2 (Cont.)

16	17	18	19	20	21	22	23	24	25	26	27	28	29	30	31	32	33	34	35	36	37	38	39	40
0	0	0	0	0	0	0	0	0	0	0	0	0	0	0	0	0	0	1	1	0	0	0	0	1
0	1	0	0	0	0	0	0	0	1	1	3	0	30	0	0	1	1	0	3	0	3	0	2	1
0	1	0	0	0	0	0	0	0	0	0	0	0	0	0	0	1	1	0	0	0	0	0	0	1
0	0	0	0	0	0	0	0	0	0	0	0	0	0	0	0	0	0	0	0	0	1	0	0	0
0	0	0	0	0	0	0	0	0	0	0	0	0	0	0	0	0	0	1	0	0	0	0	0	0
0	0	0	0	0	0	0	0	0	0	0	0	0	0	0	0	0	0	0	1	0	0	0	0	0
0	0	0	0	0	0	0	0	0	0	0	0	0	0	0	0	0	0	0	0	0	0	0	0	0
0	0	0	0	0	0	0	0	0	0	0	0	0	0	0	0	0	0	0	0	0	0	0	0	0
0	0	0	0	0	0	0	0	0	0	0	0	0	0	0	0	0	0	0	0	0	0	0	0	0
0	0	0	0	0	0	0	0	0	0	0	0	0	0	0	0	0	0	0	0	0	0	0	0	0
0	0	0	0	0	0	1	0	0	0	0	0	0	0	0	0	0	0	0	0	0	0	0	0	0
0	0	0	0	0	0	0	0	0	0	0	0	0	0	0	0	0	0	0	0	0	0	0	0	0
0	0	0	0	0	0	0	0	0	0	0	0	0	0	0	0	0	0	0	0	0	0	0	0	0
0	0	0	0	0	0	0	0	0	0	0	0	0	0	0	0	0	0	0	0	0	0	0	0	0
0	0	0	0	0	0	0	0	0	0	0	0	0	0	0	0	0	0	0	0	0	0	0	0	0
0	0	0	0	0	0	0	0	0	0	0	0	0	0	0	0	0	0	0	0	0	0	0	0	0
0	0	0	0	0	0	0	0	0	0	0	0	0	0	0	0	0	0	0	0	0	0	0	0	0
0	0	0	0	0	0	0	0	0	0	0	0	0	0	0	0	0	0	0	0	0	0	0	0	0
0	0	0	0	0	0	0	0	0	0	0	0	0	0	0	0	0	0	0	0	0	0	0	1	0
3	0	0	0	0	0	4	0	2	0	0	0	0	1	0	1	1	0	1	6	2	0	2	18	29
0	0	0	0	0	0	0	0	0	0	0	0	0	0	0	0	0	0	0	0	0	0	0	0	1
0	0	0	0	0	0	0	0	0	0	0	0	0	0	0	0	0	0	0	0	0	0	0	0	1
0	0	0	0	0	0	0	0	0	0	0	0	0	0	0	0	0	0	0	0	0	0	0	0	0
0	0	0	0	0	0	0	0	0	0	0	0	0	0	0	0	0	0	1	0	0	0	0	0	0
0	0	0	0	0	0	0	0	0	0	0	0	0	0	0	0	0	0	0	0	0	0	0	0	0
0	0	0	0	0	0	0	0	0	0	0	0	0	0	0	0	0	0	0	0	0	0	0	0	0
1	0	0	0	0	0	0	0	0	0	0	0	0	0	0	0	0	0	0	1	1	0	1	1	1
1	0	0	0	0	0	0	0	0	0	0	0	0	0	0	0	0	0	0	1	0	0	0	0	0
0	0	0	0	0	0	0	0	0	0	0	0	0	0	0	0	0	0	0	0	0	0	0	0	1
0	0	0	0	0	0	0	0	0	0	0	0	0	0	0	0	1	0	0	1	0	0	0	0	0
0	0	0	0	0	0	0	0	0	0	0	0	0	0	0	0	0	0	0	1	0	0	0	0	1
0	0	0	0	0	0	0	0	0	0	0	0	0	1	0	0	0	0	0	0	0	0	0	0	1
0	0	0	0	0	0	0	0	0	0	0	0	0	0	0	0	0	0	0	0	0	0	0	0	1
0	0	0	0	0	0	0	0	0	0	0	0	0	0	0	0	0	0	0	0	0	0	0	0	0
0	0	0	0	0	0	0	0	0	0	0	0	0	0	0	0	0	0	0	0	0	0	0	1	0
0	0	0	0	0	0	0	0	0	0	0	0	0	0	0	0	1	1	0	0	0	0	0	0	1
0	0	0	0	0	0	0	0	0	0	0	0	0	0	0	0	0	0	0	0	0	0	0	0	0
0	0	0	0	0	0	4	0	1	0	0	2	0	0	0	5	1	0	0	11	4	8	2	0	13
0	0	0	0	0	0	0	0	0	0	0	0	0	0	0	0	0	0	0	1	1	1	0	0	1
0	0	0	0	0	0	0	0	0	0	0	0	0	0	0	0	0	0	0	1	0	0	0	0	1
0	0	0	0	0	0	0	0	0	0	0	0	0	0	0	1	1	0	0	1	1	0	0	0	1
0	0	0	0	0	0	0	0	0	0	0	0	0	0	0	0	0	0	0	0	1	1	0	0	1
0	0	0	0	0	0	0	0	0	0	0	0	0	0	0	0	0	0	0	1	1	0	0	0	0
0	0	0	0	0	1	0	0	0	0	0	0	0	0	0	2	0	0	0	5	0	5	0	0	0
0	0	0	0	0	0	0	0	0	0	0	0	0	0	0	0	0	0	0	0	0	0	0	0	0
0	0	0	0	0	0	0	0	0	0	0	0	0	0	0	0	0	0	0	1	0	0	0	0	0
0	0	0	0	0	0	0	0	0	0	0	0	0	0	0	0	0	0	0	0	0	0	0	3	0
0	2	0	0	1	0	0	0	3	0	0	0	3	0	0	1	0	0	0	4	0	0	3	6	11
0	0	0	0	0	0	0	0	0	0	0	0	0	0	0	0	0	0	0	0	0	0	0	0	0
0	0	0	0	0	0	0	0	0	0	0	0	0	0	0	0	0	0	0	0	0	0	0	0	0
0	0	0	0	0	0	0	0	0	0	0	0	0	0	0	1	0	0	0	1	0	0	1	1	1
0	0	0	0	0	0	0	0	0	0	0	0	0	0	0	0	0	0	0	0	0	0	0	0	0
0	1	0	0	0	0	0	0	0	0	0	0	0	0	0	0	0	0	0	0	0	0	0	0	1
0	1	0	0	0	0	0	0	0	0	0	0	0	0	0	0	0	0	0	1	0	0	0	0	1
0	0	0	0	0-	0	0	0	0	0	0	0	0	0	0	0	0	0	0	0	0	0	0	0	0
0	0	0	0	0	0	0	0	0	0	0	0	0	0	0	0	0	0	0	2	0	0	0	0	0
0	1	0	0	0	0	0	0	0	0	0	0	0	0	0	0	0	0	0	0	0	0	0	0	0
0	0	0	0	0	0	0	0	0	0	0	0	0	0	0	0	0	0	0	0	0	0	0	1	0
0	0	1	0	1	0	0	0	0	0	0	0	0	0	0	0	1	1	1	6	0	8	0	0	4
0	0	0	0	0	0	0	0	0	0	0	0	0	0	0	0	0	0	0	0	0	0	0	0	0
0	0	0	0	0	0	0	0	0	0	0	0	0	0	0	0	0	0	0	0	0	0	0	0	0
0	0	0	0	0	0	0	0	0	0	0	0	0	0	0	0	0	0	0	1	0	1	0	0	1
0	0	0	0	0	0	0	0	0	0	0	0	0	0	0	1	0	0	0	1	0	1	0	0	1
0	0	0	0	1	0	0	0	0	0	0	0	0	0	0	0	1	0	0	1	0	0	0	0	0
0	0	0	0	0	0	0	0	0	0	0	0	0	0	0	0	0	0	0	0	0	0	0	0	0
0	0	0	0	0	0	0	0	0	0	0	0	0	0	0	0	0	0	0	0	0	0	0	0	0
0	0	0	0	0	0	0	0	0	0	0	0	0	0	0	0	0	0	0	0	0	0	0	0	0
0	0	1	0	0	0	0	0	0	0	0	0	0	0	0	0	0	0	0	0	0	0	0	0	1
0	0	0	0	0	0	0	0	0	0	0	0	0	0	0	0	0	1	0	0	0	1	0	0	0
16	17	18	19	20	21	22	23	24	25	26	27	28	29	30	31	32	33	34	35	36	37	38	39	40
0	0	0	0	0	0	0	0	0	0	0	0	0	0	0	0	0	0	0	1	0	0	0	0	0

41	42	43	44	45	46	47	48	49	50	51	52	53	54	55	56	57	58	59	60	61	62
0	0	0	0	0	0	0	0	0	0	0	0	0	0	0	0	0	0	0	0	0	0
0	0	0	0	0	0	0	0	0	0	0	0	0	0	0	0	2	1	0	0	0	0
0	0	0	0	0	0	0	0	0	0	0	0	0	0	0	0	1	1	0	0	0	0
0	0	0	0	0	0	0	0	0	0	0	0	0	0	0	0	0	0	0	0	0	0
0	0	0	0	0	0	0	0	0	0	0	0	0	0	0	0	0	0	0	0	0	0
0	0	0	0	0	0	0	0	0	1	0	0	0	0	0	0	0	0	1	0	0	0
0	0	0	0	0	0	0	0	0	0	0	0	0	0	0	0	0	0	0	0	0	0
0	0	0	0	0	0	0	0	0	0	0	0	0	0	0	0	0	0	0	0	0	0
0	0	0	0	0	0	0	0	0	0	0	0	0	0	0	0	0	0	0	0	0	0
0	0	0	0	0	0	0	0	0	0	0	0	0	0	0	0	0	0	0	1	0	0
0	0	0	0	0	0	0	0	0	0	0	0	0	0	0	0	0	0	0	0	0	0
0	0	0	0	0	0	0	0	0	0	0	0	0	0	0	0	0	0	0	0	0	0
0	0	0	0	0	0	0	0	0	0	0	0	0	0	0	0	0	0	0	0	0	0
0	0	0	0	0	0	0	0	0	0	0	0	0	0	0	0	0	0	0	0	0	0
0	0	0	0	0	0	0	0	0	0	0	0	0	0	1	0	0	0	0	0	0	0
0	0	0	0	0	0	0	0	0	0	0	0	0	0	0	0	0	0	0	0	0	0
0	0	0	0	0	0	0	0	0	0	0	0	0	0	0	0	0	0	0	0	0	0
0	0	0	0	0	0	0	0	0	0	0	0	0	0	0	0	0	0	0	0	0	0
0	0	0	0	2	6	3	0	0	0	0	0	0	0	0	0	2	8	24	3	1	2
0	0	0	0	0	0	0	0	0	0	0	0	0	0	0	0	0	0	1	0	0	0
0	0	0	0	0	0	1	0	0	0	0	0	0	0	0	0	0	1	0	1	0	1
0	0	0	0	0	0	0	0	0	0	0	0	0	0	0	0	0	0	0	1	0	0
0	0	0	0	0	0	0	0	0	0	0	0	0	0	0	0	0	0	0	1	0	0
0	0	0	0	0	0	0	0	0	0	0	0	0	0	0	0	0	0	0	0	0	0
0	0	0	0	0	0	0	0	0	0	0	0	0	0	0	0	0	0	1	0	0	0
0	0	0	0	0	0	0	0	0	0	0	0	0	0	0	0	0	0	0	1	0	0
0	0	0	0	0	0	1	0	0	0	0	0	0	0	0	0	0	0	1	0	0	0
0	0	0	0	0	0	1	0	0	0	0	0	0	0	0	0	0	1	0	0	0	0
0	0	0	0	0	0	0	0	0	0	0	0	0	0	0	0	0	1	0	0	0	0
0	0	0	0	0	0	0	0	0	0	0	0	0	0	0	0	0	1	1	0	0	0
0	0	0	0	0	0	0	0	0	0	1	0	0	0	0	0	0	0	0	0	0	0
0	0	0	0	0	0	0	0	0	0	0	0	0	0	0	0	0	1	0	0	0	0
0	0	0	0	0	0	0	0	0	0	0	0	0	0	0	0	0	0	0	0	0	0
0	0	0	0	0	0	0	0	0	0	0	0	0	0	0	0	0	0	0	0	0	0
0	0	1	0	0	4	0	2	0	0	0	0	0	0	1	0	1	1	5	1	0	0
0	0	0	0	0	0	0	0	0	0	0	0	0	0	0	0	0	0	0	0	0	0
0	0	0	0	0	0	0	0	0	0	0	0	0	0	0	0	0	0	1	0	0	0
0	0	0	0	0	0	0	0	0	0	0	0	0	0	1	0	0	1	1	1	0	0
0	0	0	0	0	0	0	0	0	0	0	0	0	0	0	0	0	1	0	0	0	0
0	0	0	0	0	0	0	0	0	0	0	0	0	0	0	0	0	0	0	0	0	0
0	0	0	0	0	0	0	0	0	0	0	0	0	0	0	0	0	0	0	0	0	0
0	0	0	0	0	0	0	0	0	0	0	0	0	0	0	0	0	0	0	0	0	0
0	0	0	0	0	0	0	0	0	0	0	0	0	0	0	0	0	0	0	0	0	0
0	0	0	1	0	5	0	0	0	0	0	0	0	1	1	0	1	34	4	48	1	8
0	0	0	0	0	0	0	0	0	0	0	0	0	0	0	0	0	0	0	1	0	0
0	0	0	0	0	0	0	0	0	0	0	0	0	0	0	0	0	0	0	1	1	0
0	0	0	0	0	0	0	0	0	0	0	0	0	0	0	0	0	1	1	1	0	1
0	0	0	0	0	0	0	0	0	0	0	0	0	0	0	0	0	0	0	0	0	0
0	0	0	0	0	0	0	0	0	0	0	0	0	1	1	0	0	1	1	1	0	1
0	0	0	0	0	0	0	0	0	0	0	0	0	0	0	0	0	0	1	0	0	0
0	0	0	0	0	0	0	0	0	0	0	0	0	0	0	0	0	0	0	0	0	0
1	0	0	0	0	0	0	0	0	0	0	0	0	0	0	0	0	0	0	0	0	0
0	0	0	0	0	0	0	0	0	0	0	0	0	0	0	0	0	0	0	0	0	0
0	0	0	0	0	0	0	0	0	0	0	0	0	0	0	0	0	0	0	0	0	0
0	0	0	0	1	10	1	0	0	1	2	0	1	0	1	0	4	2	2	1	1	0
0	0	0	0	0	0	0	0	0	0	0	0	0	0	0	0	0	0	0	0	0	0
0	0	0	0	0	0	0	0	0	0	0	0	0	0	0	0	0	0	0	0	0	0
0	0	0	0	0	0	0	0	0	0	1	0	0	0	0	0	0	0	0	0	0	0
0	0	0	0	0	0	0	0	0	0	0	0	0	0	0	0	0	0	1	0	0	0
0	0	0	0	0	0	1	0	0	0	1	0	0	0	1	0	1	0	0	1	1	0
0	0	0	0	0	0	0	0	0	0	0	0	0	0	0	0	0	0	0	0	0	0
0	0	0	0	0	0	0	0	0	0	0	0	0	0	0	0	0	0	0	0	0	0
0	0	0	0	0	0	0	0	0	0	0	0	0	0	0	0	0	1	0	0	0	0
0	0	0	0	0	0	0	0	0	0	0	0	0	0	0	0	0	0	1	0	0	0
0	0	0	0	0	0	0	0	0	0	0	0	1	0	0	0	1	0	0	0	0	0
0	0	0	0	0	0	0	0	0	0	0	0	0	0	0	0	0	1	0	0	0	0

41	42	43	44	45	46	47	48	49	50	51	52	53	54	55	56	57	58	59	60	61	62
0	0	0	0	0	0	0	0	0	0	0	0	0	0	0	0	0	1	0	0	0	0

63	64	65	66	67	68	69	70	71	72	73	74	75	76	77	78	79	80	81	82	83
0	0	0	0	0	0	0	0	1	0	0	0	0	0	0	0	0	0	0	0	0
6	0	0	0	0	1	0	0	2	0	0	0	0	0	0	0	0	2	1	9	3
1	0	0	0	0	1	0	0	0	0	0	0	0	0	0	0	0	1	0	1	0
1	0	0	0	0	0	0	0	0	0	0	0	0	0	0	0	0	0	1	1	0
0	0	0	0	0	0	0	0	0	0	0	0	0	0	0	0	0	0	0	1	0
1	0	0	0	0	0	0	0	0	0	0	0	0	0	0	0	0	0	0	0	0
1	0	0	0	0	0	0	3	0	1	1	0	0	0	0	0	0	0	0	0	0
1	0	0	0	0	0	0	0	0	0	0	0	0	0	0	0	1	0	0	2	0
0	0	0	0	0	0	0	0	0	0	0	0	0	0	0	0	0	0	0	0	0
1	0	0	0	0	0	0	0	0	0	0	0	0	0	0	0	1	0	0	1	0
0	0	0	0	0	0	0	0	0	0	0	0	0	0	0	0	0	0	0	0	0
0	0	0	0	0	0	0	0	0	0	0	0	0	0	0	0	0	0	0	0	1
0	0	0	0	0	0	0	0	0	0	0	0	0	0	0	0	0	0	0	0	0
0	0	1	0	0	0	0	0	0	0	0	0	0	0	0	0	2	0	0	2	0
0	0	0	0	0	0	0	0	0	0	0	0	0	0	0	0	0	0	0	0	0
0	0	0	0	0	0	0	0	0	0	0	0	0	0	0	0	0	0	0	0	0
0	0	0	0	0	0	0	0	0	0	0	0	0	0	0	0	0	0	1	1	0
0	0	0	0	0	0	0	1	0	0	0	0	0	0	1	0	2	0	0	1	0
0	0	0	0	0	0	0	0	0	0	0	0	0	0	0	0	0	0	0	0	1
19	7	6	0	0	0	0	0	0	1	0	1	0	1	0	0	2	0	4	30	3
1	1	0	0	0	0	0	0	0	0	0	0	0	0	0	0	0	0	0	0	0
1	1	0	0	0	0	0	0	0	0	0	1	0	0	0	0	0	0	0	1	0
0	0	1	0	0	0	0	0	0	0	0	0	0	0	0	0	0	0	0	0	0
0	0	0	0	0	0	0	0	0	0	0	0	0	0	0	0	0	0	0	1	0
1	0	0	0	0	0	0	0	0	0	0	0	0	0	0	0	0	0	1	1	0
0	0	0	0	0	0	0	0	0	0	0	0	0	0	0	0	0	0	1	1	0
0	0	0	0	0	0	0	0	0	0	0	0	0	0	0	0	0	0	0	1	0
1	0	0	0	0	0	0	0	0	0	0	0	0	0	0	0	0	0	0	0	0
0	0	1	0	0	0	0	0	0	0	0	0	0	0	0	0	0	0	0	1	0
0	0	0	0	0	0	0	0	0	0	0	0	0	0	0	0	0	0	0	0	0
0	0	0	0	0	0	0	0	0	0	0	0	0	0	0	0	0	0	0	0	0
1	0	1	0	0	0	0	0	0	0	0	0	0	0	0	0	0	0	0	1	0
1	0	0	0	0	0	0	0	0	0	0	0	0	0	0	0	1	0	0	0	0
0	0	1	0	0	0	0	0	0	1	0	0	0	1	0	0	0	0	0	1	0
0	0	0	0	0	0	0	0	0	0	0	0	0	0	0	0	0	0	0	0	0
0	0	0	0	0	0	0	0	0	0	0	0	0	0	0	0	0	0	0	0	0
0	0	0	0	0	0	0	0	0	4	0	0	0	0	0	0	0	0	0	2	0
0	0	0	0	0	0	0	0	0	0	0	0	0	0	0	0	0	0	0	2	0
1	0	0	0	0	1	0	0	0	1	0	0	0	0	0	0	2	0	7	10	1
0	0	0	0	0	0	0	0	0	0	0	0	0	0	0	0	1	0	0	0	0
0	0	0	0	0	0	0	0	0	0	0	0	0	0	0	0	0	0	1	1	0
1	0	0	0	0	1	0	0	0	0	0	0	0	0	0	1	0	0	1	1	0
0	0	0	0	0	0	0	0	0	0	0	0	0	0	0	0	0	0	1	1	0
1	0	0	0	0	1	0	0	0	0	0	1	0	0	0	1	0	0	1	1	0
0	0	0	0	0	0	0	0	0	0	0	0	0	0	0	0	0	0	1	1	0
1	0	0	0	0	1	0	0	0	0	0	0	0	0	0	1	0	0	1	1	0
0	0	0	0	0	0	0	0	0	0	0	1	0	0	0	1	0	0	1	1	0
1	0	0	0	0	0	0	0	0	0	0	0	0	0	0	0	0	0	0	0	0
4	0	0	0	0	8	0	0	0	0	0	3	0	0	7	6	0	0	18	15	1
0	0	0	0	0	0	0	0	0	0	0	0	0	0	1	1	0	0	1	1	0
0	0	0	0	0	0	0	0	0	0	0	0	0	0	0	0	0	0	1	1	0
1	0	0	0	0	1	0	0	0	1	0	1	0	0	1	1	0	0	1	1	0
0	0	0	0	0	0	0	0	0	0	0	0	0	0	0	0	0	0	1	1	0
0	0	0	0	0	1	0	0	0	0	0	0	0	0	0	0	1	0	1	1	0
0	0	0	0	0	1	0	0	0	0	0	0	1	0	0	0	1	0	1	1	0
0	0	0	0	0	0	0	0	0	0	0	0	0	0	0	0	0	0	1	1	0
1	0	0	0	0	0	0	0	0	0	0	0	0	0	0	0	0	0	0	0	0
0	0	0	0	0	0	0	0	0	0	0	0	0	0	0	0	0	0	0	0	0
0	0	0	0	0	0	0	0	0	0	0	0	0	0	0	0	0	0	0	0	0
4	0	0	1	0	2	0	0	0	0	0	1	1	0	0	0	2	0	1	11	80
0	0	0	0	0	0	0	0	0	0	0	0	0	0	0	0	0	0	0	1	0
0	0	0	0	0	1	0	0	0	0	0	0	0	0	0	0	0	0	0	1	0
0	0	0	0	0	0	0	0	0	0	0	0	0	0	0	0	0	0	0	1	0
0	0	0	0	0	0	0	0	0	0	0	0	0	0	0	0	0	0	0	0	0
1	0	0	0	0	0	0	0	0	0	0	0	0	0	0	0	0	0	0	0	0
1	0	0	0	0	1	0	0	0	0	0	0	0	0	0	0	0	0	0	0	0
0	0	0	0	0	0	0	0	0	0	0	0	0	0	0	0	0	0	0	1	0
0	0	0	0	0	0	0	0	0	0	0	0	0	0	0	0	0	0	0	0	0
0	0	0	0	0	0	0	0	0	0	0	0	0	0	0	0	0	0	0	0	1
0	0	0	0	0	0	0	0	0	0	0	0	0	0	0	0	1	0	0	0	0
0	0	0	0	1	0	0	0	0	0	0	0	1	0	0	0	1	0	1	1	0
0	0	0	0	0	0	0	0	0	0	0	1	0	0	0	0	0	0	0	1	0
1	0	0	0	0	0	0	0	0	0	0	0	0	0	0	0	0	0	0	0	0

84	85	86	87	88	89	90	91	92	93	94	95	96	97	98	99	100	101	102	103	104
0	0	0	1	0	0	6	0	0	0	0	0	0	1	0	0	0	0	0	0	0
1	0	0	0	0	0	2	0	1	1	0	0	19	12	5	0	0	0	0	0	0
0	0	0	0	0	0	0	0	0	0	0	0	0	0	0	0	0	0	0	0	0
0	0	0	0	0	0	0	0	0	0	0	0	0	0	0	0	0	0	0	0	0
0	0	0	0	0	0	0	0	0	0	0	0	0	0	0	0	0	0	0	0	0
0	0	0	0	0	0	0	0	0	0	0	0	0	0	0	0	0	0	0	0	0
0	0	0	1	0	0	0	0	0	0	0	0	2	17	0	0	0	0	0	0	0
0	0	0	0	0	0	0	0	0	0	0	0	1	1	7	0	6	0	0	0	0
0	0	0	0	0	0	0	0	0	0	0	0	0	0	0	0	1	0	0	0	0
0	0	0	0	0	0	0	0	0	0	0	0	1	1	0	0	0	0	0	0	0
0	0	0	0	0	0	2	0	0	0	0	0	2	0	0	0	0	0	0	0	0
0	0	0	0	0	0	0	0	0	0	0	0	0	0	2	0	0	0	0	0	0
1	0	0	0	0	0	0	0	0	0	0	0	0	2	1	0	0	0	0	0	0
0	0	0	0	0	0	1	0	0	0	0	0	0	1	2	0	0	0	0	0	0
0	0	0	0	0	0	0	0	0	0	0	0	0	0	0	0	0	0	0	0	0
0	0	0	0	0	0	0	0	0	0	0	0	0	0	0	0	0	0	0	0	0
0	0	0	0	0	0	0	0	0	0	0	0	1	0	0	0	0	0	0	0	0
0	0	0	0	2	0	11	1	0	0	19	0	111	11	9	0	1	2	2	1	0
0	0	0	0	0	0	0	0	0	0	0	0	0	0	0	0	0	0	0	0	0
0	0	0	0	0	0	0	0	0	0	0	0	0	0	0	0	0	0	0	0	0
0	0	0	0	0	0	0	0	0	0	0	0	0	0	0	0	0	0	0	0	0
0	0	0	0	0	0	0	0	0	0	0	0	0	0	0	0	0	0	0	0	0
0	0	0	0	0	0	0	0	0	0	0	0	0	0	0	0	0	0	0	0	0
0	0	0	0	0	0	0	1	0	0	1	0	0	0	0	0	0	0	0	0	0
0	0	0	0	0	0	0	0	0	0	0	0	0	0	0	0	0	0	0	0	0
0	0	0	0	0	0	0	0	0	0	0	0	0	0	0	0	0	0	0	0	0
0	0	0	0	0	0	0	0	0	0	1	0	0	0	0	0	0	0	0	0	0
0	0	0	0	0	0	0	0	0	0	0	0	0	0	0	0	0	0	0	0	0
0	0	0	0	0	0	0	0	0	0	0	0	0	0	0	0	0	0	0	0	0
0	0	0	0	0	0	1	0	0	0	0	0	0	0	2	0	0	0	0	0	0
0	0	0	0	0	0	2	0	0	0	0	0	1	0	2	0	0	2	0	1	0
0	0	0	0	0	0	0	0	0	0	0	0	0	0	3	0	0	0	0	0	0
0	0	0	0	0	0	0	0	0	0	0	0	0	0	1	0	0	0	0	0	0
0	0	0	0	0	0	18	1	0	1	5	0	73	2	4	0	4	2	4	3	0
0	0	0	0	0	0	0	0	0	0	1	0	0	0	0	0	0	0	0	0	0
0	0	0	0	0	0	0	0	0	0	0	0	0	0	0	0	0	0	0	0	0
0	0	0	0	0	0	0	1	0	0	0	0	0	0	0	0	0	0	0	0	0
0	0	0	0	0	0	0	0	0	0	1	0	0	0	0	0	0	0	0	0	0
0	0	0	0	0	0	0	0	0	0	0	0	0	0	0	0	0	0	0	0	0
0	0	0	1	0	0	6	0	0	0	0	0	5	2	6	0	1	0	0	0	0
0	0	0	0	0	0	0	0	0	0	0	0	0	0	0	0	0	0	0	0	0
0	0	0	0	0	0	0	0	0	0	0	0	0	0	2	0	1	0	0	0	0
0	0	0	0	0	0	1	0	0	0	0	0	0	0	0	0	0	0	0	0	0
6	0	0	47	0	0	3	3	0	0	0	0	88	6	2	0	5	0	1	0	0
0	0	0	0	0	0	0	0	0	0	0	0	0	0	0	0	0	0	0	0	0
0	0	0	0	0	0	0	0	0	0	0	0	0	0	0	0	0	0	0	0	0
0	0	0	0	0	0	0	0	0	0	0	0	0	0	0	0	0	0	0	0	0
0	0	0	0	0	0	0	0	0	0	0	0	0	0	0	0	0	0	0	0	0
0	0	0	0	0	0	0	0	0	0	0	0	0	0	0	0	0	0	0	0	0
0	0	0	0	0	0	0	0	0	0	0	0	0	0	0	0	0	0	0	0	0
0	0	0	0	0	0	4	0	0	0	0	0	0	1	1	0	0	0	0	0	0
0	0	0	0	0	0	0	0	0	0	0	0	0	0	0	0	0	0	0	0	0
0	0	0	0	0	0	0	0	0	0	0	0	0	0	0	0	0	0	0	0	0
2	0	0	0	1	0	17	0	0	0	0	1	53	4	6	1	2	1	8	0	0
0	0	0	0	0	0	0	0	0	0	0	0	0	0	0	0	0	0	0	0	0
0	0	0	0	0	0	0	0	0	0	0	0	0	0	0	0	0	0	0	0	0
0	0	0	0	0	0	0	0	0	0	0	0	0	0	0	0	0	0	0	0	0
0	0	0	0	0	0	0	0	0	0	0	0	0	0	0	0	0	0	0	0	0
0	0	0	0	0	0	0	0	0	0	0	0	0	0	0	0	0	0	0	0	0
0	0	0	0	0	0	0	0	0	0	0	0	0	0	0	0	0	0	0	0	0
0	0	0	0	0	0	0	0	0	0	0	0	0	0	0	0	0	0	0	0	0
0	0	0	0	0	0	0	0	0	0	0	0	0	0	0	0	0	0	0	0	0
0	0	0	0	0	0	0	0	0	0	0	0	0	0	0	0	0	0	0	0	0
0	0	0	0	0	0	0	0	0	0	0	0	0	0	0	0	0	0	0	0	0
0	0	0	0	0	0	0	0	0	0	0	0	0	0	0	0	0	0	0	0	0
84	85	0	0	0	0	90	0.	92	93	94	95	96	97	98	99	100	101	102	103	104
0	0	0	0	0	0	0	0	0	0	0	0	0	0	0	0	0	0	0	0	0

105	106	107	108	109	110	111	112	113	114	115	116	117	118	119	120	121	122	123	124	125
0	0	0	0	4	0	0	0	1	0	0	0	0	1	0	0	0	0	0	0	0
0	0	0	0	4	0	1	0	0	0	0	0	0	0	0	0	0	0	0	0	0
0	0	0	0	0	0	0	0	0	0	0	0	0	0	0	0	0	0	0	0	0
0	0	0	0	0	0	0	0	0	0	0	0	0	0	0	0	0	0	0	0	0
0	0	0	0	0	0	0	0	0	0	0	0	0	0	0	0	0	0	0	0	0
0	0	0	0	0	0	0	0	0	0	0	0	0	0	0	0	0	0	0	0	0
0	0	0	0	0	0	0	0	0	0	0	0	0	1	0	0	0	0	0	0	0
0	0	3	0	0	0	0	0	0	0	0	0	0	0	0	0	0	0	0	0	0
0	0	0	0	0	0	0	0	0	0	0	0	0	0	0	0	0	0	0	0	0
0	0	1	0	0	0	0	0	0	0	0	0	0	0	0	0	0	0	0	0	0
0	0	0	0	0	0	0	0	0	0	0	0	0	0	0	0	0	0	0	0	0
0	0	0	0	0	0	0	0	0	0	0	0	0	0	0	0	0	0	0	0	0
0	0	0	0	0	0	0	0	0	0	0	0	0	0	0	0	0	0	0	0	0
0	0	0	0	0	0	0	0	0	0	0	0	0	0	0	0	0	0	1	0	0
0	0	0	0	0	0	0	0	0	0	0	0	0	0	0	0	0	0	0	0	0
0	0	0	0	0	0	0	0	0	0	0	0	0	0	0	0	0	0	0	0	0
0	0	0	0	0	0	0	0	0	0	0	0	0	0	0	0	0	0	0	0	0
0	0	0	0	0	0	0	0	0	0	0	0	0	0	0	0	0	0	0	0	0
1	0	0	0	7	0	0	0	0	0	0	3	0	0	0	0	0	0	0	0	2
0	0	0	0	0	0	0	0	0	0	0	0	0	0	0	0	0	0	0	0	0
0	0	0	0	0	0	0	0	0	0	0	0	0	0	0	0	0	0	0	0	0
0	0	0	0	0	0	0	0	0	0	0	0	0	0	0	0	0	0	0	0	0
0	0	0	0	0	0	0	0	0	0	0	0	0	0	0	0	0	0	0	0	0
0	0	0	0	0	0	0	0	0	0	0	0	0	0	0	0	0	0	0	0	0
0	0	0	0	0	0	0	0	0	0	0	0	0	0	0	0	0	0	0	0	0
0	0	0	0	0	0	0	0	0	0	0	0	0	0	0	0	0	0	0	0	0
0	0	0	0	0	0	0	0	0	0	0	0	0	0	0	0	0	0	0	0	0
0	0	0	0	0	0	0	0	0	0	0	0	0	0	0	0	0	0	0	0	0
0	0	0	0	0	0	0	0	0	0	0	0	0	0	0	0	0	0	0	0	0
0	0	0	0	0	0	0	0	0	0	0	0	0	0	0	0	0	0	0	0	0
0	0	0	0	0	0	0	0	0	0	0	0	0	0	0	0	0	0	0	0	0
0	0	0	0	4	0	0	0	0	0	0	0	1	0	0	0	0	0	0	0	1
0	0	0	0	0	0	0	0	0	0	0	0	0	0	3	0	0	0	0	0	0
0	0	0	0	0	0	0	0	0	0	0	0	0	0	0	0	0	0	0	0	0
0	0	4	0	0	0	0	0	0	0	0	1	0	0	0	1	0	0	0	0	2
0	0	0	0	0	0	0	0	0	0	0	0	0	0	0	0	0	0	0	0	0
0	0	0	0	0	0	0	0	0	0	0	0	0	0	0	0	0	0	0	0	0
0	0	0	0	0	0	0	0	0	0	0	0	0	0	0	0	0	0	0	0	0
0	0	0	0	0	0	0	0	0	0	0	0	0	0	0	0	0	0	0	0	0
0	0	0	0	0	0	0	0	0	0	0	0	0	0	0	0	0	0	0	0	0
0	0	0	0	1	0	0	0	0	0	0	0	0	0	0	0	0	0	0	0	2
0	0	0	0	0	0	0	0	0	0	0	0	0	0	0	0	0	0	0	0	0
0	0	0	0	0	0	0	0	0	0	0	0	0	0	0	0	0	0	0	0	0
0	0	0	0	4	0	0	0	0	0	0	0	0	1	0	1	0	1	0	0	0
0	0	0	0	0	0	0	0	0	0	0	0	0	0	0	0	0	0	0	0	0
0	0	0	0	0	0	0	0	0	0	0	0	0	0	0	0	0	0	0	0	0
0	0	0	0	0	0	0	0	0	0	0	0	0	0	0	0	0	0	0	0	0
0	0	0	0	0	0	0	0	0	0	0	0	0	0	0	0	0	0	0	0	0
0	0	0	0	0	0	0	0	0	0	0	0	0	0	0	0	0	0	0	0	0
0	0	0	0	0	0	0	0	0	0	0	0	0	0	0	0	0	0	0	0	0
0	0	0	0	0	0	0	0	0	0	0	0	0	0	0	0	0	0	0	0	0
0	0	0	0	0	0	0	0	0	0	0	1	0	0	0	0	0	0	0	0	1
0	0	0	0	0	0	0	0	0	0	0	0	0	0	0	0	0	0	0	0	0
0	0	8	3	11	0	0	0	0	0	0	2	1	0	4	0	0	1	0	6	0
0	0	0	0	0	0	0	0	0	0	0	1	0	0	0	0	0	0	0	0	0
0	0	0	0	0	0	0	0	0	0	0	0	0	0	0	0	0	0	0	0	0
0	0	0	0	0	0	0	0	0	0	0	0	0	0	0	0	0	0	0	0	0
0	0	0	0	0	0	0	0	0	0	0	0	0	0	0	0	0	0	0	0	0
0	0	0	0	0	0	0	0	0	0	0	0	0	0	0	0	0	0	0	0	0
0	0	0	0	0	0	0	0	0	0	0	0	0	0	0	0	0	0	0	0	0
0	0	0	0	0	0	0	0	0	0	0	0	0	0	0	0	0	0	0	0	0
0	0	1	0	0	0	0	0	0	0	0	0	0	0	0	0	0	0	0	0	0
0	0	0	0	0	0	0	0	0	0	0	0	0	0	0	0	0	0	0	0	0
0	0	0	0	0	0	0	0	0	0	0	0	0	0	0	0	0	0	0	0	0
0	0	0	0	0	0	0	0	0	0	0	0	0	0	0	0	0	0	0	0	0

126	127	128	129	130	131	132	133	134	135	136	137	138	139	140	141	142	143	144	145
0	0	0	0	5	0	0	0	0	2	0	2	0	0	1	0	0	0	0	7
.	0	0	0	11	0	0	0	0	0	0	2	0	0	1	0	26	0	0	0
0	0	0	0	0	0	0	0	0	0	0	0	0	0	0	0	0	0	0	0
0	0	0	0	0	0	0	0	0	0	0	0	0	0	0	0	0	0	0	0
0	0	0	0	0	0	0	0	0	0	0	0	0	0	0	0	0	0	0	0
0	0	0	0	0	0	0	0	0	0	0	0	0	0	0	0	0	0	0	7
1	0	0	0	10	0	0	0	0	0	0	0	0	0	0	0	0	0	2	4
0	0	0	0	0	0	0	0	0	0	0	0	0	0	0	0	0	0	0	0
1	0	0	0	1	0	0	0	0	0	0	0	0	0	0	0	0	0	1	1
0	0	0	0	0	0	0	0	0	0	0	0	0	0	0	0	0	0	0	0
0	0	0	0	0	0	0	0	0	0	0	0	0	0	0	0	1	0	0	0
0	0	0	0	0	0	0	0	0	0	0	0	0	0	0	0	0	0	0	0
0	0	0	0	0	0	0	0	0	0	0	0	0	0	0	0	0	0	0	1
0	0	0	0	0	0	0	0	0	0	0	0	0	0	0	0	0	0	0	0
0	0	0	0	0	0	0	0	0	0	0	0	0	0	0	0	0	0	0	0
0	0	0	0	0	0	0	0	0	0	0	0	0	0	0	0	1	0	0	0
0	0	0	0	0	0	0	0	0	0	0	0	0	0	0	0	0	0	0	0
1	1	0	0	14	0	0	0	0	4	1	0	0	0	0	0	0	1	0	50
0	0	0	0	0	0	0	0	0	0	0	0	0	0	0	0	0	0	0	0
0	0	0	0	0	0	0	0	0	0	0	0	0	0	0	0	0	0	0	0
0	0	0	0	0	0	0	0	0	0	0	0	0	0	0	0	0	0	0	0
0	0	0	0	0	0	0	0	0	0	0	0	0	0	0	0	0	0	0	0
0	0	0	0	0	0	0	0	0	0	0	0	0	0	0	0	0	0	0	0
0	0	0	0	0	0	0	0	0	0	0	0	0	0	0	0	0	0	0	0
0	0	0	0	0	0	0	0	0	0	0	0	0	0	0	0	0	0	0	0
0	0	0	0	0	0	0	0	0	0	0	0	0	0	0	0	0	0	0	0
0	0	0	0	0	0	0	0	0	0	0	0	0	0	0	0	0	0	0	0
0	0	0	0	0	0	0	0	0	0	0	0	0	0	0	0	0	0	0	0
0	0	0	0	0	0	0	0	0	0	0	0	0	0	0	0	0	0	0	0
0	0	0	0	0	0	0	0	0	0	0	0	0	0	0	0	0	0	0	0
0	0	0	0	1	0	0	0	0	0	0	0	0	0	0	0	0	0	0	8
0	0	0	0	3	0	0	0	0	0	0	0	0	0	0	0	0	0	0	8
0	0	0	0	0	0	0	0	0	0	0	0	0	0	0	0	0	0	0	0
0	0	0	0	0	0	0	0	0	0	0	0	0	0	0	0	0	0	0	2
0	0	0	0	4	0	0	0	0	0	1	0	1	0	1	0	1	1	0	37
0	0	0	0	0	0	0	0	0	0	0	0	0	0	0	0	0	0	0	0
0	0	0	0	0	0	0	0	0	0	0	0	0	0	0	0	0	0	0	0
0	0	0	0	0	0	0	0	0	0	0	0	0	0	0	0	0	0	0	0
0	0	0	0	0	0	0	0	0	0	0	0	0	0	0	0	0	0	0	0
0	0	0	0	0	0	0	0	0	0	0	0	0	0	0	0	0	0	0	0
0	0	0	0	4	0	0	0	0	0	0	0	0	0	0	0	0	0	0	0
0	0	0	0	0	0	0	0	0	0	0	0	0	0	0	0	0	0	0	0
0	0	0	0	1	0	0	0	0	0	0	0	0	0	0	0	0	0	0	0
0	0	0	0	0	0	0	0	0	1	0	0	0	0	0	0	0	0	0	0
0	0	2	0	2	0	0	0	0	8	5	19	2	0	0	0	3	0	0	14
0	0	0	0	0	0	0	0	0	0	0	0	0	0	0	0	0	0	0	0
0	0	0	0	0	0	0	0	0	0	0	0	0	0	0	0	0	0	0	0
0	0	0	0	0	0	0	0	0	0	0	0	0	0	0	0	0	0	0	0
0	0	0	0	0	0	0	0	0	0	0	0	0	0	0	0	0	0	0	0
0	0	0	0	0	0	0	0	0	0	0	0	0	0	0	0	0	0	0	0
0	0	0	0	0	0	0	0	0	0	0	0	0	0	0	0	0	0	0	0
0	0	0	0	2	0	0	0	0	0	1	0	1	0	0	0	0	0	0	0
0	0	0	0	0	0	0	0	0	0	0	0	0	0	0	0	0	0	0	0
0	0	0	0	0	0	0	0	0	0	0	0	0	0	0	0	0	1	0	0
4	0	0	0	3	0	0	3	1	0	0	2	0	0	0	0	36	0	0	0
1	0	0	0	0	0	0	0	0	0	0	0	0	0	0	0	0	0	0	0
0	0	0	0	0	0	0	0	0	0	0	0	0	0	0	0	0	0	0	0
0	0	0	0	0	0	0	0	0	0	0	0	0	0	0	0	0	0	0	0
0	0	0	0	0	0	0	0	0	0	0	0	0	0	0	0	0	0	0	0
0	0	0	0	0	0	0	0	0	0	0	0	0	0	0	0	0	0	0	0
0	0	0	0	0	0	0	0	0	0	0	0	0	0	0	0	0	0	0	0
0	0	0	0	0	0	0	0	0	0	0	0	0	0	0	0	0	0	0	0
0	0	0	0	0	0	0	0	0	0	0	0	0	0	0	0	0	0	0	0
0	0	0	0	0	0	0	0	0	0	0	0	0	0	0	0	0	0	0	0
0	0	0	0	0	0	0	0	0	0	0	0	0	0	0	0	0	0	0	0
126	127	128	129	130	131	132	133	134	135	136	137	138	139	140	141	142	143	144	145
0	0	0	0	0	0	0	0	0	0	0	0	0	0	0	0	0	0	0	0

Appendix 2, Section 2 (Cont.)

146	147	148	149	150	151	152	153	154	155	156	157	158	159	160	161	162	163
0	0	0	0	0	0	0	0	0	0	0	0	0	0	0	16	0	0
0	1	1	0	0	0	0	10	0	0	0	0	0	0	0	78	0	19
0	0	0	0	0	0	0	1	0	0	0	0	0	0	0	0	0	0
0	0	0	0	0	0	0	0	0	0	0	0	0	0	0	0	0	0
0	0	0	0	0	0	0	1	0	0	0	0	0	0	0	0	0	0
0	0	0	0	0	0	0	0	0	0	0	0	0	0	0	5	0	0
0	0	0	0	0	0	0	0	0	0	0	0	0	0	0	15	1	3
0	0	0	0	0	0	0	0	0	0	0	0	0	0	0	1	1	0
0	0	0	0	0	0	0	0	0	0	0	0	0	0	0	1	0	1
0	0	0	0	0	0	0	0	0	0	0	0	0	0	0	10	0	0
0	0	0	0	0	0	0	0	0	0	0	0	0	0	0	3	0	1
0	0	0	0	0	0	0	0	0	0	0	0	0	0	0	1	0	0
0	0	0	0	0	0	0	0	0	0	0	0	0	0	0	11	0	4
0	0	0	0	0	0	0	0	0	0	0	0	0	0	0	11	0	2
0	0	0	0	0	0	0	0	0	0	0	0	0	0	0	5	0	0
0	0	0	0	0	0	0	0	0	0	0	0	0	0	0	2	0	0
0	0	0	0	0	0	0	0	0	0	0	0	0	0	0	7	0	1
0	0	0	0	0	0	0	0	0	0	0	0	0	0	0	11	0	1
0	0	1	0	0	0	1	0	3	0	0	0	0	0	0	128	1	40
0	0	0	0	0	0	0	0	0	0	0	0	0	0	0	0	0	0
0	0	0	0	0	0	0	0	0	0	0	0	0	0	0	0	0	0
0	0	0	0	0	0	1	0	0	0	0	0	0	0	0	0	0	0
0	0	0	0	0	0	0	0	1	0	0	0	0	0	0	0	0	0
0	0	0	0	0	0	0	0	0	0	0	0	0	0	0	0	0	0
0	0	0	0	0	0	0	0	0	0	0	0	0	0	0	0	0	0
0	0	0	0	0	0	0	0	1	0	0	0	0	0	0	0	0	0
0	0	0	0	0	0	0	0	0	0	0	0	0	0	0	0	0	0
0	0	0	0	0	0	0	0	0	0	0	0	0	0	0	0	0	0
0	0	0	0	0	0	0	0	0	0	0	0	0	0	0	0	0	0
0	0	0	0	0	0	0	0	1	0	0	0	0	0	0	0	0	0
0	0	0	0	0	0	0	0	0	0	0	0	0	0	0	2	0	0
0	0	1	0	0	0	0	0	0	0	0	0	0	0	0	16	0	2
0	0	0	0	0	0	0	0	0	0	0	0	0	0	0	7	0	1
0	0	0	0	0	0	0	0	0	0	0	0	0	0	0	1	0	1
0	0	3	0	0	0	0	0	0	0	0	0	0	0	0	48	0	5
0	0	0	0	0	0	0	0	0	0	0	0	0	0	0	0	0	0
0	0	0	0	0	0	0	0	0	0	0	0	0	0	0	0	0	0
0	0	0	0	0	0	0	0	0	0	0	0	0	0	0	0	0	0
0	0	0	0	0	0	0	0	0	0	0	0	0	0	0	0	0	0
0	0	0	0	0	0	0	0	0	0	0	0	0	0	0	0	0	0
0	0	0	0	0	0	0	0	0	0	0	0	0	0	0	16	0	6
0	0	0	0	0	0	0	0	0	0	0	0	0	0	0	0	0	0
0	0	1	0	0	0	0	0	0	0	0	0	0	0	0	0	0	0
0	0	0	0	0	0	0	0	0	0	0	0	0	0	0	2	0	1
0	0	1	0	0	0	0	0	0	0	0	0	0	0	0	116	0	12
0	0	0	0	0	0	0	0	0	0	0	0	0	0	0	0	0	0
0	0	0	0	0	0	0	0	0	0	0	0	0	0	0	0	0	0
0	0	0	0	0	0	0	0	0	0	0	0	0	0	0	0	0	1
0	0	0	0	0	0	0	0	0	0	0	0	0	0	0	0	0	0
0	0	0	0	0	0	0	0	0	0	0	0	0	0	0	1	0	0
0	0	0	0	0	0	0	0	0	0	0	0	0	0	0	0	0	0
0	0	0	0	0	0	0	0	0	0	0	0	0	0	0	5	0	0
0	0	0	0	0	0	0	0	0	0	0	0	0	0	0	0	0	0
0	0	0	0	0	0	0	0	0	0	0	0	0	0	0	3	0	0
0	11	0	0	0	0	0	36	17	0	0	0	0	0	0	37	0	50
0	0	0	0	0	0	0	0	0	0	0	0	0	0	0	1	0	0
0	0	0	0	0	0	0	0	1	0	0	0	0	0	0	0	0	0
0	0	0	0	0	0	0	0	0	0	0	0	0	0	0	0	0	0
0	0	0	0	0	0	0	0	0	0	0	0	0	0	0	0	0	0
0	0	0	0	0	0	0	0	0	0	0	0	0	0	0	0	0	0
0	0	0	0	0	0	0	0	0	0	0	0	0	0	0	0	0	0
0	0	0	0	0	0	0	0	0	0	0	0	0	0	0	0	0	0
0	0	0	0	0	0	0	1	1	0	0	0	0	0	0	1	0	0
0	0	0	0	0	0	0	1	0	0	0	0	0	0	0	0	0	0
0	0	0	0	0	0	0	0	0	0	0	0	0	0	0	0	0	0
0	0	0	0	0	0	0	1	0	0	0	0	0	0	0	0	0	0

Appendix 3

Coded Data for the Comparative Analysis of Survey Data

Section 1 Key

Survey
  Survey area (see Figure 1-1)
Km Sq
  Square kilometers surveyed
Neolithic
  Number of sites dating to the Neolithic period in the survey area. Where period subdivisions are reported, the phase with the largest number of sites represents the period total.
E Bronze
  Number of sites dating to the Early Bronze Age. Where subdivisions of EB are reported, the phase with the largest number of sites represents the period total.
M Bronze
  Number of sites dating to the Middle Bronze Age. Where subdivisions of the MB are reported, the phase with the largest number of sites represents the period total.
L Bronze
  Number of sites dating to the Late Bronze Age. Where subdivisions of the LB are reported, the phase with the largest number of sites represents the period total.
Geometric
  Number of sites dating to the phases of the Geometric Period. Where period phases are recorded, the largest number of sites of the phases represents the period total.
Archaic
  Number of sites dating to the Archaic Period (or contemporaneous, for example, Early Etruscan in South Etruria).
Classical
  Number of sites dating to the Classical Period (or contemporaneous, for example, Late Etruscan in South Etruria).
HLN/RRepublic
  Number sites dating to the Hellenistic or Roman Republican Periods.
E Roman
  Number of sites dating to the Roman Early Imperial Period.
L Roman
  Number of sites dating to the Roman Late Imperial Period, to as late as the end of the 6th century AD.
ER Farms
  Number of sites that were probably isolated farms (but not those described as villas) of the Early Roman Period. Sites less than .2 ha were included in this category.
ER Villas
  Number of Early Roman sites described as villas. Survey projects used slightly variant criteria to distinguish between ordinary farms and villas, but generally villas were identified by the presence of decorative stone, multi-colored painted plaster,

marble veneer, stucco decoration, or glass tesserae (e.g., Potter 1979: 122; cf.Dyson 1978: 257).
ER Villages
  Number of Early Roman sites variously described using terms such as hamlet, village, agglomération, and settlement, excluding farms, villas, and sites described as towns or cities (i.e. regional central places). Unless a site function is specifically reported, sites were considered to be villages when between .2 ha and 3 ha.
ER Centers
  Number of Early Roman sites described as having commercial and/or administrative functions for surrounding communities (towns and cities). Where no functional information is provided, I include in this category all sites 3 ha or larger.
ER Center ha
  Area in ha of the largest center in the survey area.
ER Cent Terr
  An estimate of the average size of the area serviced by central places in the region, including commercial central places.
LR Farms
  Number of sites that were probably isolated farms (but not those described as villas) of the Late Roman Period. Sites less than .2 ha were included in this category.
LR Villas
  Number of Late Roman sites described as villas. Survey projects used slightly variant criteria to distinguish between ordinary farms and villas, but generally villas were identified by the presence of decorative stone, multi-colored painted plaster, marble veneer, stucco decoration, or glass tesserae (e.g., Potter 1979: 122; cf. Dyson 1978: 257).
LR Villages
  Number of Late Roman sites variously described using terms such as hamlet, village, agglomération, and settlement, excluding farms, villas, and sites described as towns or cities (i.e. regional central places). Unless a site function is specifically reported, sites were considered to be villages when between .2 ha and 3 ha.
LR Centers
  Number of Late Roman sites described as having commercial and/or administrative functions for surrounding communities (towns and cities). Where no functional information is provided, I include in this category all sites 3 ha or larger.
LR Center ha
  Area in ha of the largest center in the survey area
LR Cent Terr
  An estimate of the average size of the area serviced by central places in the region, including commercial central places.

Section 2 Data

Survey	Km Sq	Neolithic	E Bronze	M Bronze	L Bronze	Geometric	Archaic	Classical	HLN/RRepublic	E Roman	L Roman	ER Farms
Capena	210	0	0	0	1	4	39	22	90	100	1	57
Sutri	84	0	0	0	0	0	1	1	32	50	1	36
Faliscus	150	0	0	1	1	27	72	104	142	123	14	86
Veientanus	250	0				16	137	127	242	327	50	175
Guadalquivir	3250									464		332
Cosanus	450	0	0	0	0	0	7	0	63	50	37	37
Rieti	22	0	1	2	1	2	18	38	52	47	21	22
Melos	34	7	11	0	0	0	26	7	4	8	27	0
Lasithi	66	15	6	37	37	1	14	3	2	2	26	1
Kavousi	21	2	2	53	30	10	11	0	0	20	20	0
W Mesara	22	9	15			2	13	26	50	50	11	
Vrokastro	35	3	14	28	44	20	20	6	7			
S Euboea	41	3	5	1	0	1	2	30	20	23	8	11
Ayiofarango	22	0	5	5	3	0	0	1	6	10	3	7
N Keos	18	4	1	6	1	1	29	40	35	8	22	0
S Argolid	44	0	32	3	37	17	38	55	110	17	57	4
Pylos	40	0	12	19	18	9	18	18	18			
Palaipaphos	73	0	0	2	1	9	3	9	16	7		0
W C R Cilicia	45	0	0	0	0	0	0	1	4	25	23	3

ER Villas	ER Villages	ER Centers	ER Center ha	ER Cent Terr	LR Farms	LR Villas	LR Villages	LR Centers	LR Center ha	LR Cent Terr
38	0	3		70	0	0	0	1		210
13	0	1		200	0	0	0	1		200
35	0	2		120	6	7	0	1		
145	0	1		250	30	20	0	0		
99	11	22		99						
12	0	1		550	26	10	0	1		550
7	16	2	5		9	3	7	2	5	
1	3	4	15		0	1	14	10	15	17
0	0	1	2.6	66	15	0	10	1		66
0	19	1	2.5		0	0	19	1	2.5	
0							0			
2	7	3	18	14	4	2	1	2	18	21
0	3				2	0	1	0		
0	8				2	0	20	0		
0	12	1	11.34		27	1	39	2	22.5	
0	9	7	10.25		0	0	3	4	16.75	
0	18	5	36.5	21	4	0	14	5	43	21

References

Alcock, Susan E.
  1993 Graecia Capta: The Landscapes of Roman Greece. Cambridge: Cambridge University Press.
  1994 Breaking up the Hellenistic world: survey and society. In Classical Greece: Ancient
        Histories and Modern Archaeologies, ed. by Ian Morris, pp. 171-90. Cambridge:
        Cambridge University Press.
Alcock, Susan E., John F. Cherry, and Jack L. Davis
  1994 Intensive survey, agricultural practice and the classical landscape of Greece. In Classical
        Greece: Ancient Histories and Modern Archaeologies, ed. by Ian Morris, pp. 137-70.
        Cambridge: Cambridge University Press.
Bagnall, Roger S.
  1976 The Administration of the Ptolemaic Possessions Outside Egypt. Leiden: E. J. Brill.
Barker, Graeme
  1991 Approaches to archaeological survey. In Roman Landscapes, ed. by Graeme Barker and John
        Lloyd, pp. 1-9. London: Archaeological Monographs of the British School at Rome No. 2.
Barker, Graeme, and John Lloyd, eds.
  1991 Roman Landscapes. London: Archaeological Monographs of the British School at Rome No. 2.
Bean, George E., and Terence B. Mitford
  1962 Sites old and new in Rough Cilicia. Anatolian Studies 12: 185-217.
  1965 Journeys in Rough Cilicia in 1962 and 1963. Wien: Osterreichische Akademie der
        Wissenschaften, Philosophisch-Historische Klasse 85.
  1970 Journeys in Rough Cilicia 1964-1968. Wien: Osterreichische Akademie der Wissenschaften,
        Philosophisch-Historische Klasse 102.
Bekker-Nielsen, Tonnes
  1989 The Geography of Power: Studies in the Urbanization of Roman North-West Europe.
        Oxford: BAR International Series 477.
Benet, Francisco
  1957 Explosive markets: the Berber highlands. In Trade and Market in the Early Empires, ed.
        by Karl Polanyi, Conrad M. Arensberg, and Harry W. Pearson, pp. 188-217. New York: Free Press.
Bintliff, John L.
  1977 Natural Environment and Human Settlement in Prehistoric Greece. Oxford: BAR
        Supplementary Series 28(i).
  1991 The Roman countryside in central Greece: observations and theories from the Boeotia
        survey (1978-1987). In Roman Landscapes, ed. by Graeme Barker and John Lloyd, pp. 122-
        32. London: Archaeological Monographs of the British School at Rome No. 2.
  1997 Regional survey, demography, and the rise of complex societies in the ancient Aegean:
        core-periphery, neo-Malthusian, and other interpretive models. Journal of Field Archaeology 24: 1-38.
Bintliff, John L., and Anthony M. Snodgrass
  1985 The Cambridge/Bradford Boeotian expedition: the first four years. Journal of Field
        Archaeology 12: 123-61.
  1988 The end of the Roman countryside: a view from the east. In First Millennium Papers:
        Western Europe in the First Millennium AD, ed. by R. F. J. Jones, J. H. F. Bloemers, S. L.
        Dyson, and M. Biddle, pp. 175-217. Oxford: BAR International Series 401.
Blackman, David, and Keith Branigan, eds.
  1977 An archaeological survey of the lower catchment of the Ayiofarango Valley. The Annual
        of the British School at Athens 72: 13-84.
Blanton, Richard E.
  1978 Monte Albán: Settlements Patterns at the Ancient Zapotec Capital. New York: Academic Press.
Blanton, Richard E., Stephen A. Kowalewski, Gary M. Feinman, and Jill Appel
  1982 Monte Albán's Hinterland, Part I: The Prehispanic Settlement Patterns of the Central
        and Southern Parts of the Valley of Oaxaca, Mexico. Ann Arbor: Memoirs of the Museum
        of Anthropology, The University of Michigan 15.
Blanton, Richard, and Nicholas K. Rauh
  1997 The Rough Cilicia Regional Survey Project. Paper presented at the annual meeting of the
        Archaeological Institute of America. Ms.
Branigan, Keith
  1970 The Tombs of Mesara: A Study of Funerary Architecture and Ritual in Southern Crete, 2800-
        1700 BC. London: Gerald Duckworth.
Braudel, Fernand
  1972 The Mediterranean and the Mediterranean World in the Age of Philip II. New York: Harper and Row.
Braun, T. F. R. G.
  1982 The Greeks in the Near East. In The Cambridge Ancient History 2nd Edition, Vol. III, Part

3, ed. by John Boardman and N. G. L. Hammond, pp. 1-31. Cambridge: Cambridge University Press.

Broughton, T. R. S.
1975 Part IV: Roman Asia. In An Economic Survey of Ancient Rome, ed. by Tenney Frank, pp. 499-918. New York: Octagon Books.

Brunt, P. A.
1971 Italian Manpower, 225 BC-AD 14. Oxford: Clarendon Press.

Burnham, Barry C., and John Wacher
1990 The Small Towns of Roman Britain. Berkeley: University of California Press.

Burns, R., and D. J. Mattingly
1980-81 The Wadi N'F'D survey. In The UNESCO Libyan Valley survey 1980, ed. by G. W. W. Barker and G. D. B. Jones, pp. 24-42. Libyan Studies 12: 9-48.

Carandini, Andrea
1989 Italian wine and African oil: commerce in a world empire. In The Birth of Europe: Archaeology and Social Development in the First Millennium AD, ed. by Klavs Randsborg, pp. 16-24. Rome: L'Erma di Bretschneider.

Chase-Dunn, Christopher, and Thomas D. Hall
1991 Conceptualizing core/periphery hierarchies for comparative study. In Core/Periphery Relations in Precapitalist Worlds, ed. by Christopher Chase-Dunn and Thomas Hall, pp. 5-44. Boulder: Westview Press.
1997 Rise and Demise: Comparing World-Systems. Boulder: Westview Press.

Cherry, John F.
1982 A preliminary definition of site distribution on Melos. In An Island Polity: The Archaeology of Exploitation in Melos, ed. by Colin Renfrew and Malcolm Wagstaff, pp. 10-23. Cambridge: Cambridge University Press.
1983 Frogs round the pond: perspectives on current archaeological survey projects in the Mediterranean region. In Archaeological Survey in the Mediterranean Area, ed. by Donald R. Keller and David W. Rupp, pp. 375-416. Oxford: BAR International Series 155.
1985 Islands out of the stream: isolation and interaction in early east Mediterranean insular prehistory. In Prehistoric Production and Exchange: The Aegean and Eastern Mediterranean, ed. by A. Bernard Knapp and Tamara Stech, pp. 12-29. Los Angeles: UCLA Institute of Archaeology, Monograph 25.
1994 Regional survey in the Aegean: the new wave (and after). In Beyond the Site: Regional Studies in the Aegean Area, ed. by P. Nick Kardulias, pp. 91-112. Lanham, MD: University Press of America.

Cherry, John F., Jack L. Davis, Anne Demitrack, Eleni Mantzourani, Thomas F. Strasser, and Lauren E. Talalay
1988 Archaeological survey in an artifact-rich landscape: a middle Neolithic example from Nemea, Greece. American Journal of Archaeology 92: 159-76.

Cherry, John F., Jack L. Davis, and Eleni Mantzourani, eds.
1991 Landscape Archaeology as Long-Term History: Northern Keos in the Cycladic Islands from Earliest Settlement Until Modern Times. Los Angeles: UCLA Institute of Archaeology, Monumenta Archaeologica 16.

Cherry, John F., Jack L. Davis, Eleni Mantzourani, and T. M. Whitelaw
1991 The survey methods. In Landscape Archaeology as Long-Term History: Northern Keos in the Cycladic Islands from Earliest Settlement Until Modern Times, ed. by John F. Cherry, J. L. Davis, and E. Mantzourani, pp. 13-35. Los Angeles: UCLA Institute of Archaeology, Monumenta Archaeologica 16.

Chisholm, M.
1968 Rural Settlement and Land Use: An Essay in Location. 2nd Edition. London: Hutchinson University.

Coccia, Stefano, and David Mattingly, eds.
1992 Settlement history, environment, and human exploitation of an intermontane basin in the central Apennines: the Rieti survey, 1988-1991, Part I. Papers of the British School at Rome 60: 213-90.

Coccia, Stefano, and David Mattingly
1995 Settlement history, environment and human exploitation of an intermontane basin in the central Apennines: The Rieti survey, 1988-1991, Part II, Land-use patterns and gazetteer. Papers of the British School at Rome 63: 105-58.

Davis, Jack L., Susan E. Alcock, John Bennet, Yannos G. Lolos, Cynthis W. Shelmerdine
1997 The Pylos regional archaeological project, Part I, overview and the archaeological survey. Hesperia 66: 3: 391-494.

de Ligt, L.
1993 Fairs and Markets in the Roman Empire: Economic and Social Aspects of Periodic Trade in a Pre-Industrial Society. Amsterdam: J. C. Gieben.

Descoeudres, Jean-Paul, ed.
1990 Greek Colonists and Native Populations. Oxford: Clarendon Press.

93

Dewdney, J. C.
1971 Turkey: An Introductory Geography. New York: Praeger.
Drachmann, A. G.
1932 Ancient Oil Mills and Presses. Det Kgl. Videnskabernes Selskab, Archaeologisk-Kunsthistoriske Meddelelser, Vol. I, No. 1.
Duncan, G. C.
1958 Sutri: notes on southern Etruria, 3. Papers of the British School at Rome 26: 63-134.
Duncan-Jones, Richard
1974 The Economy of the Roman Empire. Cambridge: Cambridge University Press.
Dyson, Stephen L.
1978 Settlement patterns in the Ager Cosanus: the Wesleyan University survey, 1974-1976. Journal of Field Archaeology 5: 251-68.
1982 Archaeological survey in the Mediterranean basin: a review of recent research. American Antiquity 47: 87-98.
Engels, Donald
1990 Roman Corinth: An Alternative Model for the Classical City. Chicago: University of Chicago Press.
Erdemgil, Selahattin, and Fatma Ozoral
1975 Antiochia ad Cragum. Teurk Arkeoloji Dergisi 2: 55-71.
Erinç, Sirri, and Necdet Tunçdilek
1952 The agricultural regions of Turkey. Geographical Review 42: 179-203
Food and Agricultural Organization of the United Nations
1959 Mediterranean Development Project. Rome: FAO.
Forbes, Hamish A., and Lin Foxhall
1978 The queen of all trees: preliminary notes on the archaeology of the olive. Expedition 21: 37-47.
Foxhall, Lin and Hamish A. Forbes
1982 Sitometreia: The role of grains as a staple food in classical antiquity. Chiron 12: 41-90.
Frederiksen, M. W., and J. B. Ward-Perkins
1957 The ancient road systems of the central and northern Ager Faliscus. Papers of the British School at Rome 25: 67-208.
Gallant, T. W.
1986 "Background noise" and site definition: a contribuiton to survey methodology. Journal of Field Archaeology 13: 404-18.
Garnsey, Peter, Keith Hopkins, and C. R. Whittaker, eds.
1983 Trade in the Ancient Economy. Berkeley: University of California Press.
Garnsey, Peter, and Richard Saller
1987 The Roman Empire: Economy, Society and Culture. Berkeley: University of California Press.
Gjerstad, Einar, John Lindros, Erik Sjöquist, and Alfred Westholm
1934 The Swedish Cyprus Expedition: Finds and Results of the Excavations in Cyprus 1927-1931. Volume I, Text. Stockholm: The Swedish Cyprus Expedition.
Goody, Jack
1972 The evolution of the family. In Household and Family in Past Time, ed. by Peter Laslett and Richard Wall, pp. 103-24. Cambridge: Cambridge University Press.
Graham, A. J.
1982 The colonial expansion of Greece. In The Cambridge Ancient History 2nd Edition, Vol. III, Part 3, ed. by John Boardman and N. G. L. Hammond, pp. 83-162. Cambridge: Cambridge University Press.
Gregory, Timothy E.
1986 Intensive archaeological survey and its place in Byzantine studies. Byzantine Studies 13: 155-75.
Haggett, Peter
1966 Locational Analysis in Human Geography. New York: St. Martin's Press.
Haggis, Donald C.
1996 Archaeological survey at Kavousi, east Crete: preliminary report. Hesperia 65: 373-432.
Hall, Thomas D.
1986 Incorporation in the world-system: toward a critique. American Sociological Review 51: 390-402.
Hayden, Barabara J., Jennifer A. Moody, and Oliver Rackham
1992 The Vrokastro survey project, 1986-1989: research design and preliminary results. Hesperia 61: 3: 293-353.
Head, Barclay V.
1911 Historia Numorum: A Manual of Greek Numismatics. Oxford: Oxford University Press.
Heberdey, Rudolf, and Adolf Wilhelm
1896 Reisen in Kilikien. Wien: Denkschriften der Kaiserlichen Akademie der Wissenschaften der Philosophisch-Historische Klasse 44.
Helburn, Nicholas
1955 A stereotype of agriculture in semiarid Turkey. Geographical Review 45: 375-84.
Hild, Friedrich, and Hansgerd Hellenkemper
1990 Kilikien und Isaurien. Wien: Osterreichische Akademie der Wissenschaften, Philosophisch-

Historische Klasse, Tabula Imperii Byzantini 5.

Hill, George Francis
1900 Greek Coins of Lycaonia, Isauria, and Cilicia. London: British Museum.

Hood, M. S. F.
1960 *Tholos* tombs of the Aegean. Antiquity 34: 166-76.

Hopkins, Keith
1978a Conquerors and Slaves: Sociological Studies in Roman History. Cambridge: Cambridge
        University Press.
1978b Economic growth and towns in classical antiquity. In Towns in Societies: Essays in
        Economic History and Historical Sociology, ed. by Philip Abrams and E. A. Wrigley,
        pp. 35-77. Cambridge: Cambridge University Press.
1983 Introduction. In Trade in the Ancient Economy, ed. by Peter Garnsey, Keith Hopkins,
        and C. R. Whittaker, pp. ix-xxv. Berkeley: University of California Press.

Hopwood, Keith
1983 Policing the hinterland: Rough Cilicia and Isauria. In Armies and Frontiers in Roman
        and Byzantine Anatolia, ed. by Stephen Mitchell, pp. 173-87. Oxford: BAR
        International Series 156.
1986 Towers, territory, and terror: how the east was held. In The Defense of the Roman and
        Byzantine East, ed. by Philip Freeman and David Kennedy, pp. 343-56. Oxford:
        BAR International Series 297.
1989 Consent and control: how the peace was kept in Rough Cilicia. In The Eastern Frontier
        of the Roman Empire, ed. by D. H. French and C. S. Lightfoot, pp. 191-201. Oxford:
        BAR International Series 553(i).

Huber, Gerhard
1967 The sites and their principal buildings. In A Survey of Coastal Cities in Western Cilicia:
        Preliminary Report, by Elisabeth Rosenbaum, Gerhard Huber, and Somay Onurkan, pp. 1-47.
        Ankara: Türk Tarih Kurumu Yayinlarindan VI, Seri No. 8.

Jameson, Michael H.
1977/78 Agriculture and slavery in classical Athens. The Classical Journal 73: 122-45.

Jameson, Michael H., Curtis N. Runnels, and Tjeerd H. van Andel
1994 A Greek Countryside: The Southern Argolid from Prehistory to the Present Day. Stanford:
        Stanford University Press.

Jones, A. H. M.
1971 The Cities of the Eastern Roman Provinces. 2nd Edition. Oxford: Clarendon.

Jones, G. D. B.
1962 Capena and the Ager Capenas, Part I. Papers of the British School at Rome 30: 116-207.
1963 Capena and the Ager Capenas, Part II. Papers of the British School at Rome 31: 100-58.

Kahane, Anne, Leslie Murray Threipland, and John Ward-Perkins
1968 The Ager Veientanus, north and east of Rome. Papers of the British School at Rome 36: 1-218.

Karamut, Ismail, and James Russell
1999 Nephelis: a recently discovered town of coastal Rough Cilicia. Journal of Roman
        Archaeology 12: 354-71.

Kardulias, P. Nick, ed.
1994 Beyond the Site: Regional Studies in the Aegean Area. Lanham, MD: University Press of
        America.
1999 World-System Theory in Practice. Lanham, MD: Rowman and Littlefield.

Kehoe, Dennis P.
1988 The Economics of Agriculture on Roman Imperial Estates in North Africa. Göttingen:
        Vandenhoeck and Ruprecht.

Keller, Donald R., and David W. Rupp, eds.
1983 Archaeological Survey in the Mediterranean Area. Oxford: BAR International Series 155.

Keller, Donald R.
1985 Archaeological Survey in Southern Euboea, Greece: A Reconstruction of Human Activity
        from Neolithic Times Through the Byzantine Period. PhD. dissertation, Indiana University.

Keswani, Priscilla S.
1993 Models of local exchange in late Bronze Age Cyprus. Bulletin of the American Schools of
        Oriental Research 292: 73-83.

Kowalewski, Stephen A., Gary M. Feinman, Laura Finsten, Richard E. Blanton, and Linda M. Nicholas
1989 Monte Albán's Hinterland, Part II: Prehispanic Settlement Patterns in Tlacolula, Etla, and
        Ocotlán, the Valley of Oaxaca, Mexico. Ann Arbor: Memoirs of the Museum of
        Anthropology, The University of Michigan 23.

Kowalewski, Stephen A.
1990 Merits of full-coverage survey: examples from the Valley of Oaxaca. In The Archaeology of
        Regions: A Case for Full-Coverage Survey ed. by Suzanne K. Fish and Stephen A. Kowalewski,
        pp. 33-85. Washington, D. C.: Smithsonian Institution Press.

Levick, Barbara
1967 Roman Colonies in Southern Asia Minor. Oxford: Clarendon Press.

Lloyd, John
  1991 Conclusion: archaeological survey and the Roman landscape. In Roman Landscapes, ed. by Graeme Barker and John Lloyd, pp. 233-40. London: Archaeological Monographs of the British School at Rome No. 2.
Magie, David
  1975 Roman Rule in Asia Minor to the End of the Third Century After Christ. New York: Arno.
Mattingly, D. J.
  1988 Oil for export? A comparison of Libyan, Spanish, and Tunisian olive oil production in the Roman empire. Journal of Roman Archaeology 1: 33-56.
  1997 Africa: a landscape of opportunity? In Dialogues in Roman Imperialism, ed. by D. J. Mattingly, pp. 117-39. Portsmouth, Rhode Island: Journal of Roman Archaeology Supplementary Series 23.
Mattingly, D. J., ed.
  1997 Dialogues in Roman Imperialism.. Portsmouth, Rhode Island: Journal of Roman Archaeology Supplementary Series 23.
McKay, A. G.
  1975 Houses, Villas and Palaces in the Roman World. Ithaca, N. Y.: Cornell University Press.
Mee, Christopher, David Gill, Hamish Forbes, and Lin Foxhall
  1991 Rural settlement change in the Methana Peninsula, Greece. In Roman Landscapes, ed. by Graeme Barker and John Lloyd, pp. 223-32. London: Archaeological Monographs of the British School at Rome No. 2.
Mitchell, Stephen
  1993 Anatolia: Land, Men and Gods in Asia Minor. Vol. I, The Celts in Anatolia and the Impact of Roman Rule. Oxford: Clarendon Press.
Millett, Martin
  1995 Strategies for Roman small towns. In Roman Small Towns in Eastern England and Beyond, ed. by A. E. Brown, pp. 29-37. Oxford: Oxbow Monograph 52.
Morley, Neville
  1997 Cities in context: urban systems in Roman Italy. In Roman Urbanism: Beyond the Consumer City, ed. by Helen M. Parkins, pp. 42-58. London: Routledge.
Morrison, John A.
  1939 Alisar: A Unit of Land Occupance in the Kanak Su Basin of Central Anatolia. Chicago: The University of Chicago Libraries.
Oakes, Harvey
  1957 The Soils of Turkey. Ankara: Republic of Turkey, Ministry of Agriculture, Soil Conservation and Farm Irrigation Division.
Onurkan, Somay
  1967 Observations on two types of buildings. In A Survey of Coastal Cities in Western Cilicia: Preliminary Report, by Elisabeth Rosenbaum, Gerhard Huber, and Somay Onurkan, pp. 69-85. Ankara: Türk Tarih Kurumu Yayinlarindan VI, Seri No. 8.
Ormerod, Henry A.
  1978 Piracy in the Ancient World: An Essay in Mediterranean History. Totowa, N. J.: Rowman and Littlefield.
Paribeni, R., and P. Romanelli
  1914 Studi e Ricerche Archeologiche nell' Anatolia Meridionale. Monumenti Antichi XXIII: 5-274.
Patterson, John R.
  1991 Settlement, city, and elite in Samnium and Lycia. In City and Country in the Ancient World, ed. by John Rich and Andrew Wallace-Hadrill, pp. 147-68. London: Routledge.
Pleket, H. W.
  1983 Urban elites and business in the Greek part of the Roman Empire. In Trade in the Ancient Economy, ed. by Peter Garnsey, Keith Hopkins, and C. R. Whittaker, pp. 131-44. Berkeley: University of California Press.
Ponsich, Michael
  1974 Implantation Rurale Antique sur le Bas-Guadalquivir. Madrid: Publicaciones de la Casa de Velázquez, Série Archéologie.
Potter, T. W.
  1979 The Changing Landscape of South Etruria. New York: St. Martin's Press.
Ramsay, W. M.
  1890 The Historical Geography of Asia Minor. London: Royal Geographic Society Supplementary Papers, Vol. 4.
Rauh, Nicholas K.
  n.d. Who were the Cilician Pirates? Ms.
Renfrew, Colin
  1972 The Emergence of Civilization: The Cyclades and the Aegean in the Third Millennium BC. London: Methuen.
Renfrew, Colin, and Malcolm Wagstaff, eds.
  1982 An Island Polity: The Archaeology of Exploitation in Melos. Cambridge: Cambridge University Press.

Rosenbaum, Elisabeth
1967a Preface. In A Survey of Coastal Cities in Western Cilicia: Preliminary Report, by Elisabeth
Rosenbaum, Gerhard Huber, and Somay Onurkan, pp. vii-x. Ankara: Türk Tarih Kurumu
Yayinlarindan VI, Seri No. 8.
1967b The cemeteries. In A Survey of Coastal Cities in Western Cilicia: Preliminary Report, by
Elisabeth Rosenbaum, Gerhard Huber, and Somay Onurkan, pp. 51-66. Ankara: Türk Tarih Kurumu
Yayinlarindan VI, Seri No. 8.
1967c A note on the churches and chapels. In A Survey of Coastal Cities in Western Cilicia:
Preliminary Report. By Elisabeth Rosenbaum, Gerhard Huber, and Somay Onurkan, pp. 67-8.
Ankara: Türk Tarih Kurumu Yayinlarindan VI, Seri No. 8.
Rostovtzeff, M.
1941 The Social and Economic History of the Hellenistic World. Oxford: Clarendon Press.
Rothaus, Richard M.
n.d. Rough Cilicia Regional Survey Project: 1997 Preliminary Ceramic Report. Ms.
Rupp, David W., Lone Wriedt Sorensen, Roger H. King, and William Fox
1984 Canadian Palaipaphos (Cyprus) survey project: second preliminary report, 1980-82.
Journal of Field Archaeology 11: 133-54.
Seton-Williams, M. V.
1954 Cilician survey. Anatolian Studies 4: 121-74.
Shaw, Brent D.
1990 Bandit highlands and lowland peace: the mountains of Isauria-Cilicia. Journal of the
Economic and Social History of the Orient 33: 200-33, 237-70.
Shipley, Graham
1987 A History of Samos, 800-188 BC. Oxford: Clarendon Press.
Small, Alastair
1991 Late Roman rural settlement in Basilicata and western Apulia. In Roman Landscapes, ed. by
Graeme Barker and John Lloyd, pp. 204-22. London: Archaeological Monographs of the
British School at Rome No. 2.
Snodgrass, Anthony M.
1990 Survey archaeology and the rural landscape of the Greek city. In The Greek City: From
Homer to Alexander, ed. by O. Murray and S. Price, pp. 113-36. Oxford: Clarendon Press.
Stirling, Paul
1965 Turkish Village. London: Weidenfeld and Nicolson.
Stratil-Sauer, G.
1933 Cereal production in Turkey. Economic Geography 9: 4: 325-36.
Tchalenko, Georges
1953 Villages Antiques de la Syrie du Nord: Le Massif du Bélus a l'Epoque Romaine, Volume I.
Paris: Institut Français d'Archéologie de Beyrouth. Bibliotheque Archéologique et Historique 50.
Tchernia, André
1983 Italian wine in Gaul at the end of the republic. In Trade in the Ancient Economy, ed. by
Peter Garnsey, Keith Hopkins, and C. R. Whittaker, pp. 87-104. Berkeley: University of
California Press.
Vallat, Jean-Pierre
1991 Survey archaeology and rural history--a difficult but productive relationship. In Roman
Landscapes, ed. by Graeme Barker and John Lloyd, pp. 10-17. London: Archaeological
Monographs of the British School at Rome No. 2.
van Andel, Tjeerd H., and Curtis N. Runnels
1987 Beyond the Acropolis: A Rural Greek Past. Stanford: Stanford University Press.
1988 An essay on the emergence of civilization in the Aegean world. Antiquity 62: 234-47.
Wagstaff, Malcolm
1978 Geographical contribution to the Vasilikos Valley project, 1978. In Vasilikos Valley project:
third preliminary report, 1978, ed. by Ian A. Todd. Journal of Field Archaeology 6: 290-4.
Wagstaff, Malcolm, Siv Augustson, and Clive Gamble
1982 Alternative subsistence strategies. In An Island Polity: The Archaeology of Exploitation in
Melos, ed. by Colin Renfrew and Malcolm Wagstaff, pp. 172-80. Cambridge: Cambridge
University Press.
Wagstaff, Malcolm, and Clive Gamble
1982 Island resources and their limitations. In An Island Polity: The Archaeology of Exploitation
in Melos, ed. by Colin Renfrew and Malcolm Wagstaff, pp. 95-105. Cambridge: Cambridge
University Press.
Wallace-Hadrill, Andrew
1991 Introduction. In City and Country in the Ancient World, ed. by John Rich and Andrew
Wallace-Hadrill, pp. ix-xviii. London: Routledge.
Wallerstein, Immanuel
1974 The Modern World-System I. New York: Academic Press.
Watrous, Livingston Vance
1974 An Archaeological Survey of the Lasithi Plain in Crete from the Neolithic to the Late

Roman Period. PhD. dissertation, University of Pennsylvania.
  1982 Lasithi: A History of Settlement on a Highland Plain in Crete. Hesperia Supplement 18. Princeton: American School of Classical Studies at Athens.
Watrous, Livingston Vance, and Harriet Blitzer, eds.
  1993 A survey of the western Mesara plain in Crete: preliminary report of the 1984, 1986, and 1987 field seasons. Hesperia 62: 2: 191-248.
White, K. D.
  1970 Roman Farming. Ithaca, N. Y.: Cornell University Press.
  1975 Farm Equipment of the Roman World. Cambridge: Cambridge University Press.
Whitelaw, T. M.
  1994 An ethnoarchaeological study of rural land-use in north-west Keos: insights and implications for the study of past Aegean landscapes. In Structures Rurales et Sociétés Antiques, ed. by Panagiotis N. Doukellis and Lina G. Mendoni, pp. 163-86. Paris: Centre de Reserches d'Histoire Ancienne.
Whittaker, Charles R.
  1978 Land and labour in North Africa. Klio 60: 331-62.
Williams, Caroline
  1989 Anemurium: The Roman and Early Byzantine Pottery. Toronto: Pontifical Institute of Mediaeval Studies, Subsidia Mediaevalia 16.
Winfield, David
  1977 The northern routes across Anatolia. Anatolian Studies 27: 151-66.
Woolf, Greg
  1990 World-systems analysis and the Roman empire. Journal of Roman Archaeology 3: 44-58.
Wright, James C., John F. Cherry, Jack Davis, Eleni Mantzourani, and Susan B. Sutton
  1990 The Nemea Valley archaeological project: A preliminary report. Hesperia 59: 4: 579-695.

Plates

Plate 3-1 Ridges NE of ER-1, LR-1, looking N.

Plate 3-2 ER-1, LR-1, looking S.

99

Plate 3-3   Detail of structure at ER-1, LR-1, with 1 m bar.

Plate 3-4   Fortified promontory, Iotape, looking SW.

Plate 3-5 Olive crushing *mortarium* at Iotape (scale bar in 10 cm segments).

Plate 3-6 Side view of *mortarium* at Iotape.

Plate 3-7 Koças massif, looking N from the hill of Selinus.

Plate 3-8 Haçimusa River E of Selinus, looking E.

Plate 3-9   Alluvial plain S of Selinus, looking NW.

Plate 3-10   Selinus, main public area, looking NE.

Plate 3-11 Selinus, the site's western extension above the river mouth (collection area 2).

Plate 3-12 Koru Dagi massif, looking NW, with Gazipasa in the background.

Plate 3-13 Coast S of Koru Dagi massif, looking SE.

Plate 3-14 North slopes of Koru Dagi massif, looking W.

Plate 3-15 Sheep herding camp near ER-15, LR-17.

Plate 3-16 The northern ridge line of Macar Kalesi massif, looking NE.

Plate 3-17 Coast S of Cestrus, looking SE.

Plate 3-18 Intensive agriculture in and around Macar village, E of Macar Kalesi, looking SE.
ER-18, LR-21 is located on the mountain summit near left beyond the village.

Plate 3-19 Güdü massif, looking NW.

Plate 3-20 Coast S of Güdü massif, looking NW.

Plate 3-21 Ridge line SE of Güdü massif, looking NW.

Plate 3-22 Quarry (ND-1) looking NW.

Plate 3-23 Partially quarried column base at ND-1.

Plate 3-24 ER-15, LR-17, looking SE.

Plate 3-25 Looted structure with exposed apse. ER-14, LR-14.

Plate 3-26 Cestrus, house remains in the vicinity of collection area 3.

111

Plate 3-27 Cestrus, monumental terrace (right) and large structure (left), looking S.

Plate 3-28 Cestrus reservoir, looking SE.

Plate 3-29 Circular structure at 28-c-02-b-2 (ND-3), looking E.

Plate 3-30 ND-4 (28-c-02-b-3), SW corner of the structure, looking NE. Wall height at the corner is .95 m.

Plate 3-31 ER-18, LR-21, terrace fragment, N edge of the site, looking SE.

Plate 3-32 House with standing doorway, ER-18, LR-21, looking S.

114

Plate 3-33 ER-18, LR-21, building complex on the hill summit, looking N.

Plate 3-34 Muz Kent ridge (left of photo), looking NW.

Plate 3-35 Coast SW of Muz Kent ridge, looking NW.

Plate 3-36 Coast E of Nephelion, looking SE.

Plate 3-37 ER-20, large house, looking N.

Plate 3-38 Acropolis area of Nephelion, looking SW.

Plate 3-39 Nephelion, acropolis area (collection area 1), looking S. To the left and below the summit is the gate-tower; below the summit near the center of the photo is a temple.

Plate 3-40 Nephelion, theater, looking E.

Plate 3-41 ER-23, on the higher of the two small peaks at the center of the photo, looking E.

Plate 3-42 28-c-09-d-6 (HLN-4), wall fragment, looking NE.

Plate 3-43 Ridge system N of Antiochia, looking NW.

Plate 3-44 Summit of the Karadag massif, looking SW.

Plate 3-45 Steep slopes S of the acropolis, Antiochia, looking E.

Plate 3-46 Lower section of the Antiochia site, looking SW.

Plate 3-47 Higher promontory at the lower section of the Antiochia site, looking NW.

Plate 3-48 Entrance to the hidden cove N of the lower promontory, Antiochia, looking SW.

Plate 3-49 Karadag site (ER-24), N corner of platform at the site's N edge, looking SW.

www.ingramcontent.com/pod-product-compliance
Lightning Source LLC
Chambersburg PA
CBHW061002030426
42334CB00033B/3332